A
DIFFERENT
KIND OF
WEB

A DIFFERENT KIND OF WEB

NEW CONNECTIONS BETWEEN ARCHIVES AND OUR USERS

EDITED BY KATE THEIMER

SOCIETY OF
American
Archivists

CHICAGO

Society of American Archivists
www.archivists.org

Printed in the United States of America

Graphic Design by Sweeney Design, kasween@sbcglobal.net

Library of Congress Cataloging-in-Publication Data

A different kind of Web : new connections between archives and our users / edited by Kate
Theimer.
    p. cm.
 Includes bibliographical references and index.
 ISBN 1-931666-39-3
1. Archives—Information technology. 2. Archives—Administration—Technological innova-
tions. 3. Archival materials—Data processing. 4. Archives users. 5. Archives—Automation. 6.
Web 2.0. 7. World Wide Web. 8. Online social networks. 9. Blogs. 10. Web sites—Design. 11.
Wikis (Computer science). I. Theimer, Kate, 1966-
 CD973.D3D54 2011
 006.7'54—dc23
                          2011027013

Table of Contents

Foreword

Both timely and timeless, Kate Theimer's volume on the challenges and opportunities of Web 2.0 sheds light on the issue we are all trying to balance—exploiting the power of technology to do our work and anticipate the needs of our users at the same time we rethink the basic principles of archival and library theory.

Of particular import in this work is the range of contributors—archivists, librarians, records managers, historians, curators, information scientists, genealogists, students, and academics. Capturing the voice of our user is key to the premise of this volume: "new connections between archives and our users."

While the tools presented in a "case study" mode are those we are now using—blogs and wikis, Flickr, Twitter, Facebook, YouTube, etc.—the lessons learned presented by the contributors provide valuable lessons for experimentation and adaptation applicable to any new and emerging technology. Particularly worthy of note is the role the end user plays in each of these studies. The effort to engage and involve the user community reflects not only our understanding of user expectations but also our belief that we can learn from our users.

The focus of the text is both user-centered and entrepreneurial and the result is an exciting journey of discovery and renegotiation of the relationship between archives and users and the evolution of our profession.

As Robert B. Townsend points out in his essay, the "breadth of . . . change and the diversity of potential users means the next stage of development in how archives use the web will need to draw heavily on input from users to be effective." Theimer and her contributors present a variety of creative approaches to this next stage of development.

David S. Ferriero
Archivist of the United States

Preface

Kate Theimer

Most of this year's incoming college freshmen will never have known a world without Google. For many of them, the concept of "Web 2.0" is confusing, because they had little experience with the world of "Web 1.0." Today's teenagers take for granted being able to access their friends—or anyone else—via their mobile phones. Using social media isn't new; it is just the way the web works.

That is not true for many of today's archivists. The archival profession successfully established itself on Web 1.0: archives have websites, online exhibits, and databases of online images; they post finding aids (whether in Encoded Archival Description or not); and they communicate with their researchers via individual e-mails and via e-mail groups and listservs. But how well is the archival profession adapting to the changes social media have brought to the way the world communicates on the web?

This book explores how archives are using the tools of Web 2.0 to reach and interact with users, old and new. In thirteen case studies archival practitioners describe their own experiences in creating blogs, wikis, and interactive websites and contributing to sites such as Flickr, YouTube, *Wikipedia,* and Second Life. The themes in these case studies are framed and explored by longer analytical essays that reflect on the larger implications of social media for archives—the "different kind of web" we are forming with our users. These essays discuss how social media are changing how archivists conduct outreach, how the concept of authority is adapting and evolving, and the opportunities social media present for enhancing and streamlining traditional archival processes. The book also provides a series of short essays presenting the viewpoints of some of the primary users of archives, such as historians, educators, students, and genealogists, as they consider the possibilities social media present for them to interact with archives in new ways. The volume concludes with a group of reflections on the larger implications of social media for archives, including the impact of Web 2.0 on diversity in the archival profession and the archival record and a cautionary reminder of the issues archivists must consider as they begin serving audiences with these new tools. In the Conclusion, I contribute an exploration of the insight these essays and case studies offer into the larger concept of "Archives 2.0."[1]

When I conceived and solicited the content for this collection, I had several goals in mind. I wanted contributions that would be relevant to readers today, but given how quickly the field of social media is evolving, I also wanted to ensure that the content would continue to be valuable even after the specifics of the tools under discussion had changed. To achieve this, I included the case studies to provide models and convey real-world experiences for archives that are considering implementing social media tools. I then chose to frame the case studies with essays to place our current Web 2.0 usage into a larger historical context and consider the broader implications of social media for the archival profession. These framing essays, as well as those that reflect on the larger implications for Web 2.0 for the profession, will provide a starting point—or many starting points—for future discussions of how the web is continuing to change our relationships with our users. A tertiary purpose of the book was to document our current thinking and use of the web for the benefit of future scholars. How were archivists thinking about social media? What opportunities and problems did it present? Many of the sites and products of web 2.0 will no doubt be ephemeral or at least will evolve so that they may bear little resemblance to the products we know today. I hope this book presents the best thinking in our profession for the readers of both today and tomorrow.

Just as this book has several purposes, it will serve many audiences as well. It is intended to benefit practitioners who are looking for reports from their colleagues on real-world implementations of social media tools. Students in archives and history programs will learn the "nuts and bolts" of implementation and management issues but will also gain insight into the broader theoretical and systemic issues raised by the use of social media. Archival educators will find both the case studies and the essays useful for illustrating how archives use technology as well as for stimulating class discussion about archives, technology, change, and the users of archives. Historians, history faculty, professionals in related fields such as libraries and museums, and those who study the use of the web will find in this book an encapsulation of the current approach of the archival profession.

This is the first resource available to archivists that provides both case studies of social media implementations and analytical and scholarly examination about the larger implications of the new web for archives. It also presents for the first time a collection of contributions representing the point of view of the *users* of archives and how they would like to see archives take advantage of social media. In addition to providing the perspectives of archives' users, the essays on the relationship between social media and diversity and on the possible shortcomings of a rush into adoption provide balance and ensure that a variety of perspectives are presented. This volume does not duplicate the information provided in recent books that seek to describe why and how archives should participate in social media. It is not intended as a "how-to" book; rather, it seeks to answer larger questions about the ways archives are using Web 2.0 and explore how this new kind of interactivity with our users will impact our profession.

The material in this book is presented in a manner intended to build on the preceding sections, although each section can also be read and appreciated on its own. Each case study follows a uniform style and is divided into seven sections:

- Overview of Repository
- Business Drivers
- Setting the Stage

- Results
- Challenges
- Lessons Learned
- Next Steps

The intent behind the case studies is not to provide detailed practical insights into using a specific Web 2.0 tool, which would be increasingly irrelevant as the capabilities and interfaces of the tools evolve over time. Instead, the case studies focus on the larger administrative and managerial issues that are likely to continue to face archives as they implement social media tools and discuss how the new web presence changed the way the archives interacts with their user community.

In the first essay, "Something Worth Sitting Still For? Some Implications of Web 2.0 for Outreach," Joy Palmer and Jane Stevenson discuss the traditional role of outreach in archives and show how this function translates into the Web 2.0 world. This essay reflects on the information presented in the five case studies that follow it, describing the use of a processing blog at the University of North Carolina; posting videos on YouTube at Iowa State University; creating a virtual archives in Second Life at Stanford University; creating individual profiles, pages, and groups on Facebook for outreach at the University of Alabama; and using Twitter to interact with users of the Jewish Women's Archive.

Elizabeth Yakel frames the next series of case studies in her essay, "Balancing Archival Authority with Encouraging Authentic Voices to Engage with Records." Yakel bases her examination of the complexities of building and maintaining authority in the online environment on existing scholarship in online communities. She uses the experiences of the case study authors to illustrate the challenges archivists face as they implement social media designed to foster contributions from and interactions with online users. The five case studies in this section include the experience of the Library of Congress sharing images on Flickr; the creation and evolution of The National Archives' *Your Archives* wiki; the National Archives of Australia's innovative Mapping Our Anzacs website and the way it allowed users to create their own scrapbooks and testimonials; and the complexities encountered by Syracuse University in contributing information about its collections to relevant articles in *Wikipedia*. The section closes with the first description in English of an innovative effort undertaken by nonarchivists in France to harvest public domain information about archival collections and redistribute it via Flickr to crowdsource additions and corrections to the descriptions created by the archival repositories.

The section that follows is unified by the theme of opportunism, or using Web 2.0 tools to achieve goals related to both management and outreach. The lead essay by James Gerencser, "New Tools Equal New Opportunities: Using Social Media to Achieve Archival Management Goals," explores this theme and uses the three case studies to demonstrate not only the viability but the potential management value of using these new technologies. The case studies document two innovative uses of blogging software—for creating a combination reference blog and reference request tracking system at Dickinson College and for creating a "catablog" to iteratively publish descriptive information at the University of Massachusetts–Amherst—and the use by archivists at the College of William and Mary of wiki software to create a "ready reference" site to serve both internal and external needs.

No publication focused on the evolving relationship between archives and our users would be complete without including pieces that capture the perspectives of some of those users. Therefore, the next section contains a more varied group of short chapters rather than uniform case studies, including a study of the use of Web 2.0 tools by high school students participating in National History Day, reflections on the use and potential use of social media by history faculty and undergraduate students interacting with archives, and a virtual "roundtable" interview with genealogists, family historians, and companies providing access to archival documents. An essay by Robert Townsend, "Old Divisions, New Opportunities: Historians and Other Users Working with and in Archives," leads off this section, placing the shorter pieces in the larger context of the evolution of user relationships with archives, reflecting specifically on the evolving relationship between historians and archives.

The essays by Terry Baxter and Randall Jimerson provide perspectives on how the changes brought by social media affect the relationship of archives and society. Baxter's essay, "Going to See the Elephant: Archives, Diversity, and the Social Web," reflects on the concept of diversity in and for the archival profession and how social media changes—or does not change—the implications for archives. In "Archives 101 in a 2.0 World: The Continuing Need for Parallel Systems," Jimerson presents a cautionary argument about the need for archives to consider the possible drawbacks of engaging with social media and the ongoing need to serve all our users, including those who continue to engage with us via traditional means.

In the volume's conclusion, I present a summary of how the evidence and themes considered in the essays and case studies illustrate a larger movement in the profession—Archives 2.0. I believe that the "different kind of web" of relationships with our users that archives are now creating through social media is just part of a larger wave of innovation and evolution in the profession. The user-centered and entrepreneurial outlook of Archives 2.0 is typified by the attitudes and actions shown by the archivists who have contributed to this volume.

I think readers will come away with an understanding of how archives are using the web today to reach new and existing users as well as to serve their own management needs. They will expand their knowledge of the function of social media for outreach and perhaps see a new perspective on the potential that social media present for changing our relationship with our users. They will gain insights into what some of the primary users of archives—historians, educators, students, family historians, genealogists, and companies offering genealogy-based services—think about the ways they would like to see archives use social media. Readers will also be reminded of the role social media serve in broadening the diversity of audiences for archival services and of the importance of remembering those whom archives continue to serve via traditional means. I hope the common philosophy of openness to experimentation and change, and the need for the archival profession to evolve to better meet our users' needs that runs throughout all the sections of the book, will inspire readers to explore emerging technologies in their own organizations and engage with their own communities of users in new and exciting ways.

Notes

[1] "Archives 2.0" is a relatively new concept. In the Conclusion I present one definition, but some of the authors in this volume use it and define it slightly differently than I do. Rather than impose my own view on the contributors, each author uses the term in the way that he or she understands and defines it.

Something Worth Sitting Still For? Some Implications of Web 2.0 for Outreach

Joy Palmer and Jane Stevenson

Introduction

In his 2008 speech about the rise of Web 2.0, Clay Shirky argued "[m]edia that's targeted at you but doesn't include you may not be worth sitting still for."[1]

Outreach has arguably been part of the archivist's core mission since the inception of the public archive, with the role of the archivist as not only one of protecting and preserving the archive but also of enabling access. The term *outreach* highlights the archivist as not just a gatekeeper, but also as a facilitator—promoting the riches of hidden or little-known collections to communities that might be encouraged to "use" the archive. Web 2.0 technologies, which are intrinsically participatory and focused on sharing, collaboration, and mutual meaning-making, are now being effectively exploited by many among us to find new ways to reach out to users and promote not only new use of the archive but also new understandings of it. In many ways, these new forms of outreach are logical extensions of existing outreach activities, but social media in particular is transforming the concept of outreach itself in positive, and sometimes challenging, ways.

This move to new forms of outreach is part of the larger movement we might call "Archives 2.0." Less about technological change than a shift in mind-set, Archives 2.0 has been characterized as a development that emphasizes openness, sharing, and collaboration and at the same time "de-privileges" archival authority.[2] As these new forms of interaction start to change our relationship with the users of archives, this chapter explores how, in turn, this impacts (traditional) outreach activities. As Timothy Ericson states, people out there will be interested in archives, *though they may not know it yet.*[3] Tools such as YouTube, Second Life, Facebook, and Twitter are all potential mechanisms for unobtrusively inviting new users to engage with the archive and to view items, or even collections, online. These case studies show how archivists can attract broader, and even global, audiences that they would never have anticipated by using more traditional means of outreach.

How, if at all, is outreach transformed with the advent of new spaces in which to reach heretofore elusive users? What are the lessons we can learn from those who are taking pioneering steps and the stories that are detailed through these case studies? The changing nature of outreach via the wealth of Web 2.0 channels available to us means that we are in a period of experimentation—discovering new ways to engage with end users and to be archivists in new spaces. As the case studies that follow demonstrate, we are in a period of flux, where we are renegotiating issues of control, authority, voice, and trust.

In this chapter we will briefly consider the more traditional notions of outreach that we have inherited as a profession and go on to discuss how new online technologies, and particularly social media or "Web 2.0," can dramatically transform the potential of outreach activities in reaching new users and attracting wider audiences. Each of our case studies pinpoints the immediate benefits that can be realized through such ventures. We will also consider how these contexts have brought with them new and sometimes unforeseen challenges, particularly those of defining and targeting an audience, establishing clear objectives, measuring successes, and delineating the personal from the professional. We will conclude with a consideration of the implications of these new spaces of interaction and meaning-making on archival authority and the role of the archivist in these new and inherently participatory models.

Perceptions of "Traditional" Outreach

The term *outreach* is a relatively new one within this sector. In his address to the UK Society of Archivists' conference of 2007, Victory Gray wryly observed how it has become one of the most overused and potentially least understood terms in archival practice: "In the new vocabulary which we have all had to learn, *outreach* must surely sit near the top of the most used words in the lexicon of current archival jargon. . . . The only puzzle to me is why it took so long to invent the word."[4] Indeed, *outreach* typically refers to a wide range of loosely related activities aimed at raising awareness and engaging with potential users: traditional activities might include large exhibitions or (more usually) small displays in modest glass-fronted cabinets, booklets, leaflets, flyers, posters, and press releases. In addition, archivists undertake public speaking engagements, collaborate with teachers in classroom-based learning, develop "tool kits," encourage "friends" groups, run evening classes, and organize open days. So many of these activities have become absolutely core to our work, but we have not necessarily taken a strategic or holistic approach to them and we have not always focused on measuring impact.

In recent years, the role of outreach has taken on much more importance in the day-to-day workings of the archival institution. But a quick perusal of professional journals over the last few decades perhaps indicates that we have not reflected on our outreach methodologies to nearly the same extent that we have theorized other aspects of archival practice. In an early reference to outreach in 1978, Elsie Freeman Freivogel defines outreach programs as synonymous with archival education and education programs, which "bring the products of archival research, the techniques of research in archives, or other aspects of humanist learning derived from primary sources to the user public, rather than to other archivists."[5] Freivogel's early definition highlighted the concept of outreach as a form of archival education, with aims that are academic and pedagogic. This characterization of outreach emphasizes loose ties with history as an academic discipline, with the archivist positioned as a type of professional historian committed to the preservation of the historical record, an authoritative scholar and a mediator. In general, archival journals have neglected to explore outreach as a professional skill and have focused on areas such as the role of archives in historical contexts, archival education, archival management issues, legislation, policy, and security.

In terms of outreach activities, in the 1980s a significant number of institutions in the United States had no outreach program at all; for those that did, the primary outreach activities were exhibitions and publications.[6] More recently, however, the concept of outreach has become intrinsically more outward-looking and benefits-led, with the Society of American Archivists defining outreach as "[t]he process of identifying and providing services to constituencies with needs relevant to the repository's mission, especially underserved groups, and tailoring services to meet those needs."[7]

Although we now embrace outreach as more intrinsic to our work, central to achieving a repository's mission, there remain real and often intractable operational realities that make undertaking truly effective outreach activities a challenge. Little attention is given to the specific skill set an archivist might require to effectively engage end users of archives or to market the archive to the broader community. To remedy this, a growing number of organizations are running training programs and workshops on marketing for archivists and other information professionals. Many of these programs highlight how such initiatives can be undertaken "on a shoestring" and with minimal resource for maximum impact—again, a reflection that there is usually little funding available to support outreach. Quite often, in grant applications, "outreach and dissemination" is a tack-on activity, consuming only a small proportion of the overall costs, and not seen as a central aspect of the project as a whole. In short, our outreach or marketing activities can often be undertaken in an *ad hoc* and nonstrategic manner. This state of affairs in the library and archival sector is effectively summed up in a recent blog post by Emily Ford: "We have the ability to be in our communities, to engage them and offer specific targeted services. Our engagement with our communities can be the defining aspect of what a library is to any given community. . . . Traditional 'outreach' services should be an integrated part of what we do, not an aside, a tacked on item."[8]

Also driving this call for a more strategic approach to outreach are the very real pressures of *demonstrating the value* of the archival institution in these economically straitened times. Professionals across the sector are looking at ways in which marketing strategies can be deployed to help institutions achieve their aims to "influence the level of institutional support for the archives, explain the need for archives, advertise for use of the material, solicit donations of material and money, and educate departments and individuals about what there is and why they should care."[9] In periods when budgets are lean and always under threat of being cut or eliminated, the need to strategically and cost-effectively market archives to the community and demonstrate their value becomes all the more critical. Web technologies can be deployed for new forms of outreach, not only reaching out to new users, but in many cases, through the intrinsically interactive nature of new social technologies, helping us to gather evidence about the use and the value of our archives. These new technologies appear to dramatically affect our ability to reach broad audiences with only minimum budget and resources, thus possibly changing the "playing field" for outreach. Indeed, each case study in this section points to business drivers that are not only concerned with promoting use of the archive's collections but also awareness of the archive itself. Throughout their accounts, the authors consistently comment on how traditional outreach was not working effectively, especially in terms of reaching new users.

New Outreach

The concept of the archive online is still a relatively new one, and as a community we are still exploring the implications of these evolving spaces for understanding. In the last decade, certain online activities have become commonplace in our outreach practices: the creation of online exhibitions and use of listservs, e-mailers, and newsletters to reach target communities. In the late 1990s, especially, issues of online access came to the forefront of our discourse, with groundbreaking work on developing electronic archival description,[10] archival networks,[11] and interface design[12] as a means to reach out to many more users and create efficiencies for existing ones. Much of this work addressed the usability of the archival discovery tool, with some attention paid to the ways in which online systems interface with the tasks of the researcher—understanding the requirements of the researcher-as-user in detail has been pivotal to this work, and online access has certainly revolutionized the concept of archival access. Arguably, though, the online description simply replicates the "physical finding aid" and does not take advantage of new opportunities for online access to information. This can be seen, for example, in the way that Encoded Archival Description (EAD) has developed to encode diverse traditional finding aids.[13] In addition, the relationship between archive, archivist, and end user has remained much the same as in a more traditional circumstance.

With the advent of new social technologies, which are low-cost and easy to implement or participate in, attention is now more focused on direct engagement and active interaction with users in online spaces. Through these approaches, archives ideally become collaborative spaces when mediated through online spaces. These new technologies of social media bring with them a rapid step-change, giving us relatively easy-to-use and easy-to-deploy software and tools for facilitating group interaction, online collaboration, network development, and individual expression. A substantial proportion of archival professionals can now easily set up and write a blog, share media, engage in online interaction such as games or debate, stay up to date with the latest news, and work in an increasingly collaborative way online. Since its inception, the web has been character-ized as "a collaborative space where people can interact."[14] But it is only with the advent of new "2.0" technologies that this appears to have been truly realized.

Hyperbole aside, it is nonetheless true that "online" is now a funda-mentally *enabling* space that supports both groups and conversation. This is a many-to-many paradigm that enables mobilization around a cause, a subject, or something of interest. As Clay Shirky states, "[g]roups that see or hear or watch or listen to something can now gather around and talk to each other as well."[15] The web thus becomes profoundly democratizing—but for whom? As these tools open wider possibilities for reaching new audiences more easily, the question of defining and understanding the user becomes all the more critical.

Who Is the User?

Perhaps the archetypal user of the archive is either the historian or "serious scholar," and, indeed, many archival institutions have a rich history of academic liaison. Historically, our outreach activities have prioritized the academic over and above the "pursuers of the trivial,"[16] and our user community has thus been quite tightly defined. Our traditional view of interaction with users is on a personal one-to-one level in the reading room, ideally giving a generous amount of time to each individual researcher or via a time-consuming exchange of letters and photocopies of selected documents. In a sense, this model is based on a perceived low level of use, which enables us to think in terms of quality rather than quantity.[17]

But this relatively singular approach is now being questioned—particularly the value judgment inherent in the concept of the "pursuit of the trivial." The emergence of the web and Web 2.0 has brought the limitations of this approach to the forefront, inviting us, perhaps even forcing us, to broaden our perspective well beyond the "scholar" in the reading room to new and unfamiliar audiences. Of course, this shift brings a broad range of challenges and tensions, not least among them the question of how we actually identify users and engage effectively within a social landscape that has changed radically from that of a few decades ago.

The case studies that follow each represent a different starting point when it comes to identifying the audience and purpose of the Web 2.0 engagement. For example, in the Facebook and Twitter case studies, the objectives were perhaps less concrete, with both projects more explicitly embarked on in the spirit of experimentation. However, both authors point to the need to raise awareness among new audiences, particularly students, through the medium (discussed below). Others began the Web 2.0 outreach activity with a much more specific audience and set of objectives in mind. For instance, Stephen J. Fletcher and his colleagues were "not motivated to use a Web 2.0 tool for the sake of using a Web 2.0 tool." Instead, the project emerged as a means to tackle the specific problem of managing the expectations of end users over a newly acquired high-demand collection of highly significant historical photography. Similarly, the "Virtual Archives" project, part of a much broader research experiment at Stanford University, was specifically aimed at using Second Life to "facilitate browsing and archival literacy" through deploying an online collaborative environment, simulating the archive as a space that "affords scholars the possibility of collaboration in real time during the discovery process."

While some of these case studies perhaps started out as more informal projects, the drive to innovate, to try something new, to learn what might occur, cuts across each of them. Identifying tangible business drivers in retrospect, then, has proven a challenge in some regards. As Stephen J. Fletcher puts it when referring to the creation of a blog about processing the Morton collection: "we faced no institutional formalities or approvals, wrote no mission statements, policies, nor measures of success." A formalized sense of business was perhaps less a motive behind these experiments than the drive to experiment and discover new modes of interacting with users and, perhaps, for new uses to drive future business cases. As these examples demonstrate, the results of such steps can be surprising, and perhaps even unpredictable, particularly in rapidly evolving social ecosystems such as Twitter, Facebook, and Second Life.

Leveraging Network Effects for Outreach

Iowa State University's use of YouTube to share its digitized film collections has proved especially successful. From the outset, this particular project articulated clear business drivers and objectives: "YouTube offered the Department a way to provide access to a collection that is not easily available to researchers." In addition: "putting the films online provided a means for ISU alumni to rediscover and share some of their moments as students by watching campus related films." The project is a particularly strong example of how archives can leverage the potential of "web-scale" systems such as Google.[18] As a Google service, YouTube has become web-scale in that it provides a "concentrated mass" of content and attention, which in turn increases gravitational pull to the resource.[19] By placing content within such a system, archives can leverage the network effects that drive traffic to content and thus dramatically increase the chances that interested parties (or accidental tourists) will discover it. This is no small feat when so many dispersed digital collections remain obscurely hidden in the "deep web," uncrawled by search engines like Google, waiting for their potential to be realized.

As a result of the YouTube exposure, Iowa State reported a dramatic increase in requests and visitations—success indicators that clearly demonstrate that the effort expended in placing the digital content into the service (which was not insignificant) was worthwhile. In particular, the activity led to use by new users, particularly former alumni of the university. The handful of comments left on several of the videos posted indicate that these users were far from traditional consumers of archives, with some stating that they were simply happy to be given the chance to watch films that brought back childhood memories: "Thanks so much for posting this video. I grew up with WOI-TV and especially enjoyed the morning show with Betty Lou. I always tried the crafts she did but they never came out very good. . . . Thanks for bringing back an early childhood memory for me. I LOVED 'Magic Window.' Just the theme song alone made my day!" (See p. 38.) These people may not characterize themselves as "archives users" in the same way as academic scholars; nonetheless, as new users they were entering into an experience with archives. Rather than undermine the "public good" proposition of the archive, they emphasize the relevancy of the archive as the harbinger for collective memory—broadening its appeal as "of the people."

The strategic significance of such feedback should not be underestimated. One result of the YouTube project was a stronger relationship with the university alumni association, which grew to recognize that the archive could play a central role in triggering nostalgic and pleasurable memories of the university. Potential benefits of this might be mapped and realized in the future; for instance, such activity might help strengthen the alumni base and perhaps even increase membership contributions. These cascading benefits might not yet be understood or realized, but it certainly indicates the possibilities, in the institutional context, where strategic marketing has become very much part of business as usual. Such activities, though not typical scholarly endeavors, strengthen the business case of the archive and bring it firmly to the funding stakeholder's attention.

Reaching Students: The Promise of Social Networking Tools

In the case of social networking technologies, both Jessica Lacher-Feldman's and Andrea Medina-Smith's projects highlight how the issue of targeting a specific audience becomes much more central, as the relationship is likely to be one of more personal or one-to-one engagement of user and archivist. Both authors point to their use of social networking tools—Facebook and Twitter—as means to reach new audiences, specifically, undergraduates and younger people. Certainly, the potential of social technologies to transform or enrich educational experiences is a significant topic in contemporary critical debate. The educational community is investigating to what extent education, especially collaborative learning, is transformed in light of new digital forms of interaction. Educators are asking how they can cater to the needs and expectations of a "born digital" generation, used to simple search, immediate access to content, and also the ability to reuse and repurpose content to their needs. A recent UK study, *Higher Education in a Web 2.0 World*, concludes that Web 2.0 has a profound effect on the behavior of students, in particular, encouraging a strong sense of communities of interest and a greater tendency to share and participate than previous generations. The report concludes that the "world they [the students] encounter in higher education has been constructed on a wholly different set of norms."[20]

Likewise, in the archival community, we are gradually shifting our expectations that users, particularly students, will come to us via our traditional channels.[21] Instead, as these projects illustrate, we are embracing the notion that to seek new audiences and engage with them effectively, we must, to echo Medina-Smith, "go where they are." In the case of university undergraduates, the social networking destination of choice is almost certainly Facebook, with Twitter also rapidly gaining momentum as a breathtakingly pervasive medium for public real-time chat.[22] Archives, museums, and libraries are exploiting the potential of social media to reach out to users, raise awareness, and potentially tap into this new "educational space" to interact with students and *teach* them about archives and historical research.

Whether social media such as Facebook or Twitter are sites for meaningful engagement with the archive, or "learning" on the part of the user, remains unproven, but these case studies demonstrate that for marketing purposes the use of social networking strategies to raise awareness of the archive repository's collections and related events has clearly been very effective–and in this, the public sector is quickly learning lessons from the commercial sector. The last few years especially has witnessed a growing mass of "fan" sites for cultural heritage institutions. Facebook users can become fans of anything from the Hoole Special Collection to the Quilt Index to the Museum of Modern Art. This approach can be very useful in developing a relationship with communities of users. Becoming a fan of a cultural heritage institution is a way for users to signify allegiance or loyalty to an organization. It is simultaneously an expression that becomes a characteristic of one's constructed online identity and a badge of allegiance in one's personal profile. The archive thus becomes collectively "owned" by those who value it. While the educational hopes for Facebook might have hinged on having interactive engagement with potential end users, the growth of such fan sites or group pages for cultural heritage organizations stand as strong examples of viral marketing tactics, aimed at increasing awareness in the short term and increased usage of the archive in the long term.

In the case of archival institutions, where experimentation is in its early phases, it is still difficult to measure the precise effectiveness of such tactics, but it is clear that each project is reaping tangible benefits, yielding results that are already being built on for further outreach work and providing valuable lessons. As Lacher-Feldman's case study indicates, her investment in developing a fan page for the W. S. Hoole Special Collections is already increasing awareness of lectures and raising numbers as a result. The Second Life project presents even more compelling positive results, with more than 200 avatars spending 30 minutes or more looking at the collections. They can now say that 400 people are more aware of Stanford's Special Collections and University Archives collections in the space of just two months.

Authors describe the unanticipated benefits of social networking tactics in similar ways–in each case, professional and peer networking opportunities were opened, enabling engagement with other cultural heritage institutions and possibilities for future collaboration or reciprocal marketing. For example, the use of Facebook to promote the Hoole Special Collections lecture series has created opportunities for creative partnerships with organizations across campus interested in collaborating on lecture series development.

In addition, social networking tools can effectively support professional learning communities, from the use of Twitter "hash tags" to track discussions of interest to the creation of online social network spaces to enable group discussion and knowledge sharing. Such tools, then, allow communities to emerge and cohere, with social ties and networks established. Thus, these channels can be used to promote the expertise and reputation of the archivist and so strengthen the reputation of the archival institution itself.

It is clear from this work that there is no one-size-fits-all solution when it comes to selecting a particular Web 2.0 tool or tools as a means for promotion and/or communication. These activities appear to highlight that the question of "which technology?" should not precede that of "which audience?" or "what are we hoping to achieve?" Indeed, several of the authors highlight the need to clarify objectives, establish measures, and put benchmarks in place before embarking on such an activity again. As Lacher-Feldman observes:

> recording quantitative information for the lecture series, such as taking quick head counts and tracking increases in traffic from before and after implementing Facebook can provide some insight, provided you regularly count heads at lectures. Comparing or documenting anecdotal information such as hearing feedback from individuals who express themselves by posting on the page, or documenting those who contact you via e-mail or Facebook, or by simply commenting that if they hadn't gotten your invitation on Facebook, they would not have known of the event. Any and all observations help to justify and rationalize this effort both to yourself as the outreach person and to your administration. (See pp. 59–60.)

The Second Life and Twitter case studies both highlight the need to more critically assess whether the targeted audience is being reached. While increased numbers in followers or "virtual visits" to the archives in Second Life are certainly positive outcomes of these activities, it is critical that with continuing work mechanisms are built in for assessing actually *who* is being reached and whether reaching a (perhaps unintended) new audience is as strategically important as reaching the community the archival institution is directly funded to serve. As Mattie Taormina notes:

> [a]lthough the Second Life team remains excited about the virtual archives, we are unsure of whether we are reaching our target audience: the Stanford community and other primary source-dependent scholars. Despite a growing awareness of virtual technologies, not many Stanford faculty or students are using SL yet, making the virtual archives still somewhat unknown to our own immediate community. Outside scholars seem to be elusive as well. Many visitors tend to be people who stumble upon the virtual archives and are unaware of what an archives is. (See p. 49.)

Medina-Smith poses similar questions as to the efficacy of Twitter in reaching the Jewish Women's Archive's target audience. Social media, she cautions, "is not a panacea for our outreach (or development) goals." While they appear to have reached many users, she asks: "does it connect us to people already in our community?" And so their next step will involve a more critical evaluation of whether they are, indeed, where the users are.

Renegotiating the Relationship between Archivist and User

> I encouraged writing about personal connections to any of the photographs so that readers could sense that photographs make connections with our lives and are not just artifacts kept in archival boxes reserved for scholarly use. Our writing styles were to reflect our personalities, but more so that of the material—the photographs of Hugh Morton. (See p. 27.)

In whatever way we choose to identify and reach out to users, those practicing outreach have essentially assumed that there is a defined relationship between the archivist as the provider and the researcher as the consumer. Typically, in the real-world context, the archivist is the "expert" who controls the environment, produces the finding aids, and guides the researcher through the process and then allows access, under strictly controlled conditions. In this scenario, the researcher is the passive consumer who listens to the message, reads the rules, and sits down quietly with the documents. The researcher then engages with the documents in a physical format. This one-way relationship is perhaps a direct result of physical constraints in the environment in which we work, particularly the reading room, with the archive safely locked away from sight and potential damage. But the space itself reflects the traditional archival paradigm that underpins our practice, in which the archivist is positioned as gatekeeper and protector. These spaces remain rarefied environments, with users requiring the expertise of the archivist to help them access and understand the documents.

The traditional connotation of the archive is of a formal and perhaps forbidding space, akin to a church or temple,[23] where relics are handled with reverence and silence reigns. This context has been about ensuring the preservation of the archive, protecting it from harm. But by protecting the archive, the archivist may be seen as "controlling the researchers" and so the "intermediary power of the archivist"[24] may effectively impede access to the material.

Perhaps the most ambitious digital project among these case studies concerns the use of Second Life. Here the aim was to recreate the experience of the archival reading room in a fully simulated online environment, which allows "patron browsing to become more interactive and three-dimensional, making the search experience more experiential." Great pains were taken to recreate the experience of being in a physical archival space, but with significant barriers removed:

> the boxes in our remote deep storage facility would be replicated virtually so that, for the first time, scholars could browse our closed manuscript collections stacks—a practice not offered in real life. Avatars could open a particular Hollinger box and see a sampling of scanned documents from that box appear along with a link to the

collection's online finding aid. It would be a method of browsing, not searching. (See pp. 44–45.)

It might be argued that such an approach perhaps simply reproduces the traditional paradigm of rarefied access, described above. Not only are barriers removed, with users able to browse stacks and virtually handle materials, new possibilities also open up—the archive is now freely accessible to all, and opportunities for collaboration and discussion of the archive emerge. The true potential for collaboration in these spaces is perhaps yet to be realized, but the early evidence is very positive, with virtual seminars already being held in the space. The trope of the traditional archival space thus becomes a meaningful anchoring point, which helps unfamiliar users of Second Life navigate the space in meaningful ways.

Interestingly, though, Taormina highlights a key challenge as one of perception—that such an approach might degrade or devalue the role of the archive, "trivializing" the experience of archival research. Concerns over authority, but also trust, quality, and credibility, begin to surface as we consider the specific value proposition of the archivist as a trusted provider and how this value gets translated, or potentially lost or diminished, in online contexts.

Such experiments indicate that we might be radically required to rethink our professional personae as we consider new mechanisms for representing not only the archive but the archivist as facilitator, getting information out to users "at the point of their information need."[25] At the heart of this change is a more collaborative relationship, more transparency and demystification of process, and a decentering of authority. This view, that we "reconceptualise our basic services and procedures from the user's point of view" is by no means a new one.[26] In 1989, Randall Jimerson stated that "visibility" was essential if we were to manage this transition.[27] These new technologies enable us to achieve this visibility more easily and in more effective ways. For instance, Stephen J. Fletcher and his colleagues chose to implement a processing blog to manage expectations about the availability of the Morton collection and also to reveal the processes of "ongoing archival work on a newly acquired collection." They hoped also to solicit comments and feedback on posted images from

the collections, which, in turn, would feed into the official documentation
of the collection:

> By sharing these challenges, we would also be providing glimpses into how photo-
> graphic archivists work. If people could understand the challenges we confronted,
> then they might understand why it would take some time before the collection could
> be made available for use. I also hoped that other photographic archivists might join
> in our discussions and share their ideas and experiences. (See p. 24.)

At the Society of American Archivists conference in 2009, in several
sessions on Web 2.0, David Weinberger's phrase "transparency is the new
objectivity" was invoked several times.[28] Projects such as *A View to Hugh*
begin to demonstrate what transparency might mean in the context of
outreach. As we move to this new way of working, rendering our processes
transparent, and making archives (and ourselves as archivists) visible, we
simultaneously move from a notion of interaction characterized by white
gloves and whispers, to one of dialogue, mutual learning, and respect. This
is a fundamental renegotiation of the archival proposition and the personae
of the archivist changes in this new context of openness and sharing. Each
case study illustrates this shift to openness, the hope for a new contract of
engagement between user and archivist—one which, to varying degrees,
decentralizes the seemingly objective authority of the archivist.

The advent of the digital means we now negotiate new spaces, more
diffuse and heterogeneous, and, as a result, the relationship between
archivist and user changes. But achieving transparency is not just a simple
case of lifting the veil and revealing the "real" archivist beneath. In the
case studies detailing the uses of social networking tools such as Facebook
and Twitter, we see that such exposure can require negotiation of the
"authentic personae"—the use of oneself as an outreach tool can surface
new tensions that challenge us to reflect on the implications of this type
of more intimate and exposed engagement.

Certainly, there is a sense in which social spaces invite a more personal
approach to outreach within a global online context. They encourage us
to combine the professional and personal, so that we engage with people
on an informal level, but at the same time, hope to interest them in what

we have to say. Jessica Lacher-Feldman, for example, describes how she decided to provide some personal information in the Facebook fan page, so that she was not a faceless individual, but instead an active member of the social network:

> I have found that one of the most significant challenges to using Facebook is striking a balance between my personal and private persona and the persona and role I play as an information provider and advocate for my repository and its holdings. My own approach to Facebook was to create a space for myself and to build on that presence by providing information and access to my repository in ways that I see fit. (See p. 62.)

This act alone highlights how the medium selected will very much affect the type of persona adopted on the part of the archival institution. Lacher-Feldman's approach required a blurring of the personal and the professional that was at times uneasy, balancing the need to be one's authentic self against that of being the face and voice of the institution. As personal friendships blur into these "professional" spaces, it can be a challenge to manage one's identity (and messages) accordingly.

A similar challenge emerges with the use of Twitter as an outreach device. In the last few years, a plethora of cultural heritage institutions and libraries have jumped onto the Twitter bandwagon as its global usage has escalated to quite staggering proportions (though this rate of growth is now showing signs of slowing).[29] Like many other organizations, the Jewish Women's Archive (JWA) opted to create an account for the institution—not an individual within it. Twitter works on the principle of people signing up to "follow" an account. Interestingly, the JWA made the decision to only follow back peer institutions and not reciprocate "follows" from individuals. This decision stemmed from concerns that to do so would make filtering the quantity of tweets extremely difficult. The JWA tweets, therefore, are more like "micro-blog" entries—relatively one-directional, "tweeted" for the purposes of information sharing as opposed to dialogue or conversation (which is perhaps at odds with their original rationale for adopting Twitter).

This trend is not universal; for instance, Nova Scotia Archives[30] and the Archives Hub[31] have consciously decided to reciprocally follow and converse (where appropriate) with the community. But this decision is perhaps not one to take lightly. What sort of voice should an institutional Twitter account adopt, and how much is this voice shaped by the personality of whoever happens to be responsible for the account at the time? How much time should be spent on Twitter and how much benefit will it bring to the institution? It is worth considering the potential risks of such a decision before undertaking it—especially because inappropriate tweets by an individual and personal voice may have an impact on the reputation of the institution. Certainly, many organizations are now having conversations about the issue of voice and thinking about a Twitter editorial policy before launching in, and the lessons learned in the last year alone have been invaluable.

Conclusion

According to Andrew Hinton, the web is "becoming the place of record for conversations, stories and even our identities, and that is because it is such a perfect medium for people to associate, connect, and discover. We know that if we do it there, it has the best chance for exposure, response and relevance."[32] Archives are, at their core, about preserving as well as mediating memory and identity. We are now working to situate archives, and archivists, within these spaces of collective memory and sharing.

Successful outreach will continue to require diverse approaches, encompassing education, interaction, communication, dialogue and reaching people who do not necessarily ever visit the archives building. Increasingly, we are not going to be directly serving the user but enabling the user to serve him- or herself.[33] Part of our role should be to stimulate ideas around memory and identity, to help create an enhanced sense of place and time and therefore to convey the importance of our role and the role of archives within our societies. Web 2.0 gives us the opportunity to think not just about promoting our collections through online and traditional finding aids but also about working to present them more imaginatively—to engage in dialogue and build communities in and around archives.

The authors of these case studies are among the pioneers of these new forms of outreach, deploying new technologies innovatively not only to raise awareness of the archive but also to encourage new forms of interaction with it. As these stories attest, we are still very much in a period of experimentation, taking calculated—and sometimes less calculated—risks to enter into these new spaces and provide an opening into the archive.[34] The authors describe the clear and tangible benefits that have been realized through their work, with outreach activities now reaching new users, raising awareness, and increasing usage of collections. But we also see notes of caution, practical points on how such activity might be undertaken more effectively in the future. There is evidence of new and interesting tensions emerging around the blurring of the personal with the professional, the challenges faced by the drive to develop a new kind of transparency and demystification of the archival process, to decenter archival authority, while at the same time balancing this against a need to maintain quality and trust and not lose sight of the value of the archivist as facilitator.

A common thread throughout these case studies concerns the power of serendipity, and each relates incidents of unexpected and positive outcomes. It is clear that while we can learn from these innovative projects as we progress with our own social media outreach projects, many of these new technologies remain in flux, as communications tools and as "social ecosystems." New audiences and new patterns of usage are emerging at a rapid pace, and perhaps it feels almost impossible to keep abreast of these shifts. But even as we negotiate this complexity, thanks to the work of these authors and others, we are also amassing an array of potential use cases for these tools—invaluable use cases that are helping us approach similar ventures. Even as we take these steps, we must accept, and even embrace, the fact that as we enter these new spaces of engagement, we often cannot predict, let alone control, the results.

Notes

1 Clay Shirky, "Here Comes Everybody," speech delivered at "Web 2.0 Expo 2008," http://blip.tv/file/855937 (accessed September 15, 2010).

2 Joy Palmer, "Archives 2.0: If We Build It, Will They Come?", *Ariadne* 60 (July 2009), http://www.ariadne.ac.uk/issue60/palmer/ (accessed September 15, 2010).

3 Timothy L. Ericson, "Preoccupied with Our Own Gardens: Outreach and Archivists," *Archivaria* 31 (1990–91): 118 (emphasis added).

4 Victory Gray, " 'Who's That Knocking on Our Door?': Archives Outreach and Community," *Journal of the Society of Archivists* 29 (2008): 1.

5 Elsie Freeman Freivogel, "Education Programs: Outreach as an Administrative Function," *American Archivist* 41 (April 1978): 147.

6 Society of American Archivists, "Reference Access and Outreach Section Administrative History," http://www.archivists.org/saagroups/rao/raohistory.asp (accessed September 15, 2010).

7 Richard Pearce-Moses, comp., *A Glossary of Archival and Records Terminology*, Society of American Archivists, 2005, http://www.archivists.org/glossary/term_details.asp?DefinitionKey=944 (accessed September 15, 2010).

8 Emily Ford, "Outreach Is (un)Dead," *The Library with a Lead Pipe Blog*, http://inthelibrarywiththeleadpipe.org/2009/outreach-is-undead/ (accessed September 15, 2010).

9 Tamar G. Chute, "Perspectives on Outreach at College and University Archives," in *College and University Archives: Readings in Theory and Practice*, ed. C. J. Prom and E. D. Swain, 145–147 (Chicago: Society of American Archivists, 2008).

10 Daniel V. Pitti, "Encoded Archival Description: The Development of an Encoding Standard for Archival Finding Aids," *American Archivist* 60 (Summer 1997): 268–283.

11 National Council on Archives, "Archives On-Line: The Establishment of a United Kingdom Archival Network" (1998), http://www.ncaonline.org.uk/materials/archivesonline.pdf (accessed December 10, 2010).

12 Wendy M. Duff and Penka Stoyanova, "Transforming the Crazy Quilt: Archival Displays from the User's Point of View," *Archivaria* 45 (Spring 1998): 44–79.

13 Elizabeth J. Shaw, "Rethinking EAD: Balancing Flexibility and Interoperability," *New Review of Information Networking* 7, no. 1 (2001): 117–131.

14 IBM developerWorks Interviews: Tim Berners-Lee, August 22, 2006, http://www.ibm.com/developerworks/podcast/dwi/cm-int082206txt.html (accessed September 12, 2010).

15 Clay Shirky, "How Social Media Can Make History," *TED* (June 2009), http://www.ted.com/talks/clay_shirky_how_cellphones_twitter_facebook_can_make_history.html (accessed September 8, 2010).

16 Felix Hill, "The Archivist and Society," *Journal of the Society of Archivists* 6 (1979): 128.

17 Timothy L. Ericson, "Preoccupied with Our Own Gardens: Outreach and Archivists," *Archivaria* 31 (1990–91): 114.

18 Lorcan Dempsey, "Web Scale," *Lorcan Dempsey's Weblog*, January 5, 2007, http://orweblog.oclc.org/archives/001238.html (accessed September 15, 2010).

19 Lorcan Dempsey, "Libraries and the Long Tail: Some Thoughts about Libraries in a Network Age," *D-Lib Magazine* 12 (April 2006), http://www.dlib.org/dlib/april06/dempsey/04dempsey.html (accessed September 15, 2010).

[20] Committee of Inquiry into the Changing Learner Experience, *Higher Education in a Web 2.0 World* (March 2009), 9, http://www.jisc.ac.uk/media/documents/publications/heweb20rptv1.pdf (accessed September 15, 2010).

[21] Stephen Abrams, "Web 2.0, Library 2.0 and Librarian 2.0: Preparing for the 2.0 World," *Online Information Conference* (December 4, 2007), http://www.online-information.co.uk/online08/files/freedownloads.new_link1.1080622103251.pdf (accessed September 8, 2010).

[22] Danah Boyd, "Viewing American Class Divisions Through Facebook and MySpace," *Apophenia Blog Essay* (June 24, 2007), http://www.danah.org/papers/essays/ClassDivisions.html (accessed September 15, 2010).

[23] See Eric Ketelaar, "Archival Temples, Archival Prisons: Modes of Power and Protection," *Archival Science* 2 (2002): 221–238.

[24] Randall C. Jimerson, *Archives Power: Memory, Accountability and Social Justice* (Chicago: Society of American Archivists, 2009).

[25] Ann M. Lally and Carolyn E. Dunford, "Using Wikipedia to Extend Digital Collections," *D-Lib Magazine* 13, no. 5/6 (May/June 2007), http://www.dlib.org/dlib/may07/lally/05lally.html (accessed September 12, 2010).

[26] Randall C. Jimerson, "Redefining Archival Identity: Meeting User Needs in the Information Society," *American Archivist* 52 (Summer 1989): 338.

[27] Ibid., 339.

[28] David Weinberger, "Transparency Is the New Objectivity," *JOHO The Blog*, July 19, 2009, http://www.hyperorg.com/blogger/2009/07/19/transparency-is-the-new-objectivity/ (accessed September 9, 2010).

[29] "Twitter's Tweet Smell of Success," *Nielsen Wire Online*, March 18, 2009, http://blog.nielsen.com/nielsenwire/online_mobile/twitters-tweet-smell-of-success/ (accessed September 8, 2010).

[30] See http://twitter.com/ns_archives (accessed September 15, 2010). See also Kate Theimer, *Web 2.0 Tools and Strategies for Archives and Local History Collections* (London, England: Facet Publishing, 2010), 121–136.

[31] See http://twitter.com/archiveshub (accessed September 15, 2010).

[32] Andrew Hinton, "The Machineries of Context: New Architectures for a New Dimension," *Journal of Information Architecture* 1 (2009): 41.

[33] Online Computer Library Center, "Perceptions of Libraries and Information Resources: A Report to the OCLC Membership" (2005), http://www.oclc.org/reports/pdfs/Percept_all.pdf (accessed September 15, 2010).

[34] Chute, "Perspectives on Outreach at College and University Archives," 145–147.

A View to *A View to Hugh*: Reflections on the Creation of a Processing Blog

Stephen J. Fletcher

Overview of Repository

The Hugh Morton Collection of Photographs and Films is the largest and perhaps most significant photographic collection in the North Carolina Collection Photographic Archives, which is part of the North Carolina Collection at the University of North Carolina at Chapel Hill Library. The North Carolina Collection comprises a research library, gallery, and photographic archives and is one of the departments within the Louis Round Wilson Special Collections Library. The North Carolina Collection documents the history, literature, and culture of the state by actively collecting, organizing, and providing access to publications, photographs, and artifacts to build a comprehensive and lasting collection that represents the diversity of North Carolina and its people. The North Carolina Collection encourages use of its holdings by the university community, citizens of North Carolina, and other researchers throughout the world, regardless of affiliation.

The Morton collection contains an estimated 500,000 photographic items and 60,000 feet of moving image material. The North Carolina Collection Photographic Archives contains an estimated 1.5 million photographic and other pictorial items. As the North Carolina Collection Photographic

Archivist with direct curatorial responsibility for the Morton collection, I report to the curator of the North Carolina Collection. Elizabeth Hull is the Hugh Morton Collection Archivist, hired specifically to process the collection for a term of two to three years. She is a member of the Wilson Library Special Collections Technical Services Department.

Business Drivers

We were not motivated to use a Web 2.0 tool for the sake of using a Web 2.0 tool. The idea of creating a "processing blog"—a blog that would share with an audience the ongoing archival work on a newly acquired collection—emerged as a possible solution for a specific problem: the acquisition of a voluminous and mostly unorganized collection with minimal or no documentation that would in all certainty be in high demand, yet would take two to three years to make available to researchers—even using the principles of "More Product, Less Process" (MPLP) advocated by Mark Greene and Dennis Meissner.[1]

The challenge we faced was the photographic archive of Hugh MacRae Morton (1921–2006), a widely known and influential twentieth-century North Carolinian, promoter, businessman, conservationist, public servant, and prolific photographer and filmmaker. Within the state of North Carolina and regionally in the Blue Ridge Mountains, Morton is known as the developer of Grandfather Mountain, a major tourist attraction that Morton's surviving family donated to North Carolina in 2008 and is now a state park. Morton also had a deep love for the University of North Carolina at Chapel Hill, which he attended as a member of the class of 1943 until he enlisted in the military in the autumn of 1942 and served as a combat newsreel cameraman in the South Pacific. Made first when Morton was a student and later when he was a supporter and sports enthusiast, his photographs of the university span decades. Over the years he became well connected politically and briefly ran in the Democratic gubernatorial primary from December 1971 to mid-February 1972.

Before we acquired the Morton collection, we had reason to believe that there was no identifying information about what was depicted in the photographs and negatives. (To paraphrase something the photographer's wife often said: "He has it all in his head!") Though not as bad as we feared, a very high percentage of the photographs and negatives are completely unidentified, though some, such as UNC campus scenes and views of Grandfather Mountain, are recognizable. Fortunately and unfortunately, Morton only wrote minimal topical information on negative sleeves and slide boxes when he did label them; for example, a sleeve with negatives might be labeled with the name of an event, but the people represented in the individual images are not identified. So while it was not *all* in his head, a great deal of it was.

With that scenario, my immediate hopes were that a processing blog would let interested parties know why the collection was such a challenge to process and that as we worked on the collection we could inform them about our progress. In doing so I believed we could also discuss problems we would encounter and present our solutions in a manner that nonarchivists could understand. By sharing these challenges, we would also be providing glimpses into how photographic archivists work. If people could understand the challenges we confronted, then they might understand why it would take some time before the collection could be made available for use. I also hoped that other photographic archivists might join in our discussions and share their ideas and experiences. I further believed that, if we could highlight discoveries we made along the way, we could slowly promote the collection and thus begin to garner underlying support for the collection. With growing interest, we could also solicit information about selected images from the blog's eventual readership or even from casual visitors who might find the site through their web searches on topics that had been discussed in the blog. All of this would, hopefully, foster continuing discussion with input from readers and build additional awareness of the richness of the Morton collection.

Setting the Stage

For the temporal context of *A View to Hugh*, I had the idea of creating a processing blog for the Morton collection sometime during the spring of 2006, probably subconsciously after driving back from Grandfather Mountain near Linville, North Carolina, surrounded by boxes in a fully packed passenger van. It was on that trip that Robert Anthony, curator of the North Carolina Collection, and I met with members of the Morton family to discuss the collection's future. We saw the collection in its raw state for the first time and learned that the collection—or at least what we could take back with us in two vans on the first of two trips—was heading to its new home in Chapel Hill. (The second trip required two more vans.) I certainly remember talking about a processing blog in a general sense with colleagues during the Society of American Archivists' annual meeting that summer. Formal acquisition of the Morton collection occurred in February 2007, and Elizabeth Hull began work that September. She and I began to create the blog very soon after her arrival.

The above time line illustrates the informal roots of the Morton processing blog, and we were in experimental mode from the start. We faced no institutional formalities or approval processes and wrote no mission statement, policies, nor measures of success. We did, however, need to work through the Library Systems Department, which first began using blogs for its own internal needs in May 2005. Starting in January 2006, Library Systems began servicing other internal library blogs on the staff intranet. Sometime during that year, Library Systems began using WordPress.[2] That history predetermined the software platform for creating the blog.

A View to Hugh (http://www.lib.unc.edu/blogs/morton/) debuted on November 1, 2007, the third public blog published by the university library. The North Carolina Collection's *North Carolina Miscellany* (http://www.lib.unc.edu/blogs/ncm/), begun in June 2005, was the first public blog created by a library department, but it was not brought under Library Systems' managed hardware until a year later. That blog features items from the North Carolina Collection, typically with a few descriptive or contextual sentences. The second predecessor to *A View to Hugh* is *Carolina Science Concourse* (http://www.lib.unc.edu/blogs/science/), first published in mid-July 2007 but with only seven posts by the time *A View to Hugh* went live three-and-a-half months later.

For the developmental context of *A View to Hugh*, I looked at numerous blogs for design ideas and to get a sense of how people used them. I had a little bit of experience using a WordPress-hosted blog to help manage my daughter's soccer team but not enough exposure to the various ways people used or contributed to blogs. During my explorations, I did not limit my survey to archival blogs; I looked at all types, including photoblogs where a photograph rather than writing takes center stage. During this process I discovered a useful presentation by Matt Mullenweg, the founding developer of WordPress.[3] Mullenweg recommends that blog designers take a pencil and paper, go to a quiet place away from daily distractions, and start sketching. So I did, drawing several sketches of what I thought the blog might look like based upon all the blogs I surveyed. The final design for *A View to Hugh* looks very little like anything I sketched, but the process made me think about the visual elements and organizational structure of the blog.

One of the first design decisions we needed to make was to determine the role for images. The Morton collection is a photographic collection, but I quickly dismissed the photoblog format, which focuses almost entirely on a single image and leaves little room for narrative or discussion. We soon developed a preference for a three-column layout, which would allow us to feature photographs in the center column but at the same time allow for extensive writing when we wanted that option and provide better overall searching, navigation, and linking within either of the side columns. As we examined WordPress "themes" (design templates), we selected a three-column layout called "Blue Zinfandel." Having completed the sketching process, that theme just felt right to me when I saw it. Elizabeth chose a Morton photograph from which she cropped a panoramic detail for the banner, while two members of the Library Systems staff adapted Blue Zinfandel to meet our needs. She and I chipped in with refinements, but essentially information technology (IT) staff did IT stuff. We considered one final design element: a small representative gallery of thumbnails in one of the columns. We investigated gallery plug-ins but decided to wait until we had a sufficient number of images posted on the blog to revisit that possibility, in part because implementation would prolong the blog's publication.

We did little testing other than making sure that the programming worked offline on a web development server. There were no formal usability studies. We developed two simple goals while working on the blog: create a clean, simple design, and write in a conversational tone (i.e., not academic) that would foster broad readership and participation. I encouraged writing about personal connections to any of the photographs so that readers could sense that photographs make connections with our lives and are not just artifacts kept in archival boxes reserved for scholarly use. Our writing styles were to reflect our personalities, but more so that of the material— the photographs of Hugh Morton. At first Elizabeth and I shared writing duties, but as her knowledge about the collection grew she did most of the writing. Eventually other writers contributed posts, including some graduate students working with the collection and a devoted volunteer who knew Hugh Morton and frequently offered comments on the blog.

Results

Results and success are very difficult to gauge with blogs. Another of Mullenberg's recommendations is "Have Metrics for Everything You Do." In his presentation he states, "if you're not measuring the things that your users are doing and the metrics of your success, you're never going to know when you get there." He recommends asking yourself, "What is it that there will be more of or less of that means you're successful," adding that we might not know yet what makes for "successful blogging" and suggesting that the answer may be rooted in the number of page views and comments a post may receive.

Despite Mullenweg placing high value on metrics, WordPress has limited statistical tools. Web usage statistics are, unfortunately, also very problematical because in terms of page views, "bots" (computer programs that harvest information from web pages) and RSS feed aggregators wildly inflate the number of "hits" a website receives. Estimating the number of "visits" is a different statistical measurement designed to counter that inflation. In terms of the library's web statistics for its managed blogs, *North Carolina Miscellany* consistently ranks first in hits and *A View to Hugh* is second. (See Figure 1.) As measured by "visits," however, *A View to Hugh* surpassed *North Carolina Miscellany* in June 2008 and, with the

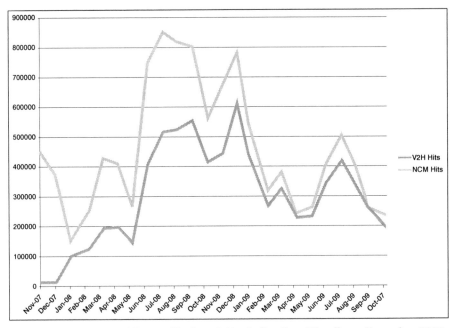

Figure 1: "Hits" on *A View to Hugh* and *North Carolina Miscellany*, November 2007–
October 2009.

exception of July 2009, has continuously ranked first through October 31,
2009.[4] (See Figure 2.)

After exactly two years, we had written 131 posts—an average of 5.5
posts per month. The blog received 903 "approved" comments and 1,480
instances of "comment spam," which is spam masquerading as a comment
that may or may not sound like it is pertinent to the post. WordPress does
an admirable job of capturing comment spam in a holding area for review.
Some of the filter's approved comments, however, still "smell like spam." We
delete the obvious ones that get past the spam filter, but we let some stay if
they sound genuine just in case they are real. With those caveats concerning spam and comments, each post averages about seven comments. We do
not moderate comments, meaning that readers' comments appear online
instantaneously. This helps enliven discussion, especially if we have written a post related to a current topic in the news. The downside of this decision is the need to sift through comments daily and delete spam not caught
by the spam filter. As with tallying hits and visits, counting comments is

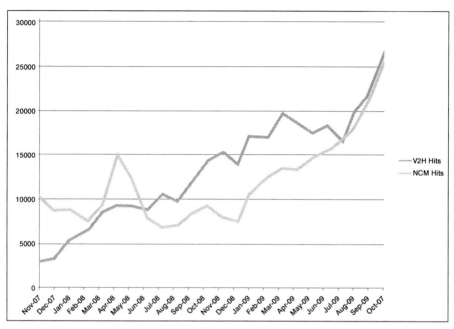

Figure 2: "Visits" to *A View to Hugh* and *North Carolina Miscellany,* November 2007–October 2009.

only a relative measure of success; total readership is significantly greater than those who leave comments.

So if counting page hits, visits, and comments are not good metrics for evaluating a blog's successfulness, what is it that "there is more of or less of" that proves the blog has been successful? Here are some examples that are more like "intangibles" than the results of metrics. One of our goals was to provide readers a glimpse into processing the Morton collection so they might have a better understanding about what archivists do. We have thus far created 27 categories that we assigned to posts, and the most frequently used has been "Behind the Scenes" (44 posts). That category means that a post focuses on or includes some discussion that relates to processing the collection, so a third of our posts address that goal. The blog led to our dedicated volunteer who has helped us immensely with identifications. The blog has given graduate students who work with the collection an opportunity to share their insights and experiences. Blog readers have identified many photographs, enhancing future access to those images. Sometimes we stir up enthusiasm without even trying: ten minutes before leaving work on a UNC–Duke basketball game day, I quickly mounted a post using an unidentified color slide from a past game with minimal text. It remained the blog's most-commented-on post more than a year and a half later. Other library departments saw what a blog could do and created their own. And perhaps most satisfying of all: we have not received a single e-mail or telephone call wondering why the Morton collection has taken so long to process. So despite the lack of hard-and-fast statistics, we know we have broadened awareness about the Morton collection.

One tangible accomplishment undoubtedly contributed to increased readership. In February 2008, *A View to Hugh* won *ArchivesNext*'s Best Use of Web 2.0 Technologies Award.

Challenges

Our first challenge emerged after writing a post that unwittingly touched on a contentious topic, revealed to us by reader comments. We decided to let the comments play out in the spirit of scholarly debate and to focus our writing on the photographs of Hugh Morton and not the person of Hugh Morton. Less dramatic but equally important is the responsibility of coming up with content on a consistent basis. If posts are added sporadically, readers will drift away. To retain readers, our posts usually have substantive writing, which takes time—time that could be spent processing the collection. Determining the appropriate amount of time to spend creating a post is very subjective, with some topics meriting longer text and other subjects relatively little. And sifting through the spam issues noted above is a bit annoying, but not burdensome.

One disappointment has been that archivists, photographic or otherwise, seemingly do not contribute comments. We know many archivists and colleagues read the blog because they tell us how much they enjoy it when we see them at professional meetings and other gatherings.

Lessons Learned

"Think 1.0" is another Mullenweg guideline that means get your blog out there as soon as possible. Learn from user feedback. You'll make mistakes and encounter unexpected situations; learn from them, too. Pay attention to details: unless the situation does not permit, we always have a second pair of eyes look at a post before posting, with an eye for things such as typographical errors and improper punctuation, style issues (I turn to the *Chicago Manual of Style* when in doubt), and nonfunctioning links. Involve other staff to share the limelight and recruit other contributors for a variety of voices—but at the same time keep a harmonious style. This also parcels out the workload, helping to negate the time spent away from collection processing. Follow up on blog comments—at least the useful ones—and say thanks or even send a separate e-mail offline. This creates an atmosphere of dialog and encourages future readership and participation.

As I've thought about the question on what I wish I had know before I got started, I've honestly concluded that I'm glad I knew very little. This kept the excitement and enthusiasm levels high as we explored a new endeavor.

Next Steps

Our overarching idea for the Morton collection is to leverage *A View to Hugh* to capitalize on its success. We have yet to develop a gallery for images used within the blog, but recent developments by the library's web team utilizing Media RSS may allow us to do so. A CONTENTdm collection (http://www.lib.unc.edu/dc/morton/) has been created to showcase highlights from the collection, and we now make connections between blog entries and records in the CONTENTdm collection. Now clicking on an image in the blog opens a doorway into more than 2,000 scanned Morton images at the time of this writing. We incorporated a feedback form into the digital collection, but to date we have not made it function like blog comments.

More significantly, we developed a successful proposal funded by the North Carolina Humanities Council to hire humanities scholars to write essays based around selected images in the Morton collection. The essays, 1,000 to 1,500 words long, will analyze predominate subjects and themes within the collection. Authors will be drawn from a pool of interdisciplinary scholars and writers who are established authorities on their topic. The essays will be added to a special section of *A View to Hugh*.

From a design standpoint, advancements in WordPress (and the inevitable conflicts with web browsers that result) will likely cause us to select a different template than Blue Zinfandel and thus redesign the site. Tampering with success can be risky. Finally, the library is looking at Omeka as a possible tool for developing online exhibits. It is a program that is very similar to WordPress, so it may be possible to make connections between posts in *A View to Hugh*, online exhibits, and CONTENTdm records.

Notes

[1] Mark A. Greene and Dennis Meissner, "More Product, Less Process: Revamping Traditional Archival Processing," *American Archivist* 68 (Fall/Winter 2005): 208–263.

[2] The software can be acquired from http://www.wordpress.org; www.wordpress.com is a website for hosted blogs.

[3] Matt Mullenweg, "The First 100K Users Are Always the Hardest," presentation at BayCHI (San Francisco Bay Area chapter of the Association for Computing Machinery, Special Interest Group on Computer-Human Interaction), August 8, 2006, http://www.baychi.org/calendar/20060808a/ (accessed December 10, 2010).

[4] A visit is defined as "a sequence of requests from a uniquely identified client that expired after a certain amount of inactivity" (see the entry for "web analytics" on http://www.wikipedia.org). The UNC Library uses Webalizer to compile its web usage statistics and visits are determined by the Webalizer "total entry pages" calculation.

"Broadcast Yourself": Putting Iowa State University's History on YouTube

Michele A. Christian and Tanya Zanish-Belcher

Overview of Repository

The Special Collections Department was created at the Iowa State University Library in 1969. Its mission is to identify, select, preserve, create access to, provide reference assistance for, and promote the use of rare and unique research materials that support major research areas of Iowa State University. The department maintains active public service, outreach, and tour programs for both on- and off-campus groups, including academic classes, the Center for Excellence in Learning and Teaching, the Honors Program, ISU Learning Communities, Extension and 4-H groups, and K–12 student groups such as National History Day. The seven-member department serves more than 150 researchers per month and responds to nearly 15,000 reference requests annually, in addition to hosting hundreds of other on-site visitors.

The collections include some 17,000 linear feet of archival materials documenting agriculture, natural history, statistics, veterinary medicine, and women in science and engineering. Included are manuscript collections donated by individuals and organizations not necessarily connected with ISU but reflective of the university's mission. The department also includes the University Archives, consisting of official records and faculty papers; more than 1,000,000 photographs; and 50,000 rare books dating back to

1475, with strengths in agriculture and the natural sciences. Finally, there are 10,000 motion picture films (dating from 1940 to 1980), the majority produced by the Iowa State Film Production Unit and WOI-TV. The collection also includes film footage that is related to manuscript collections, such as the Roswell Garst Family and the Rath Meat Packing Company.

Business Drivers

As noted above, the Special Collections Department has always been focused on outreach and public service. As efforts continued to digitize important parts of the collection, we at the department were pressed to find a new way to share this material outside of the Library's website, and Web 2.0 appeared to be a viable solution. Of particular concern was access to the department's 10,000 16mm motion picture films. With hundreds of millions of international users watching videos each day, YouTube was the obvious choice of the video sharing sites. We use YouTube in conjunction with our other Web 2.0 tools, such as Flickr and Scribd, which allow us to share photographs and documents easily. These tools have increased the department's visibility, not only outside of Iowa State University but, surprisingly, also on campus.

YouTube offered us a way to provide access to a collection that is not easily available to researchers. Until now, anyone wanting to watch the films had to visit the department's Reading Room and use specialized equipment for viewing archival film. YouTube gives the department an outlet to highlight many of the unique films in the collection and also removes the onus of providing storage and access for digitized films through the Library's servers. These films provide a means for ISU alumni to rediscover and share some of their moments as students by watching campus-related films.

Setting the Stage

After experiencing success using Flickr for its photograph collections, we decided that using YouTube would be an excellent way to provide access to the department's films. We organized the account in January 2008. The first technical issue was to determine how to best upload the films to YouTube. For the past few years, the university's Information Technology Services had been digitizing and transferring the department's 16mm films to DVD. Departmental staff had requested that some films be digitized based on the frequency of reproduction requests from patrons and researchers. As a general policy, a duplicate copy was always created for the department's collections as well. Because these films were already in a digital format, we selected them as the highest priority for YouTube. Once these initial films were loaded, we selected additional films based on varying factors, such as patron use, content and appeal, and requests. We have thus far focused on uploading films documenting Iowa State University, the state of Iowa, and agriculture.

Because we selected YouTube as our platform, we followed their requirements and suggestions for uploading videos. YouTube has limits on the size and length of the videos to be uploaded; the video cannot be more than 1 GB in size or more than ten minutes long.[1] YouTube also offers suggestions about what formats are most compatible, including .avi, .mov, .mp4, and .swf.[2] We elected to use .mp4, because these files could also be loaded to the department's iPods, which were purchased for patrons to listen to oral history interviews.

Because most of the films in the department are more than ten minutes long, we used software to edit the films into segments and create the .mp4 files. We selected Adobe Premiere for editing the films. Once we loaded the video into the computer, we edited the films into ten-minute segments. We created a simple set of text templates for titling each segment, which included the call number and title of the video and the segment number. We inserted text at the end to let the viewer know how he or she could acquire a reproduction.

After saving the segments, we loaded the videos into YouTube. Loading them backward, with the last segment uploaded first, puts the video segments for each film in the right order. When loading the films to YouTube, we included brief metadata about each film, such as the title, date, description, and names of key individuals in the film. YouTube also allows for the tagging of each video, and we chose terms as basic and specific as possible so researchers could easily locate what they needed. YouTube offers many features, such as allowing comments and ratings by viewers and allowing users to embed the videos to websites. To deter spammers from leaving comments, we selected the option to have the viewer comments be approved before they are posted on the web. We also chose not to allow the videos to be embedded in order to control their use.

Results

We have been pleased with the results thus far. After uploading more than fifty films to YouTube, patrons had viewed our videos more than 52,000 times and viewed our channel more than 4,000 times. According to YouTube's Insight program, the videos have attracted YouTube viewers from around the world, including countries such as Mozambique, Russia, Uruguay, and Indonesia. So far, sixty individuals have subscribed to our channel; we gain approximately two to four new subscribers each month. The department has also become "friends" with Iowa Public Television, Silos and Smokestacks National Heritage Area, ISU Athletics, ISU News Service, and ISU Extension. In YouTube a friends list is a contact list.[3] We chose to use the friends list as a way to connect the department's channel viewers to channels of other cultural institutions and Iowa State University units.

Some of the most popular films include several produced by the Iowa State University Film Production Unit and CINE Eagle Award winners, *When We Farmed with Horses* and *The Last Pony Mine*. Patrons have visited these two films 2,846 and 1,225 times, respectively. Other films that have received numerous hits include episodes of television shows produced by WOI-TV. The Fort Madison Prison episode of *In Our Care* is the most viewed video on the department's YouTube channel; it has received 7,144 views. It received nearly 5,000 views its first day and continues to get a few hundred views each month. Episodes of *The Magic Window*, a local children's show, are also popular. We had included several episodes of *The Whole Town's Talking*, a show from the 1950s dedicated to helping communities talk about some of the more pressing issues they faced,

Figure 1: "Bells of Iowa State" video on the ISU Library Special Collections Department YouTube channel.

including school consolidation, youth recreation, school funding, and Native American rights.

Thus far, the videos have been well received, and many viewers have contacted the department to ask for more episodes to be added. The best comments have come from those who seem to be emotionally attached to the videos. Several comments were made about the episodes of *The Magic Window*. They include:

> I loved this show as a kid. And that was some pretty snappy dialogue between Betty Lou and the puppets. My favorite line is "It would be a shame if you died and missed Christmas!"

> Oh my gosh!! I am so happy to find this on You Tube. I remember watching this when I was little!!! So funny to see it now that I am older. . . . Thanks again for posting it.

Thanks so much for posting this video. I grew up with WOI-TV and especially enjoyed the morning show with Betty Lou. I always tried the crafts she did but they never came out very good.... Thanks for bringing back an early childhood memory for me. I LOVED "Magic Window." Just the theme song alone made my day![4]

Many viewers have also contacted the department to request reproduction copies, and the department has experienced a major increase in the number of requests. Before uploading these films to YouTube, we had received, at the most, no more than a dozen requests each year. Currently, between three and six requests per month are received and we have adjusted our policies accordingly.

Throughout the ISU campus community, the department's YouTube channel has received some positive press, including being advertised to Iowa State University alumni through the ISU Alumni Association's newsletter. Articles have also appeared in the university's newsletter for faculty and staff, and the films' accessibility on YouTube have been emphasized in presentations for Alumni Weekend.

Challenges

The department has faced several minor challenges since starting the channel on YouTube. The first was the dedication of staff time to select and work with the films as well as keeping abreast of YouTube's new features. While the department has seven staff members, only two spent time working on these efforts. The department head supervised the project, prioritized film for digitizing, and provided needed feedback and support. The archivist spent considerable time learning software and managing the process of selecting and uploading film, which could be between fifteen and thirty minutes of prep work for the software to convert the file to .mp4. It takes approximately one to one and a half hours per ten-minute segment for the software to convert the file and an additional fifteen to thirty minutes to upload the video to YouTube. For a busy department, this dedication of staff time is a significant commitment.

The department's channel frequently received spammed comments. Many of these comments were invitations to other sites that were oftentimes obscene. This issue was easily handled by selecting the option to approve all comments before they went live and became available to all viewers.

Our most significant challenge concerns copyright issues. The majority of films were produced by the university and, consequently, the department has rights to reproduce and make them available. However, in some cases, nonexclusive reproductive rights had been given to a third party such as a distributor. This was especially true for the most popular films, such as *The Last Pony Mine* and *When We Farmed with Horses*. Although patrons were unable to download a high-quality film, the distributor remained convinced that the availability of even a low-resolution copy on the web would result in descreased demand for fee-based reproductions by the distributor. In reality, one could argue just the opposite—that a YouTube copy with an explicit link to the distributor could actually increase the film's visibility and marketability. After seeking guidance from the university's Information Technology Services, we decided to maintain access to the films in their entirety.

Another copyright challenge had to do with the uploading of the department's one episode of *Seventeen*, a popular local teenage dance show from 1958 produced by WOI-TV. YouTube decided to remove or mute videos containing Warner Music Group (WMG) music after negotiations with the company broke down in December 2008.[5] Unfortunately, WMG owned the copyright to many of the songs the teenagers danced to in the video, although they were of extremely poor quality, and in February 2009 the video had a copyright challenge. To be compliant, we could either remove audio for these selected songs or remove the entire film from YouTube. For the time being, we have decided to remove the film in its entirety but may add the portions back at a later date with the copyrighted sound removed. This is simply another Web 2.0 learning experience.

Lessons Learned

The greatest lesson we learned from this experience is the amount of time, effort, and labor involved with digitizing films, uploading them, and making them available on YouTube. While not difficult, it did require staff research and experimentation to learn the process, as it is not simply uploading an already existing file. Despite the time commitment, this experience has been worth it. As an outreach tool, YouTube has provided the department with a worldwide audience we never would have had otherwise.

Next Steps

We plan to continue to expand efforts with YouTube, as well as Flickr, iTunesU, and Scribd. In particular, we will focus on adding to YouTube some of the department's more critically acclaimed films, such as digitizing and uploading the remaining episodes of *The Whole Town's Talking*. The first several episodes were digitized using a grant from the National Television and Video Preservation Foundation (NTVPF). The series was funded by the Ford Foundation with the goal to "achieve a new and broader sort of audience participation program—through the involvement of the whole community. . . . It is trying to show that it can use the colorful limelight of a television setup to spark entire communities to a discussion of their problems." The discussions touch not only on school consolidation but also on the relationships between farm and town dwellers, services in the community for youth, and manufacturing.

We will also explore digitizing more of *In Our Care*, a series of documentaries filmed inside Iowa's mental hospitals, prisons, and other institutions. The series was awarded the National Sylvania Television Award for Production Excellence. These films provide perspectives and issues faced by Iowans in the mid-twentieth century that may enlighten those facing similar issues today.

Finally, we will be working collaboratively with the university's Information Technology Services, which has recently entered into a partner account with YouTube. We will also explore opportunities relating to grant funding and curriculum development utilizing film and video footage.

Notes

[1] "YouTube Help," Google, http://www.google.com/support/youtube/?hl=en (accessed December 14, 2010).

[2] "YouTube Help," Google, http://www.google.com/support/youtube/?hl=en (accessed December 14, 2010).

[3] "YouTube Glossary: Friends," Google, http://www.google.com/support/youtube/bin/answer.py?hl=en&answer=95408 (accessed May 18, 2009).

[4] "Magic Window with Betty Lou" (12/16/1955), http://www.youtube.com/watch?v=tMdolODeYDU (accessed December 14, 2010).

[5] Richard Koman, "YouTube Takes Down Thousands of Fair-use Videos," *ZDNet News & Blogs*, http://government.zdnet.com/?p=4484 (accessed April 13, 2009).

The Virtual Archives: Using Second Life to Facilitate Browsing and Archival Literacy

Mattie Taormina

Overview of Repository

Stanford University's Special Collections and University Archives department is located in the Green Library on Stanford's campus in Palo Alto, California. Our department comprises seventeen staff members: nine professionals and eight paraprofessionals. Five of the seventeen staff members work part-time. Many are grant funded. In 2008, we answered approximately 2,500 reference questions and circulated 81,000 items. In addition to rare book collections, these circulated items come from our department's approximately 35,000 linear feet of manuscript materials and 25,000 linear feet of university archival materials serving the Stanford community as well as the general public. Additionally, we have a robust instruction program resulting in approximately 177 classes being held in Special Collections, serving more than 2,000 students.

Business Drivers

In 2006, Stanford University Libraries and Academic Information Resources (SULAIR) created a Second Life (SL) team to explore virtual world technology and its potential impact on the future of libraries and on outreach. The all-volunteer team, led by Deni Wicklund, manager of the Stanford

University Libraries Tech Support Group, consists of representatives from different parts of the library and includes me in my role as the head of Public Services for Special Collections and University Archives.

Virtual reality is an emerging field that allows discovery and collaborative research opportunities that enables patron browsing to become interactive and three-dimensional, making the search experience more experiential. Second Life (SL) is a virtual world where individual users create avatars—or online personas—to travel throughout SL and interact with other people in real time. In fact, in August 2009, one source reported that there are approximately 1 million people with accounts and almost 60,000 users online at any given time.[1] Joining SL is free and conversations between avatars occur in real time through online chat or microphone use.

The team chose Second Life specifically because, at the time, there were very few well-developed virtual worlds that were not based on gaming programs. Virtual-world technology, more than the traditional method of a static list of scanned books on a web page or database, affords scholars the possibility of collaboration in real time during the discovery process. For example, if one scholar in France is browsing R. Buckminster Fuller materials and another Fuller scholar in Texas walks up and sees this, the two can spontaneously begin discussing their research. And, like traditional websites, having our digital content in SL makes parts of Stanford's rich library resources browseable to any scholar, anywhere, regardless of Stanford affiliation, without compromising the safety and security of the original resource.

Setting the Stage

Realizing how incredibly powerful this new virtual-world technology could be for collaborative research, by early 2007 Stanford library's island in Second Life had become a sophisticated gathering of virtual buildings and complexes specifically designed as meeting places. Although classes and lectures were held on the island, there were no educational resources, so there was little reason for visitors to return on their own.

The SL team approached my department and asked for unique content that could be featured in the virtual buildings. Ideally, this unique content would draw visitors back to the island and showcase Stanford's extensive educational resources. One SL team member, Digital Collections Project Manager Michael Olson, suggested constructing a virtual archives that would create a new opportunity for scholars to discover and use our primary resources online. Michael's idea offered direct and unmediated access to primary source materials, without a curatorial overlay, and circumnavigating the real-life concerns of material damage, theft, and fluctuating climate conditions while providing a new way for scholars to collaborate in real time. Additionally, I saw the experiment as a way to replicate the richness of the real-life reading room experience in order to promote archival literacy and familiarity.

We conceived a test site that would contain the following features: the boxes in our remote deep storage facility would be replicated virtually so that, for the first time, scholars could browse our closed manuscript

Figure 1: Stanford University's Virtual Archives in Second Life features manuscript boxes on reading tables, ready for browsing and research from virtual patrons.

Figure 2: A sampling of scanned images from each box appears when the box is opened. These images detail the impact that the 1906 San Francisco Earthquake had on the Stanford campus.

collections stacks—a practice not offered in real life. (See Figure 1.) Avatars could open a particular Hollinger box and see a sampling of scanned documents from that box appear, along with a link to the collection's online finding aid. (See Figure 2.) It would be a method of browsing, not searching.

To build this test site, team member Jessie Keck had to create an original script in order to replicate the Hollinger boxes, because one did not already exist in Second Life. I would provide all the digital content and bibliographic information for the featured collections. Because team members had limited time to devote to the test site, we decided that instead of scanning the entire contents of a collection (something that would have taken a great amount of time), we would offer a sampling of documents based on the reproduction requests public services had received over the years. This way, the images could be repurposed and no new labor would be required

Figure 3: Each Second Life manuscript box exactly replicates the appearance of the real-life box it represents, including the box's labels.

for that part of the project. Additionally, the actual boxes' contents and labels were photographed to capture and replicate the appearance of the physical box. (See Figure 3.)

This realism plays a key role in furthering our goal toward archival literacy and removing some of the perceived barriers to using Special Collections.[2] For inexperienced researchers, seeing the manuscript boxes and folders virtually familiarizes them with the physical reading room. Going through the boxes online makes the process of primary source research less intimidating, and they get a sense of the time needed to conduct archival research. For more experienced scholars, the ability to quickly survey the contents of a collection allows them to make a more informed decision about whether or not a trip to Stanford University is necessary or if ordering photocopies will suffice. (See Figure 4.)

Because reference is a key component to any archives, we created a virtual bulletin board where patrons can post reference questions that are then sent to Public Services and answered via e-mail. (See Figure 5.)

Results

From the outset, we created the virtual archives as an experiment—a test site—and so the results and outcomes are still being tabulated and considered. Thus far, however, the feedback has been overwhelmingly positive. The virtual archives' official opening was July 2009 with an open house specifically geared toward archivists and special collections librarians. The open house produced success that we were not prepared for: bloggers wrote about their experiences, thereby giving us more exposure. Less than three hours after the open house, a participant made a video of his visit to

Figure 4: By seeing the actual box's contents, scholars can quickly assess the thickness of folders, note the condition and housing of materials, and compare the finding aid's listing to the actual box contents.

the virtual archives and posted it on Flickr, thereby making us realize we
needed to create an "official" video as well. That same evening, a professor
from a nearby university brought his class to our site and held a virtual
seminar there centered on our materials. The following business day, a
reporter from the *Chronicle of Higher Education* wrote an article on the
archives that was later reprinted in the American Library Association's
(ALA) online news. Last, we were taken aback by the numerous requests we
received for a second open house, which occurred in August and included
museum professionals as well. From July to the beginning of September
when this article was written, almost 200 avatars visited the virtual
archives, with each person spending approximately thirty minutes looking
at our collections. Those new avatars, coupled with the number of hits the
unofficial Flickr video of our site received (208), resulted in approximately
400 more people aware of Stanford's Special Collections and University
Archives' collections in two months.

Figure 5: Visitors can send their reference questions to staff by posting messages on the
virtual message board.

Following are some of the comments we received:

- Stanford's work has shown they are also focused on finding ways to increase the value of their collections simply by providing new means of access. (E-mail received by the author)

- I like how the virtual archives are meant to look like the real archives, at least in terms of the containers, photo of what is in them, and sample content. (Live feedback from July 31, 2009, SL open house)

- First, it seems a new and interesting way to both provide access and outreach, a good way to introduce students and other visitors to what closed stack material is like. (E-mail received by the author)

- I really like the out-of-the-box thinking for this project. It is just the kind of thinking that is needed to keep the Special Collections and Archives worlds relevant in the 21st century. (Blog post)

More surprisingly, it is not only information professionals that seem to enjoy our archives. The earliest feedback we received was from newspaper reporters writing articles on Second Life or social networking technologies. The reporters wrote favorably about the virtual archives portion of our online resources. More specifically, they delighted in selecting a box, opening the lid, and seeing a Mark Twain letter that they could zoom in on rather than the thumbnail image most e-databases provide.[3]

Although the Second Life team remains excited about the virtual archives, we are unsure of whether we are reaching our target audience: the Stanford community and other primary source-dependent scholars. Despite a growing awareness of virtual technologies, not many Stanford faculty or students are using SL yet, making the virtual archives still somewhat unknown to our own immediate community. Outside scholars seem to be elusive as well. Many visitors tend to be people who stumble upon the virtual archives and are unaware of what an archives is. To remedy this, we need to be more aggressive in our advertising and outreach efforts to the Stanford community and to other scholars. Additionally, a fuller representation of the archives' holdings potentially could draw in more visitors as well.

Challenges

The main challenges we faced in placing primary source material in Second Life were SL construction knowledge and a lack of devoted full-time project staff. SL construction can be time-consuming and requires some technological expertise. For example, it takes me about thirty minutes to review previously scanned items, quality-check their metadata, and make any needed adjustments to the image (crop, resize, etc.) before it can go into Second Life. Additionally, it takes me approximately forty-five minutes to create a new virtual box and match it with its corresponding scanned images. Thus, each manuscript box takes almost one and a half hours to create.[4]

Without staff specifically dedicated to building and augmenting the Second Life island, individual projects tend to move slowly. Our virtual archives potentially could have more end users if more collections were represented in SL, but limited staff time devoted to this project stymies this. Despite the lack of staffing, our team still has successfully created more than twenty boxes representing fourteen collections. This is due solely to the passion and dedication of the team members who often give up their personal time on nights and weekends to make the island fuller and richer.

More difficult challenges that we are addressing are those based on perceptions. Some of my colleagues are resistant to the project because they view Web 2.0 tools as either a "time drain" or as a conflict between games and research.[5] While it is true that SL requires significant time to create items in the virtual world, these staff members may see the value in exerting such efforts when statistics support a solid return, be that in online class visits, reference requests, in-person visits, and/or individual online visits. One colleague remarked that viewing information in a 3-D, interactive manner seemed to trivialize the research process, making primary sources look like computer games. Because Second Life is still "gaming" driven, the average visitor may not consider or realize that the island is a learning environment.

In fact, many in the information profession share this point of view as well. One comment posted on the popular blog *ArchivesNext* concerned our first open house: "interesting idea . . . would think that the choice of second life as platform might not be serious enough for the archives of Stanford."[6] Additionally, several archivists commented via e-mail that they were not able to access Second Life from their work computers because their employers prohibited them from using any social networking sites such as Second Life, Facebook, and Twitter, because their administrations did not view these technologies as business-related or appropriate.

Although it is true that most scholars today are not yet using this method to conduct their research, there is a strong possibility that our not-too-distant-future end users will. Virtual-world technology could likely be the next incarnation of the web, but it will take society some time to absorb and adopt it into their everyday lives. This delay is part of the natural process of introducing people to something new. That said, society is well into this cultural shift as virtual worlds are the natural next step in our ongoing relationship with technology. We are already absorbing three-dimensional, interactive computer interfaces into our daily lives: Google maps, iPhone applications, personal GPS navigation in cars, augmented reality, and Wii videogames used for fitness (not games!). Why would we assume that this technology would not spill over into the field of primary source research in the near future? Using virtual worlds to conduct research is a paradigm shift, a new way of thinking about scholarship, which requires a new approach to research. The perceived barriers to using this technology for scholarly endeavors will ebb with time and increasing familiarity.

Next Steps

The future holds endless possibilities for our island, but significant additions to the virtual archives will remain on hold, however, until we can assess our visitors' feedback and how they use that part of the island. We have to be patient and allow time for people to discover and use the archives. If we see interest in the resources there and receive reference questions, we will add more archival collections.

In the meantime, we continue to focus our efforts on publicizing the virtual archives' existence. First, we will produce an official, informational video introducing the archives to users. We will post this video on Flickr and YouTube for greater public dissemination. Second, we will create a traditional web page on the Special Collections and University Archives website and list the collections we have in SL with the island's address. We will add an RSS feed option on that page to alert subscribers when new collections are added. The aforementioned informational video will be featured there as well. Because SL is not crawled by search engines, the traditional web page will allow users to discover the archives using popular search tools. Next, bookmarks advertising the archives will be placed at each of Green Library's entrance doors in an effort to reach the Stanford community directly. Additionally, we held an open house for the scholarly community in winter 2010 in an effort to increase awareness among scholars and to solicit their direct feedback.

Last, because so many online visitors to the island are unfamiliar with an archives, we will create a virtual billboard that explains what these materials are and how people use them. We see this as a wonderful opportunity to introduce our profession to a larger audience while getting them excited about our resources.

Although Second Life may not be the ultimate platform for virtual research in the future, our early exploration of this virtual-world technology allows us to forecast how our users will want to discover primary sources in the not-too-distant future. It has provided us an essential launching pad to experiment with these new concepts and see what is effective and engaging to our patrons. We are excited about the future of our island and look forward to virtual scholars using our materials as creatively online as they do in real life.

Notes

[1] "Linden Lab," *Crunchbase*, http://www.crunchbase.com/company/secondlife and http://secondlife.com/statistics/economy-data.php?d=2009-09-01 (both accessed September 3, 2009).

[2] Alice Schreyer, "From Treasure Room to Research Center: Special Collections in the United States," (2005), 7, available at http://www.initiativefortbildung.de/pdf/sondersammlungen2005/schreyer.pdf (accessed June 2, 2009). In this piece, Schreyer describes some of the barriers to using special collections: "The labor-intensive nature of cataloging and describing rare and unique materials meant that vast quantities of it remained invisible, while the need for security and preservation measures created significant barriers to use. Thus, when library budgets were cut in the 1970s, administrators began to question the value of acquiring and maintaining high-cost, low-use collections. In 1980, historian Neil Harris called special collections "atavistic": "they are fussier, less accessible, more resistant to rationalization than other parts of the academic library. They are costly to operate, seemingly inefficient and unpredictable; they present special preservation, storage, and cataloging problems."

[3] Sue Dremann, "The Not So Real World," *Palo Alto Weekly*, July 23, 2008.

[4] As an aside, there is a charge for building in SL; each of our boxes cost approximately $4.50 (U.S. dollars) to create.

[5] "We tend to think of videogames as frivolous activities—something we do to kill time, not to improve productivity. But a new generation of designers is taking a different tack: Like Reeves, they're using the principles of videogame design to transform everyday activities—helping people work more efficiently, use less energy, and get healthier. Turn the world into a game, they argue, and it works better." Clive Thompson, "How Game Design Can Revolutionize Everyday Life," *Wired.com Reports*, May 26, 2009, http://www.wired.com/techbiz/media/news/2009/05/games_wired (accessed June 2, 2009).

[6] Post by R. Porter, posted on *ArchivesNext*, July 28, 2009, http://www.archivesnext.com/?p=317#comment-51579 (accessed September 3, 2009).

Making Friends and Fans: Using Facebook for Special Collections Outreach

Jessica Lacher-Feldman

Overview of Repository

The W. S. Hoole Special Collections Library is part of the University Libraries at The University of Alabama, a public university founded in 1831 and located in Tuscaloosa, Alabama. With a student body of around 30,000, including undergraduate, graduate, and professional students, the campus is diverse and dynamic. The University of Alabama Libraries is a member of the Association of Research Libraries[1] and is considered the flagship academic institution in the state of Alabama. The W.S. Hoole Special Collections Library is an academic special collections library, serving as the university's institutional archives as well as a manuscript repository and a rare book and published materials library. The library holds more than 2,700 manuscript collections, including major congressional papers, plantation and farm records, business and church records, and papers of authors, artists, and others. The library also holds significant book collections, including rare books, Alabamiana, and several other important print collections. Other significant holdings include rare maps, extensive photographic collections, and other materials that reflect Southern history and culture, popular culture, folk life, and American vernacular music.

The Hoole Library serves more than 3,000 patrons per year both virtually and on site. More than forty classroom visits a year, public events, and an active exhibit calendar bring people from across campus and around the community to the library for reasons besides individual research projects. The library staff includes eleven full-time employees (five faculty members, one professional staff member, and five support staff positions) and is the physical home for the University Libraries' digital program. In addition to staff, the Hoole Library employs more than thirty undergraduate and graduate students year-round in various capacities.

The primary audience of the Hoole Library is University of Alabama faculty, staff, and students. The Hoole Library also serves a variety of other constituencies, including researchers and scholars from Alabama and around the world.

Business Drivers

I joined Facebook rather reluctantly, primarily because a Facebook presence centers on exposing one's personal life for the entire world to see. My interest in joining did not originate within my repository or as part of a larger discussion on outreach, but rather developed out of my personal interest in outreach. I finally decided to sign up for Facebook during the Society of American Archivists' annual meeting in August 2008, when colleagues strong-armed me into joining. Sitting in my hotel room on my laptop computer, I created my profile and began to explore the site.

My primary motivation was to simply tap into the very powerful social network that is Facebook and to see how traditional and progressive outreach endeavors might be furthered through the use of this medium. Outreach has always been a fundamental professional interest of mine and a motivating factor in much of my work as an archivist, and it was clear both on a personal and professional level that joining Facebook was critical in moving outreach endeavors forward and in finding new audiences and making greater contacts. To determine if this would work for outreach endeavors, and to determine how my repository and my outreach endeavors might benefit from this medium, I had to actually join Facebook.

Figure 1: A screenshot of the W.S. Hoole Special Collections Library's fan page, February 21, 2011.

My interest in developing a Facebook presence for the Hoole Special Collections Library and other library and academic outreach endeavors under my purview was multifaceted. (See Figure 1.) One factor revolved around gaining exposure for the University Libraries' lecture series for which I am responsible. Finding a way to get the lecture series to a broad range of students has always been extremely appealing, especially because we are always competing for audiences, as any large academic institution might be.

Conventional methods of promoting lectures, readings, and events, such as press releases, fliers, the use of community calendars and conventional e-mails to potentially interested parties has been critical, but despite a loyal following and all efforts, many people have not found out about an event. Anecdotal feedback from "friends" and constituents has indicated that without receiving invitations and information from Facebook, they would not have known about something that is of great personal or professional interest to them. Even further, many have grown to rely on Facebook to find out about cultural events in their community.

And while we know that we cannot always reach everyone using one method, it is an ongoing quest for anyone doing outreach and promoting events to finding better, cheaper, faster, and more efficient ways to spread the word.

Setting the Stage

With some trepidation, I carefully considered my own Facebook profile as the foundation for what I would be doing and how I would represent myself to the public. In setting up my Facebook presence, I made a mental note that I did not want to reveal a great deal of personal information. (That is really less about Facebook and more about my own concern about privacy.) Instead, I chose to create a more skeletal presence that would be scalable and recognizable but not exposing too much beyond what one would expect of someone using Facebook for work purposes. I left out some of the general profile information—which may seem like it is mandatory to complete when in fact it is not. In talking to several people about their own profile information, I found that people often complete whatever information is requested of them. This means the ordinary user sometimes reveals personal information that they might not ordinarily share, including home address and phone number.

While I wanted and continue to want my Facebook presence to reflect who I am, I made a conscious decision not to expose my own political or religious beliefs in my profile. I also chose to accept and seek out friends of all stripes to have the widest exposure to others who might be interested in the kinds of things I promote and work with in my repository. I continue to seek out friends, especially among the students and faculty at my university.

As my presence on Facebook grew, I chose to join "groups" and become a "fan" of things that reflect both my personal and my professional interests. I did this to see what others are doing on Facebook and to learn from what I see.

In addition to paying close attention to other repositories and other archivists/curators, I began to create some of my own groups, which has allowed me to help promote my repository and the work that we are doing. This includes a group called "Cool @ Hoole: The Blog of the W.S. Hoole Special Collections Library." The group is directly related to the Hoole blog, *What's Cool@Hoole,* which was created to allow the author to highlight "the collections, events, items, happenings, ideas, new acquisitions, discoveries, initiatives, and everything else that's Cool @ the W.S. Hoole Special Collections Library at The University of Alabama."[2] All blog postings become Facebook "notes" and generate more interest and comments. Additionally, these postings become status updates, increasing exposure for the blog, the Facebook page, and the Hoole Library in general.

I created this group page without much consideration for what others on Facebook were doing that might be similar. I made the decision to create this group as a means to promote another Web 2.0 resource, namely the *What's Cool@Hoole* blog. I did not want the Facebook presence to become additional work, but rather a tool to promote the blog. The group page, which had more than 250 members as of December 2010, has provided new opportunities to promote both the blog itself and the collections of the Hoole Special Collections Library to a still broader audience.

The most successful and active group that I have created on Facebook is "University Libraries Lecture Series | The University of Alabama." This group allows me to promote each lecture and event separately and to share these events with a broader and broader audience. This group has more than 200 members. All members receive information on each of the individual events announced on the site, but, additionally, I am able to promote individual events more broadly. I can send invitations to each lecture or reading separately to a targeted audience and informally ask those who wish to share this invitation with other interested parties.

To further promote lectures and events, I use my status update in Facebook to remind friends that something is happening, especially the day before or the day of the event. For example, I might write "We hope to see you today at 4 p.m. in Gorgas Library Room 205 for a reading with poet Jane Doe," and provide a link to the Lecture Series Facebook group, or a picture, or something that further promotes the event. This method of promoting a lecture or event has proven useful as it reminds interested parties that something they might want to attend is happening in the very near future and it solicits comments and energy. Sometimes I find that someone might comment about a particular speaker or film we are promoting, saying something like "I saw her in New York and her work is very moving." These impromptu critiques help to fuel the energy surrounding an event.

One final group that I created is called, "Publishers' Bindings Online, 1815–1930: The Art of Books." This group, with more than 200 members, was created as an opportunity to promote the digital project of the same name, for which I served as project manager. Again, this is just another way to get the word out in a different venue.

In addition to these groups, I created a fan page for our library, The W.S. Hoole Special Collections Library. As of December 2010, this page had more than 300 fans, and I have used the opportunity to promote this fan page by using a widget on the *What'sCool@Hoole* blog.

Results

Using Facebook for outreach has had some excellent results, namely, in making certain that people and organizations are finding out about the lectures, activities, and endeavors that we are trying to promote. Each endeavor using Facebook has proven to be a success, as it requires minimum effort for setup and upkeep, but there clearly are benefits, starting with providing new paths to exposure. Measuring these benefits can be difficult, but not impossible, and it is worth tracking on some level. Recording quantitative information for the lecture series, such as taking quick head counts and tracking increases in traffic from before and after implementing Facebook can provide some insight, provided you regularly count heads at lectures. Comparing or documenting anecdotal information such as hearing feedback from individuals who express themselves by posting on the page, or documenting those who contact you via e-mail or Facebook, or by simply commenting that if they hadn't gotten your invitation on Facebook, they would not have known of the event. Any and all observations help to justify and rationalize this effort, both to yourself as the outreach person and to your administration.

By regularly checking the number of members of my groups and scanning them for names and faces that I do not recognize, I can keep track and understand the impact this form of promotion is having. I have been thanked both in person and via Facebook for updates and information, including a very welcome statement from a colleague in the Art Department, who said, "if it weren't for your updates and events, I would never know what was happening on campus!" Audiences continue to grow, and, additionally, I am asked more and more about my methods for promoting and am often contacted about opportunities for readings and book signings by authors.

Facebook has allowed the forging of new collaborative relationships with other academic and support units on campus. For example, the UA Libraries lecture series now has a new creative partner in the form of one of the most active endowed series on campus, the Bankhead Visiting Writers Series in the Department of English. For the first time, in fall 2009, all of the public Bankhead readings were held in Gorgas Library and were cross-promoted as part of the UA Libraries lecture series, bringing still broader audiences to our events. I believe that this was initiated after the faculty member who was then in charge of coordinating the series found that what we had been doing on Facebook was a success and wanted to work collaboratively. This collaboration has been fruitful and successful.

My role in promoting materials via Facebook has also led to positive outcomes for other organizations with which I am affiliated. For example, as a new member of the executive board of the Alabama Folklife Association, I was able to provide some key anecdotal information and advice about embracing this new technology and medium, which ultimately led to the creation of a page for the organization on Facebook. I have also provided advice and guidance to other colleagues from other special collections repositories that are uncertain about Facebook's role in promoting their own repositories and having difficulties in addressing this medium and its potential impact to their own administrators. While much of my advice and guidance is very informal, as is the resulting feedback, I have seen and heard the positive results that this information has netted, which includes the embracing of this medium by administrators in archival repositories and anecdotal feedback and commentary about the added positive exposure that Facebook provides.

In thinking about outreach, I chose to use tools within Facebook in different ways, depending on my needs. For example, by creating a Facebook page specifically for the W.S. Hoole Special Collections Library, I created opportunities for people to become "fans" and opportunities for me to give Hoole "fans" and others specific and basic information about the overall repository, such as hours and information about new collections, while at the same time providing a venue for posting announcements about the repository. As of February 2011, this repository page had 332 fans. The Cool@Hoole Facebook presence, as a group page, creates a greater sense of collaboration and potential participation, which is reflective in the venue it represents, a blog. It is for that same reason that I chose to create a group rather than a fan page for the University Libraries Lecture Series at The University of Alabama. Semantically, I believe that the notion of "group" creates a sense of community in a different way than a Facebook "fan page" might, though the purpose is largely the same. A "fan page" on Facebook is more informational and less participatory, though I find that the level of participation from "fans" or "group members" is about the same and what is key is to have a place for people on Facebook who appreciate and are interested in what you are doing.

On a personal/professional level, Facebook has provided me with a much larger network of colleagues than was previously accessible without this tool. It has been easier to identify like-minded colleagues and to build on professional relationships in several ways, including the opportunity to write this case study. I have used this network to communicate, share information, explore what other repositories are doing, and continue to shape my professional and cultural networks.

Challenges

I have found that one of the most significant challenges to using Facebook is striking a balance between my personal and private persona and the persona and role I play as an information provider and advocate for my repository and its holdings. My own approach to Facebook was to create a space for myself and to build on that presence by providing information and access to my repository in ways that I see fit. Though Facebook requires a user to have a personal account in order to create groups and fan pages, the social network may be offering new ways to create space and information that can exist without ties to a personal account.

One solution might be to create one account that is used just for work while keeping a private account to serve as a personal communication tool. This would allow for a clear separation between public and private.

Lessons Learned

With more than 1,000 Facebook "friends" from several different parts of my life, it was necessary to make a conscious decision about the types of personal information that are displayed. Because I, like many, hope to keep one of my primary uses for Facebook centered around special collections outreach endeavors, I have found it both critical and necessary to be conscious of this notion at all times. My Facebook "friends" range from long-lost friends from elementary school and summer camp, to distant and close relatives, to a spouse, and friends from high school, college, and graduate school, mixed in with donors and potential donors and colleagues from around the world. Embarking on the use of Facebook as a communication tool is truly an opportunity to bring one's private and public life together. Anyone approaching the idea of using Facebook as an outreach tool and linking professional endeavors so closely with such personal information should think carefully about the personal information that they share and the presence that they put forth. While opportunities to share political, religious and social views may be readily available using Facebook, it is important to consider potential ramifications in sharing opinions publicly with such a wide range of "friends."

My established network on Facebook has proven to be a critical tool in several areas, including communication, collection development, outreach, and as a learning tool. By joining groups and becoming a "fan" of my colleagues' repositories and endeavors as they are presented on Facebook, both informal and formal best practices can be developed, ideas can be shared, and collaboration can be fostered through this dynamic and rich virtual environment.

Using Facebook to promote lectures and events, my repository, my repository blog, and the digital project I managed for more than five years have all been very positive experiences. If I could do this again, I might pay greater attention to the "before" and "after" and find better ways to track the success and impact of these endeavors. I believe this in a way speaks to the ease in which we can come to Facebook and use it to our advantage. In going from complete nonparticipation to an active user in the matter of one evening, I found that developing metrics and measuring tools did not seem like a priority at the time. Much of my feedback has been anecdotal and, in fact, positive, but I would like to identify more concrete measures of success. I believe that anyone approaching the use of Facebook as an outreach tool should keep in mind methods of measuring outcomes and success.

Next Steps

In the near future, I would very much like to gather concrete feedback and compile statistics about how the use of Facebook has had an impact on outreach and collection development endeavors and how it has helped me fulfill my roles as a curator and lecture series coordinator. The documentation of anecdotal feedback, doing short surveys, or soliciting comments will help build a greater understanding of how Facebook is furthering outreach and can help focus my endeavors in the future.

Additionally, I plan to incorporate some of the more frivolous but extremely "viral" applications for Facebook, including creating a "gift" application focusing on nineteenth-century publishers' bindings from the Hoole Library and a second gift application that uses images from the *What's Cool@Hoole* blog, including University of Alabama historical images and other campus-related images. This will allow information sharing to a broader audience by providing Facebook users who are not necessarily interested in the library but rather interested in The University of Alabama an opportunity to share virtual gifts with their friends, thus exposing them to materials from the Hoole Library's collections and the mission and goal of the library. This has been done with success at Albion College and William and Mary. For example, the William & Mary Gifts application, created by Amy Schindler, has sixty-seven choices that range from the historical to the ironic.

I am confident that the use of Facebook as an outreach tool for archives and special collections is one that is useful, practical, and effective. While using Facebook as an outreach tool does require thought and planning, some of the information shared here should provide groundwork for making intelligent and pragmatic decisions about blending the public persona of your repository and special collections outreach endeavors along with your own private information when using this powerful and dynamic Web 2.0 tool.

Notes

[1] Association of Research Libraries, http://www.arl.org/ (accessed February 21, 2011).

[2] *What's Cool@Hoole*, http://coolathoole.blogspot.com/ (accessed February 11, 2011).

Going Where the Users Are: The Jewish Women's Archive and Its Use of Twitter

Andrea Medina-Smith

Overview of Repository

The Jewish Women's Archive, located in Brookline, Massachusetts, is a national nonprofit organization founded in 1995 to chronicle the stories, struggles, and achievements of Jewish women in North America. We develop partnerships, sponsor programs, conduct and support original research, create educational materials, and maintain an innovative website, all designed to help us understand our past and shape our future. Our collections are entirely digital and comprise 225 oral histories, hundreds of digital images, a "virtual archive" guide to manuscript collections around the country, and *Jewish Women: A Comprehensive Historical Encyclopedia*, one of the most in-depth reference guides to the lives and work of Jewish women available. Staff at the Jewish Women's Archive includes fourteen men and women whose backgrounds range from museum administration to education, academia to typesetting; together they form the dynamic team that has created a website that averages 60,000 unique visitors each month. These visitors are from all walks of life.

Our purpose is to invite people to share stories, express opinions, and pose questions. Some seek insight into a collective history; others yearn for a stronger sense of community. Many hope to explore more fully the richness of Jewish culture. A great number share our passion for making the world a more just and equitable place. The Jewish Women's Archive focuses on women in the Jewish community because for much of history the men around them have subsumed their stories. Husbands, fathers, or brothers, supported and assisted by women, were the ones who were chronicled, and their stories were shared. The Jewish Women's Archive is an institution dedicated to their inclusion in the future of history.

Business Drivers

Our decision to start using Twitter was based on the need to grow our audience. Currently, we identify our audience as "seekers"; a seeker is a user who wants to connect to some part of him- or herself through our site. The audience can be divided into four sections: continuity seekers, knowledge seekers, connection seekers, and identity seekers. Very few of our users are researchers who traditionally use archival materials, and the Primary Sources section of our website (http://jwa.org/teach/primarysources/) is geared toward primary and secondary school teachers. Currently, we do not have more information on the demographics of our web users, but we are undertaking a program to find out more about them in fiscal year 2010.

For several years we have used other Web 2.0 technologies (including our blog, *Jewesses with Attitude,* and Facebook) to strengthen our position among college students and young professionals. Twitter was seen as one more way of putting our resources in front of that audience. It also filled our desire to create the space for interaction with our users. Like other 2.0 technologies, Twitter allows for a two-way conversation between users— whether they are institutions or individuals. The goal was to identify other cultural institutions and users with whom we were not connecting on other platforms. In the past, when a user wanted to share a story with us, it was nearly impossible to do so in a public and unmediated way. The user could send the story via e-mail to one person, who hopefully would remember to send it to other interested parties on staff, and the interaction with our user was delayed often by weeks. Now using Twitter and the comment feature on many of the sections of the website, personal stories can be shared with other users and the world. Yes, sometimes it takes more than 140 characters, but the interaction is initiated in that short post and can be followed up by e-mail.

Through Twitter, we are hoping to reach the coveted group of potential new users—twenty- and thirtysomethings. According to the recent Pew Internet & American Life Project's memo on Twitter, the median age of Twitter users is thirty-one.[1] As an institution we want to grow this portion of our base because they represent two important factors in our work. First, they are a connection to other generations; these might be their parents, who are possibly computer users, but they are also the connection to members of the older generation, who are less likely to be computer literate but who retain many of the stories we aim to preserve. Second, they are an opportunity for the Jewish Women's Archive to connect with future donors.

Setting the Stage

Setting up an account on Twitter is simple, takes less than ten minutes, and costs nothing (as of now). Twitter started as an experiment for the Jewish Women's Archive. On a whim our director of Online Strategy, Ari Davidow, signed us up for an account and began "tweeting" our "This Week in History" articles as daily tweets with a link back to our site and the full article. "It was like creating a master RSS feed, and one result was to create an ongoing ambient presence, communicating that the Jewish Women's Archive is doing lots of interesting stuff," says Davidow. At first it was just about getting our feet wet, so to speak, but we were quickly reminded by members of our Technology Advisory Committee that doing something without a goal or purpose, no matter how little time it took, was a waste of precious resources. (The Technology Advisory Committee is a group of outstanding professionals in the library, archives, and information technology [IT] world. They act as a sounding board and brainstorming group for our technology programs and initiatives. Once a year we meet to review past activities and generate ideas for upcoming projects.) We then revisited our decision to use Twitter, to see if it was a tool we wanted to continue to use. Twitter gives us access to many "micro" communities at one time;

it allows us to dialog with our users and expand our base. Looking back at the technology plan we wrote in late 2007, we were reminded that one of the goals outlined in the plan was to "meet users where they are." Twitter fit this bill perfectly, as does our use of other social networking sites such as Facebook and Flickr. These points were all evidence that we should continue with Twitter.

The range of individuals and organizations that follow our feed is broad and includes women's organizations, museums, Jewish organizations and

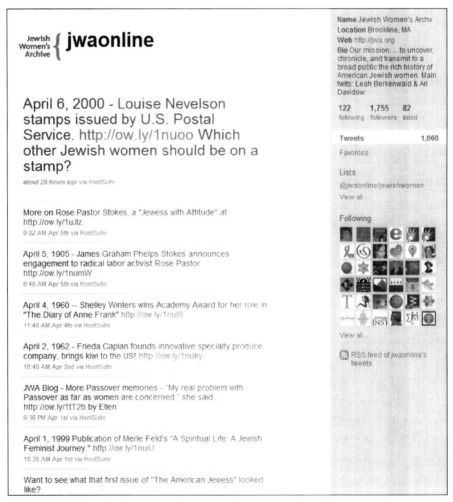

Figure 1: An example of tweets on the Jewish Women's Archive Twitter page. For a current view, visit http://twitter.com/jwaonline.com.

institutions, social justice groups, and other archives. We have chosen not to follow everyone who follows us; if we did, the volume of posts would be impossible to deal with, given the limited time we devote each day to Twitter. People we follow automatically are those who start a conversation with us; if they have "re-tweeted" (re-posted) a post or asked a question, we follow their feed and continue the dialog. The casual follower is like the casual user of our website; we have yet to bring them into the circle of users who interact with us, but as we develop new strategies for interaction, we can hopefully build on the casual relationship. At this time we are developing more formal policies, but so far we have merely tested new ideas as they came to us and watched the results.

Our posts fall into three categories: content from our website, questions for the crowd, and stories of our successes. For example, a content-related tweet often consists of a "This Day in History" fact, such as "Aug 24, 1861—Eugenia Levy Phillips was arrested as a Confederate spy! http://bit.ly/E9l5q."[2] As new blog posts go up, we add an announcement to the Twitter feed, such as "Ellen's first blog post! 'Do Jews Celebrate Thanksgiving?' includes a celebration of the life of Hilda Meltzer."[3] The most personal posts are those that cover our successes, which range from the technical ("So many little things to fix on the Enc. Feel very proud that we did the accents on people's names in Titles, etc. No more mere ASCII. [Ari]"[4]) to the programmatic ("Excellent planning meeting 4 our 'American Jewish Women & WWII' Flickr Commons proj w/both Hartford, New Haven Jewish Hist Socs. Stay tuned!"[5]). Future posts will build on these three common types and include more "retweets" and responses to our followers and those we are following.

Results

When we started our Twitter feed in November 2008, we didn't expect too much—a mention here or a chance to quickly share a success there. Now we know that the expectation of the technology team (composed of the director of Online Strategy, our web application's developer, and myself) were too low. As Twitter expands through different demographics, we expect our content to reach new users and we can experiment with our feed with ease.

As of December 21, 2010, we have posted more than 1,700 tweets and have more than 2,400 followers. This has resulted in a small bump to our blog readership, which we can't attribute entirely to Twitter, but nothing else has changed about how we promote the blog in the time since we started our Twitter feed, thus lending credibility to our assumption. Using Twitter has not resulted in a general rise in the number of unique visitors to our site each month over the previous year. This does not mean that the experiment has been unsuccessful; any time we have 700 people reading "This Day in History" or seeing what we are blogging about, we are inserting ourselves into those followers' circle of "ambient intimacy."[6] We are becoming part of their everyday experience. Our Twitter feed is deemed successful because we have seen steady growth of followers (those reading our feed), which has led to increased readership of our website and blog.

Internally, we have had a slow warming to Twitter. At first, many on staff thought it would be another flash-in-the-pan trend (which it may still turn out to be), but as our number of followers continues to rise (as we report monthly at staff meetings), and as our budget tightens, it has become a favorite, fast, and fun way to communicate new ideas and content to this "micro-community" of users.

Challenges

While I was employed by JWA, there were three main "twits" (as we call them), the online communication specialist, our director of Online Strategy and myself, the digital archivist. I joined the mix because of my personal experience using Twitter; my "co-twits" had organizational reasons for participating at the highest level. The online communication specialist is in charge of "This Week in History" and blogs frequently, so it seemed a natural fit for her to begin posting. The director of Online Strategy had jumped in feet first by starting our account and has continued to be one of its biggest supporters and posters. In addition to the three main posters, everyone on staff was encouraged to join in; we wanted more voices in the mix so that we could sustain interest among the niche groups who are following us: the educators, the archives and cultural institutions, and the legacy seekers. Our biggest challenge was incorporating tweeting into the everyday tasks for those not directly charged with maintaining the Twitter account. For instance, in my work as digital archivist I did so many non-content-related tasks that I sometimes wanted to post about but didn't. Why? I didn't want to alienate the followers (who make up the majority of our community) who I assumed were not interested in the nitty-gritty of digital repository work. (I did, and continue to tend to post more detailed tweets on digital repositories and archives theory in my personal Twitter feed.) For others, like our online communication specialist, putting up content on Twitter is just another step in her workflow of content broadcasting. (See Figure 1.)

However, for most of the already busy staff, another daily task can seem like the tipping point. Questions such as "I don't get this Twitter, why do they want to know what we're eating for lunch?", "Do I need to be pithy and witty?", and "Why would our users be interested in what I do?" were heard over and over again in one form or another. The answer to the first question is this: That's not the type of feed we developed. Yes, many people have personal sites on which they discuss the minutiae of everyday life, but our feed, like our whole site, would be one of substance. For the second question the answer is this: Of course not; our site should be well written and under 140 characters (though this may be a definition of *pithy*), but witty and pithy aren't requirements. For the third question, our answer is this: If our users know what is going on "under the hood," as it were, they will be more likely to see us as a group of interesting individuals collectively doing great work versus seeing us as an institution that magically pops out content with little to suggest otherwise.

One final question needed to be answered for the staff and our board: Would this help our development numbers? To date, the answer is no, but we are not currently using Twitter as a platform to solicit donations or cultivate donors. I have looked for other cultural institutions that are using Twitter in this way. There are none that I know of, but human services organizations like The Salvation Army[7] have used Twitter to raise funds through microdonations. The Salvation Army's "Red Kettle" Twitter account has a modest $10,000 goal, and as of this writing they have raised approximately $2,000. Other smaller organizations like Well Wishes and Christmas Future[8] have created accounts with TipJoy[9] to fund-raise for their organizations. TipJoy is a third-party business that is dedicated to helping charities and nonprofits earn online. Some of these fund-raising projects are time-bound, such as Christmas Future's Tweetmas Future (now under the name uend:Poverty), which ran for two weeks before Christmas 2008,[10] while others like the Salvation Army's campaign are ongoing.

Lessons Learned

The greatest lesson we've learned is that for the Jewish Women's Archive, Twitter, and other social media sites, is not a panacea for our outreach (or development) goals. Twitter is great for pushing content to users we wouldn't have necessarily reached before, but does it connect us to people already in our community? We're not sure, and for right now we are okay with that. The upcoming expansion of our Web 2.0 presence and evaluation of our use of Twitter will help us answer these questions and find strategies for leveraging our connections.

Another lesson we have learned is that we need to better prepare staff and members of our advisory boards to use all new technologies. Those of us on the technology team started full-steam ahead, and we were a bit stunned that not everyone could see Twitter's utility at first glance. If we had managed our expectations and enthusiasm better as we launched our project, we might have had more staff on board more quickly. It took a bit of time to come to the conclusion we reached above, and had those realizations happened before, we might have raised the volume of tweets posted over the seven months I was involved in the project.

Next Steps

Current plans for our future on Twitter include testing the platform as a way to bring in new donors by posting more links to our donation page and expanding our dialog with other users. Other ideas include finding better ways to evaluate our Twitter use through figuring out who our followers are and looking beyond posting links to our donation page. Questions we would like to answer about our users include: Are they already part of the Jewish Women's Archive circle? Are they transitioning to being donors? What do they do with our posts? Do they retweet them or pass them on in other ways, or do they come to our site for more information? What do they get from following our feed? As for expanding our fund-raising efforts on Twitter, we are currently tracking how TipJoy is working for organizations like those mentioned previously, and we are in the process of deciding if we will be one of the first cultural institutions to test it out.

Our new online communications specialist has taken the Twitter account under her wing and made several changes to the way we will handle it in the future. First, she has begun using the Twitter app TweetDeck to manage our account. TweetDeck allows one to work on the computer offline or in another window and still view the Twitter feed. It is part of her duties to expand our use of Web 2.0 technologies by responding in a timely manner to the range of comments, questions, and suggestions we receive on Twitter, Facebook, and Flickr. This new attention to our 2.0 presence will allow an expanded dialog with users, both old and new.

Notes

[1] Amanda Lenhart and Susannah Fox, "Pew Internet Project Data Memo," Pew Internet & American Life Project, February 12, 2009, http://www.pewinternet.org/~/media//Files/Reports/2009/PIP%20 Twitter%20Memo%20FINAL.pdf (accessed December 21, 2010).

[2] Jewish Women's Archive Twitter post, August 24, 2010, http://twitter.com/jwaonline/status/ 22024314325 (accessed December 21, 2009).

[3] Jewish Women's Archive Twitter post, November 25, 2008, http://twitter.com/jwaonline/status/ 1023466079; blog post, November 25, 2009, http://jwablog.jwa.org/do-jews-celebrate-thanksgiving (both accessed December 21, 2010).

[4] Jewish Women's Archive Twitter post, March 4, 2009, http://twitter.com/jwaonline/status/1280986926 (accessed December 21, 2010).

[5] Jewish Women's Archive Twitter post, June 24, 2009, http://twitter.com/jwaonline/status/2310167499 (accessed December 21, 2010).

[6] The term "ambient intimacy" describes the ability to keep in touch with many people—generally, those you wouldn't necessarily have the same level of access to without social platforms—in a regular manner using applications such as Twitter, Facebook, and blogs. Leisa Reichelt originally described it on her blog *Disambiguity* on March 1, 2007, http://www.disambiguity.com/ ambient-intimacy/ (accessed December 21, 2010).

[7] Salvation Army, *Online Red Kettle* (2008), http://give.salvationarmyusa.org/site/TR/ RedKettleCampaigns/RedKettle?team_id=12090&pg=team&fr_id=1200 (accessed July 25, 2009).

[8] *Christmas Future*, http://www.christmasfuture.org/dt/ (accessed December 21, 2010).

[9] TipJoy, http://tipjoy.com/ (accessed July 27, 2009).

[10] Leif Baradoy, "TweetmasFuture: Starting the Conversation," *Christmas Future*, December 11, 2008, http://www.christmasfuture.org/2008/12/11/tweetmasfuture_start/ (accessed July 25, 2009).

Balancing Archival Authority with Encouraging Authentic Voices to Engage with Records

Elizabeth Yakel

"Findability is at the center of a quiet revolution in how we define authority, allocate trust, and make decisions."[1]

Increasing the engagement of individuals and communities with archival collections has been a goal of archival repositories for decades. A century ago in the United States, an archival researcher had to be a graduate student or faculty member and present a letter of introduction to gain entrance to many archives. The selection of researchers paralleled collecting practices focusing on major figures, institutions, and events. Many repositories judged the researcher's ability to carry out a project, as well as his or her demeanor and institutional pedigree. Those researchers whom archivists deemed less qualified or whose questions did not meet approval were sent away. If allowed to enter the archives, some researchers, most notably genealogists, were deemed inferior even by such archival luminaries as T. R. Schellenberg and Howard Peckham.[2] Peckham went so far as to advocate that those researchers he termed "incompetent scholars ... whose research [the archivist] believes will be superficial or of no real significance" be excluded from manuscript repositories in research libraries.[3] The role of the archives was seen as not only the preservation but also the defense of records against misuse. The archivist's role was to protect the records, and one way to do this was to limit access to the records.

In the 1960s, archives began to open up. The practice of judging the capabilities of researchers declined, letters of introduction went by the wayside, and collecting policies transformed. Following calls from other archivists and historians, archivists began seeking records that documented daily life and individuals or groups who previously had been absent from the archives space. This could be considered the "First Great Opening" of archives. Archivists' fears that archives would be overrun by inexperienced researchers damaging documents or that researchers would be overwhelming reference archivists with inane questions have been unfounded. Archivists added a new fundamental value to archival work—access—and they adapted to a broader range of researchers through a series of mechanisms, such as subject guides, lectures, and orientations. External influences, such as the "Roots phenomenon" in the 1970s that greatly expanded the number of genealogists using archives, also played a role in this expansion and further opened archives' doors. I begin here because this era is waning in our memory. Collectively, we are forgetting the time when access was routinely denied due to such criteria as status and affiliation. The focus on archives and access is largely concentrated on government archives, particularly at the federal level.[4] Yet, the era of the 1960s and 1970s was when archivists reexamined their underlying mission and made a series of decisions that altered the balance between preservation and access and changed the relationship between archivists and researchers forever.

The rise of user studies followed this new focus on the researcher. This began as a trickle in the 1980s and became a flood in the 1990s and 2000s, making this area of research one of the most vibrant in archives.[5] These studies have used a variety of quantitative and qualitative methods—citation analysis, interviews, focus groups, surveys, observations, and content analysis. As a result, we now know more about the people who use archives than ever before. This research does have gaps: more is known about some types of researchers, such as historians and genealogists, than others.[6] More is also known about how researchers engage in certain activities, such as searching online finding aids[7] and viewing digital images.[8] However, all of the user studies in both the physical/analog environment or in virtual space point to surprisingly similar results. Researchers have trouble with archival terminology and are unfamiliar with the hierarchical and provenance-based organization of archives and the search processes in archives. In one way or another, these studies all point to the significant role mediation plays in archives and the key role of the archivist, whether omniscient or not, as mediator between researchers and records.[9] In 2004, Katharine Salzmann argued that archivists will retain this role; fast-forward six years and the picture is far from clear.[10] As discussed throughout this chapter, the role of the archivist as mediator is waning and is in some ways anathema to Archives 2.0.

Elsie Freeman was one of the early advocates of this perspective, arguing that archivists should change from their materials-focused mind-set to one that was user-centric.[11] She also posited that if archivists did not change their approach to reference service, people would go elsewhere for the information or change their projects.[12] Freeman's comments are even more pertinent today, with the proliferation of information on the web and the blurring of boundaries between archives, libraries, and museums in the digital realm.[13] Archives and archivists have to work harder to get and retain researchers' attention spans.

Today, we are facing an even more fundamental change in the relationship between researchers and archivists. What perhaps makes archivists fear the onslaught of Web 2.0 technologies is that we are facing a change in the relationships between the records and the researchers that leaves out archivists. Web 2.0 applications accelerate the process of engagement and invite participation and collaboration in ways that are often not imagined by website developers. The addition of multiple voices, through such mechanisms as commentary, tagging, and ratings to manuscripts, archival records, and finding aids on the web, has the potential to add new information and contexts to records in formal archival custody as well as to link materials that are both inside and outside of formal archival institutions. This is the "Second Great Opening" of the archives, and, although it furthers the focus on access begun in the "First Great Opening," it more directly encroaches on the authority of the archives/archivist to represent the collections.

Authority is a major issue that is both at the center of and challenged by Archives 2.0. I begin this essay with some thoughts on archives and authority, followed by an introduction to the concept of "cognitive authority" and a discussion of how this relates to archives and archivists. The essay then highlights several dimensions of archival authority that become salient in the Archives 2.0 environment as seen through the lens of the five case studies in this section as well as in other Archives 2.0 sites on the web. The goal of the essay is to foster deeper discussion rather than to solve the core questions surrounding how archivists can best navigate through the social web while balancing the core archival issue of authority with the mantra of the wisdom of crowds. In this essay I will not talk about Web 2.0 technologies per se; rather I will discuss the implicit social process of authority that is at work when Web 2.0 technologies are implemented to enable peer production. By "peer production," I mean a way of "producing goods and services that relies on self-organizing communities of individuals who come together to produce a shared outcome. In these communities the efforts of a large number of people are coordinated to create meaningful projects."[14] There are two aspects of this definition, both explicit and implicit, that should be noted. The first is the term "self-organizing communities," which indicates several things, but, in essence, peer production involves responsibility and agency on the part of the online community itself. The second element is the idea of a shared outcome or outcomes with all members of the community working toward a goal. In Archives 2.0 peer production systems, the process of construction, (re)creation, and verification of authority is an underlying theme and one on which this essay focuses.

Archives and Authority

Social computing technologies in archives challenge the fundamental social contract under which archivists have operated for millennia. In the social contract, archives maintain the authenticity of records through a chain of custody and retain a certain moral authority by representing these records accurately. The SAA *A Glossary of Archival and Records Terminology* defines *authenticity* as "the quality of being genuine, not a counterfeit, and free from tampering, and is typically inferred from internal and external evidence, including its physical characteristics, structure, content, and context."[15] Yet, there are deeper roots to this term and more nuances to its meaning. In her book *Trusting Records*, Heather MacNeil argues that as early as the days of ancient Rome, trust transferred from the record to the archives, giving the archives an "authenticating function."[16] Since that time, the legal system has changed even more to imbue authenticity in records through the bureaucratic system in which records were created and/or maintained (i.e., the chain of custody).[17] Authenticity is also derived from the methods archivists use to protect records from manipulation in the chain of custody. Authenticity of archives is predicated on a culture of evidence based on fixity and the idea of records as static. The meaning of content can be reinterpreted over time, but the physical (or now virtual) record itself is fixed. Likewise, provenance and respect des fonds both guard against manipulation of the context, asserting that there is evidence of the original context. Peter Van Garderen has noted that authenticity is a concern in the social web:

> I assume, of course, that professional archivists will have issues with blurring the lines between institutionally managed archival materials and descriptions and those contributed, enhanced or re-used by patrons. Copyright and restrictive access conditions placed on material by donors are a concern. Another legitimate concern would be to protect the authenticity of archival materials and the context of their original creation and use.[18]

Archives are imbued with authority. In the SAA *A Glossary of Archival and Records Terminology,* "authority" is defined in relation to "authority control," "authority file," and "authority record" and, when applied to an organization, it is applied narrowly, such as in "disposition authority" or "certificate authority."[19] Yet, authority is central to archives as an institution as well as the records. In her reflection on institutions that published digital resources, Abby Smith notes, "The only reason that we expect [an] image to be a truthful representative of the original is that we can rely on the integrity of the institution that has mounted the files and makes them available to us."[20] In spite of the spate of postmodern discussions challenging the "authority of the archive," these claims are predicated on an authority of the archives as an institution as well as the authority-giving function of the archives to the records it holds and, as an extension, the withholding of authority from records it does not hold.

Cognitive Authority

Patrick Wilson refers to the trustworthiness and reliability that people grant to texts, records, institutions, and people as cognitive authority.[21] Wilson argues that knowledge can be grossly divided into two types: firsthand and secondhand knowledge. Firsthand knowledge is what we know from our own experience and learning. But there are limits to what we have learned and experienced firsthand. So we rely on others to inform us about other things, such as the Society of American Archivists' 2009 meeting in Austin, Texas; a new archival descriptive standard; or the best restaurant in Washington, D.C. This latter type of knowledge is secondhand knowledge, and we use a variety of criteria (prior correct information, expertise of the individual, role of the organization) to select who we will rely on for this knowledge. When we select someone or someplace to rely on in this way, we endow the person, institution, or text with cognitive authority.[22] This differs from administrative authority in which people acknowledge a hierarchical relationship within an organization.[23] Cognitive authority also applies to an area of activity and can emanate by degree: given a serious health crisis, one can trust one's physician's opinion up to a certain point, until one asks for a second opinion. Finally, cognitive authority is related to credibility—for example, competence and trustworthiness.[24] Cognitive authority applies to archives and manuscripts on three levels: the institution, the record, and the archivist.

Wilson focuses less on institutions as the object of cognitive authority than on people. When he treats institutions, his focus is on disciplinary communities (e.g., scientists) as an institution or libraries. Still, his discussion, while incomplete, is important. Wilson argues that there is a "liberal library" that is characterized by its broad collecting policies encompassing works that have and do not have cognitive authority. This is opposed to a "didactic library," which would only select trusted or authoritative works in an area. An example might be a school library or a library in a doctor's office. While he acknowledges that all libraries have selection policies that exclude items, the basic idea is that the liberal library collects widely across the spectrum of works with varying degrees of cognitive authority. Furthermore, he posits that it is consumer demand that drives these selection policies. Unfortunately, he does not explain the nature of the cognitive authority of libraries as institutions. I would propose that it is people's belief that these libraries collect materials representing a variety of perspectives and engage in some type of balancing that is the source of their cognitive authority.

This extrapolation of Wilson's ideas to archival and manuscript repositories may be a stretch; he discounts historians as having cognitive authority and dismisses the notion that there are any institutions associated with the production of history.[25] This is a difficult and controversial section of Wilson's book. At the same time he discounts historians, he simultaneously argues that scientists make up an "institution of science" and that this scientific institution does have cognitive authority. Given debates about global warming and creationism, this argument seems less persuasive than it perhaps did in 1983 when Wilson wrote the book. However, I would argue that his views on the production of history are wrong. There are institutions associated with the production of history—archives and manuscript repositories—and these institutions do have cognitive authority. Furthermore, this authority of archives is partly attributable to the nature of the selection processes and the attempt to document some realm of experience. It is also due to the function of archives to ensure accountability, protect the rights of citizens, and preserve cultural heritage. The opening up of archives has potentially increased the identification of archives as sites of authority. Wilson makes a similar claim that a publishing house known for good books gains cognitive authority that is passed along to new texts it prints.[26] Archives also possess authority to represent collections (an authority again that the postmodernists acknowledge while challenging the representations themselves). In general, most researchers rely on archival representations (finding aids) to locate materials and have complained most about the lack of representations—thus the recent focus on "hidden collections."

Many of the attributes by which people judge the cognitive authority of texts can also be applied to records and manuscripts as well as to
finding aids. In addition to association with an archives, as noted above,
authorship (provenance), publication history (custodial history), and intrinsic plausibility are all associated with the cognitive authority of texts.
Yet, for archival materials cognitive authority and credibility are slightly
different because they are used differently from texts. Archival materials are used as evidence and do provide information on facts; archival
materials also present perspectives and accounts that are not necessarily
true but are still valuable for insight into contemporary attitudes, values,
and beliefs. This split between authority and truthfulness when assessing
records and manuscripts differs from credibility judgments for other information media. Finding aids, along with archivists themselves, are perhaps
the major means of findability of archival materials and can also be viewed
as texts that have cognitive authority and which reflect that of the archives
and the archivist. As a representation of the collection, the finding aid
serves as an authoritative mapping of a collection's content and context.

Wilson primarily discusses how cognitive authority is ascribed to
people. Again his discussion centers on librarians, but the application of
his ideas to archivists is possible. Wilson considers whether a librarian can
be an "authority on authorities" or "one who can be trusted to tell us who
else can be trusted,"[27] but he ultimately decides this role is impossible.
Librarians cannot possibly know each text and information source about
all the subjects represented in their collections. Yet, this is just what is often
expected of the "omniscient" archivist.[28] Given the amount of mediation
and necessity of intercession by archivists in analog archives, researchers
often endow archivists with cognitive authority. At the same time, this
authority is fragile; some researchers are constantly assessing how much
they can rely on and trust archivists.[29]

Archival Authority and Peer Production

The difficulties inherent in peer production in archives become apparent
when thinking about the frequently mentioned and successful instances of
peer production; websites, such as *Wikipedia*; and open-source software

development, such as Linux. *Wikipedia* and Linux are often cited as the exemplars. Neither of these instances of peer production is within a formal institution. Yet, both have achieved cognitive authority with an internal structure and a small but existent hierarchy to support the "self-organizing communities" within *Wikipedia* and Linux. This small hierarchy consists of a limited number of people (kernal) who make mission-critical decisions and facilitate the work of others. Still, the organizational structure of *Wikipedia* and Linux is far less hierarchical and formal than that of archives and special collections and the institutions in which they reside. Yochai Benkler argues that the structure of peer production in *Wikipedia* and Linux resembles a hub-and-spoke model with a core of dedicated workers who are involved in such activities as directing policy and managing the technology. Creating the core set of rules and standards is done in the kernal as well as in the commons through peer production.[30] While the hub is involved in major decisions and managing the technology, the work of peer production is carried on in the spokes where work is highly compartmentalized. *Wikipedia* and Linux are so successful because the commons does take responsibility in managing the pieces. Interdependencies are limited, such as in *Wikipedia*, where work on one article does not affect other articles. This differs greatly from archives, which have more interdependencies among archival functions, and many of these are related to the maintenance of authenticity. Furthermore, archives and manuscript repositories are generally hierarchical; even those with a small staff are located in institutions that tend to be organized around hierarchical models. How well archives and special collections can incorporate and support the work of "self-organizing communities" is an open question. How much authority can peer production activities be given before fundamental assumptions about archival institutions and the nature of archival authority are called into question. Can archives remain trusted institutions if they share authority over the representation of records? Will participants be able to "self-organize" and thrive in an environment with greater control and limitations to the wisdom of crowds?

We see one possible answer to this question in the PhotosNormandie case study. The creators of this project, Patrick Peccatte, an information scientist, and Michel Le Querrec, an amateur historian, have created a Flickr photostream of photographs originally from the U.S. National Archives and Library and Archives Canada but more recently published online by the Regional Council of Lower Normandy to commemorate the sixtieth anniversary of the liberation of Normandy from the Nazis. When the Regional Council declined to cooperate, Peccatte and Le Querrec copied photographs that were no longer under copyright from the Regional Council's site and created their own photostream on Flickr. They purposefully recreated the archives content in Flickr because it was not possible to interact with it on the original site. Their motivations were a passion for the materials and the challenge of the work. Is this loss of control a loss of authority for the archives or the texts?

Researchers have noted the transition of authority in participatory websites. In discussing digital libraries, David Lankes notes that participatory information networks allow visitors to assess the credibility of information through "conversations" with other users.[31] This, in turn, decreases the need for pre-established information authority (in Lankes case–digital librarians). Andrew Flanagin and Miriam Metzger posit that in Web 2.0 sites credibility and authority are decoupled. This calls into question "our conception of authority as being centralized, impenetrable, and singularly accurate" thus changing "the model of single authority based on hierarchy to a model of multiple authorities based on networks of peers."[32]

How should the conflicting archival impulses of opening up the archives and remaining the one authoritative archival voice be balanced in the emerging peer production environment? Can coherent representations be presented with multiple voices and perhaps conflicting information? When multiple voices become part of the record and/or its metadata, what is the nature of the authoritative record?

Negotiating Authority

Negotiation of authority is a characteristic of peer production systems. Authority quickly comes to the fore when archives use external services. Services such as Flickr and websites such as *Wikipedia* exert authority through highly developed mechanisms for maintaining themselves and the social web within their sites. Among the interesting aspects of the chapter by Michele Combs (Syracuse University) and the chapter by Helena Zinkham and Michelle Springer (Library of Congress) are their experiences in peer production systems that are not of their own making. The Syracuse University Archives case study stands out from the others in that it does not primarily solicit user-generated content but provides additional information and links to primary sources within *Wikipedia*. In essence, the Syracuse project adds the cognitive authority of the archivist to *Wikipedia*. Combs goes into great detail about how the *Wikipedia* commons debated whether archival institutions adding links to collections in their custody was a public good or self-promotion (spurred by Ann M. Lally and Carole Dunford's article in *D-Lib*),[33] summarizing the "Discussion" sections, which appear on the *Wikipedia* site as well as in every article. It is here that major debates, discussions, and differences of opinion are presented. The thinking around the role of cultural heritage professionals continues to evolve, and over the summer of 2010 new guidelines emerged.

> Museum curators, librarians, archivists, art historians, heritage interpreters, conservators, documentation managers, subject specialists, and managers of a special collection (or similar profession) are encouraged to use their knowledge to help improve Wikipedia, or to share their information with Wikipedia in the form of links to their resources.[34]

By understanding the social system in *Wikipedia*, Combs and her colleagues at Syracuse University identified a means of working within *Wikipedia*'s social norms to integrate information about their collections into *Wikipedia*. As a result, the Syracuse University archivists have become a part of the social web in a way that the archives-generated sites have not. Combs explains the social mores of *Wikipedia*:

> [e]ditors wishing to add such links would do well to respect the spirit of *Wikipedia* by contributing substantively to its content as well. This discussion gave me the idea for our project and also led directly to our two guidelines: add content whenever possible, not just a link; and only link if our collection (as represented by our finding aid) has something unusual or significant to offer. (See p. 145.)

There are other models of participation with *Wikipedia*. In an interesting negotiation between authorities, the National Library of Germany's naming authority (Personennamendatei [PND]) is cooperating with the German version of *Wikipedia*. The German naming authority has developed systematic methods of linking authority records to Wikipedia entries.[35] This example is one of truly lending the authority of the institution to *Wikipedia*.

Zinkham and Springer recount the Library of Congress's (LOC) discussions with Flickr. These discussions led to the development of a special area of Flickr for cultural heritage institutions, the Flickr Commons. Before the discussions with the LOC, Flickr had established norms for expressing copyright. Through negotiation, the LOC convinced Flickr to add more categories to more accurately express the copyright status of some LOC photographs. Flickr, however, would not change any of its rules about deletion of comments. As a result, Springer and Zinkham note that they had to be "familiar with any community guidelines. Members referee each other's behavior, but occasionally inappropriate content may need to be deleted." (See p. 113.) This aligned with Flickr's "play nice" philosophy. Ceding control and authority and trusting the social web was an important lesson. The LOC's influence on Flickr's social norms is not typical. Few archives could do this. More common is the Syracuse University case, which shows the archives adapting to the social norms systems. Noteworthy in both essays, however, is the initiation into and understanding of social norms in these peer production systems. Both the Library of Congress (Flickr) and Syracuse University (*Wikipedia*) learned these social conventions in order to participate.

The Not-So-Social Web of Archives

Discussions of archival authority pervade four of the five chapters in this section. Combs, Zinkham and Springer, Guy Grannum, and Tim Sherratt are concerned with the cognitive authority of the archives or the perception that the archives deliver authoritative information (whether in terms of finding aids or actual archival materials). Yet, in some of these articles cognitive authority is not linked to the archivist, but rather to the archives' reputation, trust, and (in an anthropomorphic way) identity. The authors see these as key attributes that archives convey to the public and which help archives to fulfill their role in their communities and/or society at large. At the same time, these case studies demonstrate the care being taken to develop relationships and engage new audiences, much in the same way they have worked to foster users in the physical repository. Throughout these essays one sees how the impetus for authority and maintaining authoritativeness gets in the way of these sites fulfilling their true potential as part of the social web and enabling peer production to work to its fullest. The institution in each of these four case studies has made decisions about how to manage its participation in the social web. Interestingly, the three national institutions—The National Archives (TNA) in the United Kingdom, the National Archives of Australia (NAA), and the Library of Congress (LOC) in the United States—appear on the surface to be more concerned about maintaining authority than community.

While the goals of PhotosNormandie mirror those of the archives— to provide greater exposure for the photographs and to generate better descriptive information—PhotosNormandie has also carefully crafted a space for visitors to discuss the photographs, a Flickr group called "Discussions sur PhotosNormandie" (http://www.flickr.com/groups/ discussionphotosnormandie), where discussions, negotiations, and decisions about description are made.[36] However, in actuality the independent project PhotosNormandie imposes the greatest amount of control and does not have an interest in the long-term preservation of the contributions or the online community engaged with the site.

Two of the techniques used to maintain cognitive authority are separation and moderation. In the case of The National Archives (TNA) in the United Kingdom, the National Archives of Australia (NAA), and PhotosNormandie, the project's descriptive products are separated from the social space created for users. The National Archives utilizes wiki software (MediaWiki, the same platform used by *Wikipedia*) for users to expand on, comment on, transcribe documents, and so on. In turn, *Your Archives* contains links to the official catalog. TNA also does not implement the "Discussion" function, allowing no discussion in conjunction with the article pages. User pages do have a "Talk" page that allows for discussion, although it is disconnected from the page (subject) of discussion. Perhaps because of the more specialized nature of archives and the large but still limited collections at TNA, the site appears to be much more controlled than *Wikipedia*. When asking for contributors, a list of types of pages to contribute to are listed, but there is no structure, as in *Wikipedia*, where people are responsible for pages. Visitors are given responsibility for content but not management of the site, making contributors not quite peers in the production process.

The archivists are also the most visible in this site. TNA archivists seem to monitor content and add information, primarily linking online finding aids and other information in the official catalog to the entries. These interventions both assert the authority of the archivists as well as add authority to the articles in the peer production system.

The National Archives of Australia adopts the scrapbook metaphor, which is not only separate from the finding aids but also purposefully different in form.

> We needed to make it clear where public contributions began and archival data ended. . . . A "scrapbook" was also something quite different to a finding aid. The informality helped to make the boundary clear between record and response. The separation was physical as well as intellectual. . . . (See p. 131.)

This explicit need to separate peer production from the "official" finding aid is ubiquitous in Archives 2.0 instances. This is the best articulation of the separation with some indication of the thinking behind it. The separation appears to be a way to protect the authority of the archives (in this case, the catalog) while allowing peer production on the periphery.

The separation between record and response is just one of the separations apparent in Archives 2.0 sites. The other and perhaps more important separation is between the archivists and the community. This is starkly seen in the chapter on PhotosNormandie. Would there have been a different result if the regional council had agreed to participate in the project? How best for archivists to be of, but not totally in, the community still needs to be worked out. In almost all cases of Archives 2.0, the archivist is a distinct, omniscient, and controlling authority, rather than a member of the community working toward shared goals.

Archivists face a conundrum: foster peer production processes with shared responsibility that impinges on, changes, and recontextualizes the records, or restrict user-generated content to a virtual space controlled by the archives? Archivists are currently doing the latter; but are we losing more in the long run? Are we also giving up something when we maintain cognitive authority at the cost of creating communities that might contribute in unforeseen ways to the archives? What is also worrisome is whether these practices actually negate peer production. By relegating user contribution to special areas and, more importantly, not trying to delegate any responsibility for the site to the community, are archives actually engaging in the social web?

Negotiating between incorporation and separation is difficult and the archival literature presents a diversity of opinions. Robert Middletown and Julie Lee note that archivists have

> deep-seated concerns about authority once user-generated content is brought into the mix. The concept of external parties editing the content of an institutional site is problematic from both a brand and a "trusted organization" perspective.[37]

Others, such as Wendy Duff and Verne Harris, have argued for greater openness and transparency:

> We need to create descriptive systems that are more permeable. In doing so archivists will have to relinquish some of their power to control access to, and interpretation of, their records. . . . We need to create holes that allow in the voices of our users. We need descriptive architectures that allow our users to speak into them. Architectures, for instance, which invite genealogists, historians, students, and other users to annotate the finding aid or to add their own descriptions would encourage the leaking of power.[38]

Both of these passages raise issues about cognitive authority and the implicit power relationships that are part of this concept. They also demonstrate an almost irreconcilable difference of opinion. Furthermore, both focus on user-generated content as a point of authority. Neither consider

the communities that form around Archives 2.0 sites and this larger context
in which authority is negotiated.

Authenticity and Credibility: User-generated Content

Four of the projects described in this section actively moderate user-
generated content. Interestingly, in the case of the LOC and the Flickr
Commons, the moderation is less geared toward inappropriate posts and
more in relation to "distracting" notes, at times obscuring the actual image.
Furthermore, it is members of the LOC Flickr community who are calling
for these deletions.

Authority and authenticity collide more drastically on *Your Archives*:

> Post-moderating has also raised concerns from some users and staff about the control
> of content before publishing, issues surrounding trust and the accuracy of content,
> and questions on whether it is appropriate for a government department and trusted
> archive to more or less relinquish editorial authority to the user. (See pp. 120–121.)

Grannum's case study of *Your Archives* shows the uneasiness that can
arise when the world of archives and social media intertwine. Each page
of *Your Archives* features a disclaimer: "The National Archives does not
vouch for the accuracy of information appearing in *Your Archives*." This
disclaimer is interesting for two reasons. First, it explicitly separates wiki
content from "official" content. Second, the implication is that all the other
information (archival records or the finding aids) in The National Archives
is accurate. Is this a measure to support cognitive authority? Why is it
necessary to flag wiki content in this way? Is trust in archives or public
institutions so fragile? What assumptions are archivists making about
users of the social web?

The most heavily edited and filtered site is the PhotosNormandie presence on Flickr, which is also the only project not implemented by archivists.
There is no provision for maintaining the discussion around the photographs
and despite an active Flickr group, "Discussions sur PhotosNormandie,"
there seems little thought to maintaining the community. This seems to
go against the ethos of the social web. An editor synthesizes "information

collected in a discussion or from other sources and write[s] a precise and coherent caption. According to our process, anyone may propose new descriptions to the group, but it is the editor alone who decides the final text based on the collected information." (See p. 155.) While this process may result in better captions overall, much context, a vital element for archives, is lost.

While Patrick Peccatte explicitly discusses what happens to user-generated content in PhotosNormandie, other sites are less explicit. In a separate report on the Flickr project, Springer and her colleagues discuss the utilization of user-generated content and adding it to existing meta-data.[39] As for the TNA and the National Archives of Australia, it is hard to understand how user-generated content will be saved or incorporated into the "official" venues.

Authority as a Non-rival Good

A critical question for archivists is whether Web 2.0 applications challenge, enhance, or remain neutral in regard to archival authority. In the physical repository, decisions about content, description, and representation are made in processing (back) rooms and transparency is low. Michelle Light and Tom Hyry have long argued for increased transparency in the development of finding aids, using annotations about the processing process and the processor him- or herself.[40] Web 2.0 applications are about openness and transparency, so revealing decision making and process can be scary, and putting this information out there in a mutable form invites commentary, if not challenges.

The concerns expressed about authority also seem to indicate a deeper, more fundamental assumption that authority is a finite property. If we believe this, participating in the social web means that archives either give up authority or their authority is called into question by competing and erroneous information about their collections. By enabling wider participation, the legitimacy of those "in authority" (e.g., archivists) to control representations, may be partially undermined. The experience of the archives in these case studies does not support these fears.

In a 2007 article, Max Evans argues that archives should be considered public goods, and he argues that in the online environment, they are non-rival.[41] Non-rival goods are those that can be consumed by many people simultaneously. For example, we can both use the park and enjoy it without taking away each other's pleasure in the experience. In Archives 2.0, we can both examine and tag a Library of Congress photograph on Flickr at the same time and then benefit from each other's interaction with the online photograph.

But consider a different application of this concept in the Web 2.0 environment: What if authority is not a finite property and, when authority for the description and representation of digital objects is shared, it simply means that more parties are drawing on the limitless available supply of authority? In economic terms this would be a non-rivalrous good. In this way the archives is not only sharing authority but also creating a ubiquitous authority that could lead to an undiscovered power of the social web for cultural institutions. The next section discusses the ways in which individuals and communities interact with archival materials and descriptions in these case studies and the unexpected benefits of archival participation in online communities.

Participating in the Social Web

User-generated comments are not new for archives; however, the social web provides a means of systematically collecting, discussing, and making these comments available to others in a structured way. Both the Library of Congress and The National Archives discuss their long traditions of user feedback on collections and finding aids and the difficulty of capturing this information in an orderly manner.

In all cases, providing a venue for user feedback and commentary has opened a floodgate of contributions. At the Library of Congress,

> by July 2009, Flickr members had submitted more than 17,000 comments (from 6,000 accounts) and more than 104,000 tags on the photos. The crowd-sourcing benefit of user-generated tags and requests for photos to join subject-based Flickr groups has resulted in increased discovery of our photographs. The high level of

accuracy in both the additional information we have verified and the spelling of the tags has been reassuring. (See p. 109.)

The incredible numbers generated on the web is staggering for archives. Reflecting on the Flickr Commons experience of the Powerhouse Museum in Australia, Sebastian Chan reported that

> In the first 4 weeks of the Commons we had more views of the photos than the same photos in the entirety of last year on our own website. It wasn't as if we made the images on our own website all that hard to find—they were well indexed on our own site by Google, they were made available to the national federated image search/repository *Picture Australia*, and they also existed in our OPAC. Still, that was no match for Flickr.[42]

Yet, the feedback from users extends well beyond error detection and identification. The social web has opened up new ways for individuals and communities to interact with archives and archival collections. In the case of *Your Archives:*

> the user community has been using *Your Archives* in ways we hadn't considered: researchers have been writing transcripts, abstracts, and indexes of digitized sources, opening up the archives in a way that wasn't possible before. (See pp. 123–124.)

This is one mark of success and a transformative moment for the site: not only is adaptation and appropriation by the common[43] possible, but it is an evolution into a more recognizable form of peer production.

Many of the comments generated also go well beyond the records:

> We are enjoying the many different ways that users define their own experiences and regularly invent new ways to engage the photographs. Many comments are fan mail, ranging from "Beautiful!" to "I happened across this account tonight. What treasures! Thank you for adding them to Flickr. They are pictures I might not have ever seen otherwise." Flickr members also contribute then-and-now pairings of images, combine photos with maps, make jokes inspired by the images, and suggest new collections they'd like to see. Other comments discuss history in general, recollect personal experience and grandparents' lives, and recreate photo scenes in modern settings. (See p. 107.)

These types of comments have no place in our current descriptive metadata for images and records, yet it is just these types of comments that recontextualize the records and change both the records and their context forever. These comments also add another layer of authenticity to the records with their "authentic voices." The LOC and PhotosNormandie appear to be the case studies that elicited most of these types of comments, but these are exactly the types of comments that indicate a community that both revolves around and extends beyond the records. These comments also show how close to the records some visitors can be and are more characteristic of well-defined sites, such as Beyond Brown Paper, which draws a more limited but devoted audience.[44] Beyond Brown Paper is a collaboration between three departments at Plymouth State University: the Lamson Library's Michael J. Spinelli Jr. Center for University Archives and Special Collections, the Karl Drerup Art Gallery, and the Center for Rural Partnerships. The project documents the Brown Company of Berlin, New Hampshire, a major manufacturing company in the region, from the nineteenth century until it closed in the mid-1960s.

The impact of Archives 2.0 sites is substantial. In the case of the Flickr Commons (which hosts the LOC photographs), a group called the Indicommons (http://www.indicommons.org) has emerged.

> Flickr community members who felt passionately about the value of The Commons created a robust discussion group within Flickr and also opened a blog site to highlight collections. They curate exhibits that gather thematically related photos from across The Commons, interview Commons users as well as archivists, develop applications to help both public users and image contributors, and post news of events at the physical repositories. (See pp. 108–109.)

Still, fostering online communities is not discussed in great depth in these case studies and is one feature that no Archives 2.0 site has dealt with very effectively. One of the earliest cultural institutions using Flickr was the National Library of Australia with Picture Australia, which began in 2000.[45] Picture Australia has two parts: 1) a federated search service for cultural institutions in Australia, and 2) the Flickr account where individuals can comment or link additional pictures.[46] Picture Australia has done substantial work to build the number of contributors (both institutions and individuals) and to create a community around the project. For a time, Picture Australia sponsored annual meetings of contributors to link the virtual and physical participants.

The daily work of community building in Archives 2.0 space is difficult, and there are few precedents to follow. Archives and special collections are only beginning to understand how to sustain online communities. The structures of the communities that will emerge around records and the norms for peer production in online cultural heritage communities are still evolving. One thing is clear, though: the community around the sites must be engaged, committed, and regenerative to sustain sites by distributing much of the work. Even successful and established sites, such as *Wikipedia*, must deal with challenges that emerge as the sites mature.[47] What we see in all the archival sites mentioned in this chapter is that the brunt of the work in managing and maintaining the sites is assumed by the archives itself. What I envision is a social structure characterized by a shared approach to governance, authority, and concern for sustainability of the communities (rather than the sites).

Appropriation and adaptation in the peer production process are key factors in having a vibrant and evolving site. It demonstrates both uptake by the community and responsibility for shared innovation on the site. For these transformations to occur, though, archivists need to share more authority with the online community and responsibility for the management of the site. A vision of the type of transformation required is best articulated in Mapping Our Anzacs: "Instead of merely being markers on a map, the records will start to overlay and inform the very spaces in which we move. The stories they contain will become part of our journeys; the people they document will have found their way home." (See p. 138.) The PhotosNormandie case study, although based on appropriation, provides a theoretical framework for this type of transformation, which the author calls *redocumentarisation*, a collective re-description of objects that is only possible through the social web. This leads me to think there are more types of authority and more possibilities to extend archival authority through the social web than we have yet imagined.

A final lesson from these case studies is that library and archives staff cannot simply post items on the web and sit back and watch users reinterpret their collections. For example, Syracuse University's use of *Wikipedia* is predicated on an open give-and-take in editing, consistent participation over time, and the establishment of a reputation on the web that is distinct from that in the physical repository. Engagement on the social web works both ways. The success of these sites cannot be measured only by the number of contributors or the number of new subject headings repositories are able to incorporate into their catalogs. The projects described in the case studies are successful because they interact with the online community forming around their archives and manuscripts. As Zinkham and Springer write, "The level of engagement provided by the archives or library helps shape the amount of involvement from the community." (See p. 113.) Despite reservations about maintaining authority, archivists are committed to experimenting in order to figure out what it means for archives to be part of the social web.

Conclusion

More than twenty years ago, Terry Cook argued that "archivists must transcend mere information, and mere information management, if they wish to search for, and lead others to seek, 'knowledge' and meaning among the records in their care."[48] Archives 2.0 and the ensuing Second Great Opening is the latest step and perhaps greatest challenge in this process. Archives and archivists face substantial challenges to their authority but also tremendous benefits in terms of how archives, archivists, and records are viewed in society.

The contrast between the relationship between researchers, archivists, and documents in the First and Second Great Openings is best articulated in an article by Angèle Alain and Michelle Foggett.[49] In their comparison of Library and Archives Canada's site Moving Here, Staying Here: The Canadian Immigrant Experience[51] and the National Archives' (UK) website Moving Here: 200 Years of Migration to England,[51] which both employ Archives 2.0 features, the authors uncover challenges with each approach. Working indirectly with communities through genealogy centers, historical societies, and subject experts, Library Archives Canada found gaps in documentation and poor coverage of some immigrant groups. The National Archives (UK) went so far as to offer computer literacy classes for immigrant communities to increase participation, but community members were disappointed that their contributions were not immediately available online. Archivists on the social web are only too often reminded of their obligations.

In the past, archives have been heavily mediated. This has privileged the role of the archivist and placed the archivist at the center of findability. Essentially, find the archivist, find the source. Archives 2.0 challenges this hegemony and gives everyone the power to be an archivist by creating his or her own online collections, describing records through tagging and commenting, and providing reference to others on the site. While the First Great Opening increased access to records, the Second Great Opening opens the archives as well as the records.

Reading these case studies makes me want to create a research agenda focusing on issues arising from Archives 2.0. There is a great need to study the nature of cognitive authority of archivists and of archives and the dynamics of the emerging shared authority structures. More research showing the nature of use, the volume of the comments, and the resulting conversational threads is needed to understand the dynamics of peer production in the archival social web. Additional research is also needed on the effects of the Second Great Opening, particularly vis-à-vis the relationships between remote researchers and archivists and researchers and the records. We also need to know more about how researchers want to interact with materials and whether any form of mediation is acceptable and under what circumstances.

Many institutions are currently being questioned in our society. Archives are among the institutions whose authority is being challenged, both by those who have been traditionally disenfranchised and underrepresented in the collections and by the digital natives who view authorship and authority very differently.[52] Ironically, at the same time that archives are being challenged by the push toward more open access and Archives 2.0 features, they are also being squeezed from the other side by commercial ventures, such as Ancestry[53] and Footnote,[54] which are providing enhanced access to archival materials for a fee, which consumers seem to be willing to pay. The actions of PhotosNormandie creators Peccatte and Le Querrec may be just the tip of the iceberg. We are at the beginning of a transformation in these relationships—perhaps it is the scariest time. We are not used to thinking in expanded ways about the nature of archival authority and we are still quite anxious about the effects of sharing that authority. The question is not whether materials will remain open and accessible on the web, but how they are embraced by new communities and whether these new communities forming around the digital records accept the mantle of cognitive authority that comes from participating in the social web of archives.

Notes

[1] Peter Morville, *Ambient Findability: What We Find Changes Who We Become* (Sebastopol, CA: O'Reilly Media, 2005), 15.

[2] T. R. Schellenberg, *Modern Archives: Principles and Techniques* (Chicago: University of Chicago Press, 1956); see pages 232–235 for the relevant passages. Howard H. Peckham, "Aiding the Scholar in Using Manuscript Collections," *American Archivist* 19 (July 1956): 221–228.

[3] Peckham, "Aiding the Scholar," 225.

[4] Randall C. Jimerson, "Archives for All: Professional Responsibility and Social Justice," *American Archivist* 70 (Fall/Winter 2007): 252–281.

[5] For a review of user studies, see Anneli Sundqvist, "The Use of Records—A Literature Review," *Archives & Social Studies* 1, no. 1 (2007): 623–653, http://socialstudies.cartagena.es/images/PDF/no1/sundqvist_use.pdf (accessed September 1, 2010).

[6] Given the Sundqvist review cited above, I will not go into detail on these studies here. To begin an investigation of historians, see Helen R. Tibbo, "Primarily History in America: How U.S. Historians Search for Primary Materials at the Dawn of the Digital Age," *American Archivist* 66 (Spring/Summer 2003): 9–50. For genealogists, see Elizabeth Yakel and Deborah A. Torres, "Genealogists as a 'Community of Records,' " *American Archivist* 70 (Spring/Summer 2007): 93–113.

[7] For example, see Christopher Prom, "User Interactions with Electronic Finding Aids in a Controlled Setting," *American Archivist* 67 (Fall/Winter 2004): 234–268.

[8] For example, see Karen Collins, "Providing Subject Access to Images: A Study of User Queries," *American Archivist* 61 (Winter 1998): 36–55.

[9] Wendy M. Duff and Allyson Fox, "You're a Guide Rather Than an Expert: Archival Reference from an Archivist's Point of View," *Journal of the Society of Archivists* 27, no. 2 (2006): 129–153.

[10] Katharine A. Salzmann, " 'Contact US': Archivists and Remote Users in the Digital Age," *Reference Librarian* 41, no. 85 (2004): 43–50.

[11] Elsie Freeman, "In the Eye of the Beholder: Archives Administration from the User's Point of View," *American Archivist* 47 (Spring 1984): 111–123.

[12] Elsie Freeman, "Buying Quarter Inch Holes: Public Support Through Results," *Midwestern Archivist* 10, no. 2 (1985): 89–97.

[13] Paul F. Marty, "An Introduction to Digital Convergence: Libraries, Archives, and Museums in the Information Age," *Archival Science* 8, no. 4 (December 2008): 247–250.

[14] "Peer Production," *Wikipedia*, http://en.wikipedia.org/wiki/Peer_production (accessed February 23, 2010).

[15] Richard Pearce-Moses, comp., *A Glossary of Archival and Records Terminology*, Society of American Archivists, 2005, http://www.archivists.org/glossary/term_details.asp?DefinitionKey=9 (accessed August 31, 2009).

[16] Heather MacNeil, *Trusting Records: Legal, Historical, and Diplomatic Perspectives* (Dordrecht, Netherlands: Kluwer Academic Publishers, 2000), 2.

[17] Ibid., 56.

[18] Peter Van Garderen, "Archival Institutions and Web 2.0," *archivemati.ca blog*, May 8, 2006, http://archivemati.ca/2006/05/08/web-20-and-archival-institutions/#more-34 (accessed September 15, 2010).

[19] Pearce-Moses, "Glossary."

[20] Abby Smith, *Why Digitize?* (Washington, DC: Council on Library and Information Resources, 1999), 5.

[21] Patrick Wilson, *Second-Hand Knowledge: An Inquiry into Cognitive Authority* (Westport, CT: Greenwood Press, 1983), 81.

[22] Wilson, *Second-Hand Knowledge*, 3–10

[23] Herbert Simon, *Administrative Behavior*, 2nd ed. (New York: Free Press, 1965), Chapter 7, passim.

[24] Wilson, *Second-Hand Knowledge*, 13–16.

[25] Ibid., 96.

[26] Ibid., 168.

[27] Ibid., 179.

[28] Mary Jo Pugh, "The Illusion of Omniscience: Subject Access and the Reference Archivist," *American Archivist* 45 (Winter 1982): 33–44.

[29] Elizabeth Yakel and Deborah A. Torres, "AI: Archival Intelligence and User Expertise," *American Archivist* 66 (Spring/Summer 2003): 67–68.

[30] Yochai Benkler, "Coase's Penguin, or Linux and the Nature of the Firm," *Yale Law Journal* 112 (2002): 369–446.

[31] R. David Lankes, "Credibility on the Internet: Shifting from Authority to Reliability," *Journal of Documentation* 64, no. 5 (2008): 667–686.

[32] Andrew J. Flanagin and Miriam J. Metzger, "Digital Media and Youth: Unparalleled Opportunity and Unprecedented Responsibility," in *Digital Media, Youth, and Credibility*, ed. Miriam J. Metzger and Andrew J. Flanagin, 5–27 (Cambridge, MA: MIT Press, 2007), 17.

[33] Ann M. Lally and Carolyn E. Dunford, "Using Wikipedia to Extend Digital Collections," *D-Lib Magazine* 13, no. 5/6 (May/June 2007), http://www.dlib.org/dlib/may07/lally/05lally.

html (accessed August 22, 2009). For an update, see Ann Lally, "Using Wikipedia to Highlight Digital Collections at the University of Washington," *Interactive Archivist*, http://lib.byu.edu/sites/interactivearchivist/case-studies/wikipedia-at-uw/#footnote10 (accessed February 23, 2010).

[34] To read the 2007 *Wikipedia* discussion about the propriety of archivists adding links to archival materials, see "Wikipedia talk: WikiProject Spam/2007/Unusual University Spam Archive Jul," *Wikipedia*, http://en.wikipedia.org/wiki/Wikipedia_talk:WikiProject_Spam/2007_Archive_Jul#Library_links_discussions (accessed September 1, 2010). By August 2010 the following statement appeared on the web page titled "Wikipedia: Conflict of Interest" in the section "Subject and Cultural Heritage Professionals": "Museum curators, librarians, archivists, art historians, heritage interpreters, conservators, documentation managers, subject specialists, and managers of a special collection (or similar profession) are encouraged to use their knowledge to help improve Wikipedia, or to share their information with Wikipedia in the form of links to their resources," http://en.wikipedia.org/wiki/Wikipedia:Conflict_of_interest#Subject_and_culture_sector_professionals (accessed September 1, 2010). This was a result of an April 2010 discussions such as "Wikipedia talk: Conflict of Interest," http://en.wikipedia.org/wiki/Wikipedia_talk:Conflict_of_interest#Requesting_opinions:_conflict_of_interest.3F (accessed September 1, 2010).

[35] "Name Authority File," *Wikipedia*, http://translate.google.com/translate?hl=en&sl=de&u=http://de.wikipedia.org/wiki/Personennamendatei&ei=YLZ6S4T4OtOMnQfPrZHQCQ&sa=X&oi=translate&ct=result&resnum=3&ved=0CBYQ7gEwAg&prev=/search%3Fq%3DPersonennamendatei%2B%28PND%29%2Bwikipedia%26hl%3Den (accessed September 1, 2010). This article links to a page entitled "Help: PND," which describes the process. National Library of Germany's naming authority [Personennamendatei (PND)] is analogous to the Library of Congress's Name Authority Cooperative Program (NACO).

[36] "Discussions sur PhotosNormandie," Flickr, http://www.flickr.com/groups/discussionphotosnormandie (accessed February 23, 2010). There is also an English-language group, "Discussions in English on PhotosNormandie," Flickr, available at http://www.flickr.com/groups/discussionsinenglishonphotosnormandie (accessed February 23, 2010).

[37] Michael R. Middleton and Julie M. Lee, "Cultural Institutions and Web 2.0," paper presented at the Fourth Seminar on Research Applications in Information and Library Studies (RAILS 4), November 30, 2007, RMIT University, Melbourne, p. 19, http://eprints.qut.edu.au/10808/ (accessed September 1, 2010).

[38] Wendy Duff and Verne Harris, "Stories and Names: Archival Description as Narrating Records and Constructing Meanings," *Archival Science* 2, no. 3/4 (2002): 279.

[39] Michelle Springer, Beth Dulabahn, Phil Michel, Barbara Natanson, David Reser, David Woodward, and Helena Zinkham, "For the Common Good: The Library of Congress Flickr Pilot Project," October 30, 2008, http://www.loc.gov/rr/print/flickr_report_final.pdf (accessed September 1, 2010).

[40] Michelle Light and Tom Hyry, "Colophons and Annotations: New Directions for the Finding Aid," *American Archivist* 65 (Fall/Winter 2002): 216–230.

[41] Max Evans, "Archives of the People, by the People, for the People," *American Archivist* 70 (Fall/Winter 2007): 387–400.

[42] Sebastian Chan, "Commons on Flickr—A Report, Some Concepts and a FAQ—The First 3 Months from the Powerhouse Museum," Powerhouse Museum, July 21, 2008, http://www.powerhousemuseum.com/dmsblog/index.php/2008/07/21/commons-on-flickr-a-report-some-concepts-and-an-faq-the-first-3-months-from-the-powerhouse-museum/ (accessed July 1, 2009).

[43] By *commons*, I mean the resources that are commonly owned. Many social computing sites (e.g., Flickr, *Wikipedia*) have commons.

[44] Beyond Brown Paper, http://beyondbrownpaper.plymouth.edu/ (accessed February 23, 2010).

[45] Picture Australia, http://www.pictureaustralia.org (accessed February 23, 2010).

[46] "Contributing to Picture Australia," Picture Australia, http://www.pictureaustralia.org/contribute/index.html (accessed February 23, 2010).

[47] Julia Angwin and Geoffrey A. Fowler, "Volunteers Log Off as Wikipedia Ages," *Wall Street Journal,* November 27, 2009, http://online.wsj.com/article/SB125893981183759969.html (accessed February 23, 2010). For a response by Jimmy Wales, the founder of *Wikipedia,* see "Wikipedia's Volunteer Story," http://blog.wikimedia.org/2009/11/26/wikipedias-volunteer-story/ (accessed February 23, 2010).

[48] Terry Cook, "From Information to Knowledge," *Archivaria* 19 (Winter 1984–1985): 49.

[49] Angèle Alain and Michelle Foggett, "Towards Community Contribution: Empowering Community Voices On-line," in *Museums and the Web 2007: Proceedings,* ed. Jennifer Trant and David Bearman (Toronto: Archives & Museum Informatics, 2007), http://www.archimuse.com/mw2007/papers/alain/alain.html (accessed February 23, 2010).

[50] Library Archives Canada, Moving Here, Staying Here: The Canadian Immigrant Experience, http://www.collectionscanada.gc.ca/immigrants/index-e.html (accessed February 23, 2010).

[51] National Archives (UK), Moving Here: 200 Years of Migration to England, http://www.movinghere.org.uk (accessed February 23, 2010).

[52] Peter Williams and Ian Rowlands, "Information Behavior of the Researcher of the Future," British Library/JISC, 2007, p. 10, http://www.jisc.ac.uk/media/documents/programmes/reppres/ggworkpackageii.pdf (accessed February 23, 2010).

[53] Ancestry, available at http://ancestry.com (accessed February 23, 2010).

[54] Footnote, available at http://footnote.com (accessed February 23, 2010).

Taking Photographs to the People: The Flickr Commons Project and the Library of Congress

Helena Zinkham and Michelle Springer

Overview of Repository

The Library of Congress, based in Washington, D.C., is the national library for the United States.[1] Founded in 1800, it is also the oldest federal cultural institution in the United States. The Library's mission is global in scope—"to make its resources available and useful to the Congress and the American people and to sustain and preserve a universal collection of knowledge and creativity for future generations." The collections offer nearly 142 million items, including printed books and electronic databases, manuscripts and maps, movies and music, photographs, and sound recordings. Its reference services respond to more than 500,000 inquiries each year.

Within that context, the Prints & Photographs Division (P&P)[2] serves a wide variety of user communities, from the general public and K–12 teachers to advanced scholars and documentary filmmakers. Approximately 4,000 people visit P&P in person each year to work with the collections on site, while 12 million off-site search sessions tap into the Prints & Photographs Online Catalog. A staff of 40 people preserves and provides access to the 14 million architectural designs, cartoons, documentary drawings, fine art and historical prints, photographs, and posters in our care.

Business Drivers

Like many archives and libraries, our key motivation for trying Web 2.0 was the goal of reaching new audiences and increasing the discovery and use of collections. We also wanted to become more approachable; the sheer size of our collections can be unintentionally off-putting. Our challenges include limited institutional resources to describe collections; competition for the attention of an online community that has ever-expanding choices of where to pursue their interests; a technical infrastructure that does not easily allow users to comment, share, and interact with content; and concerns about exposing collection content to social networking environments that have a reputation for snarky humor and disrespectful dialog.

We chose photographs for an experiment with user-generated activity because images appeal to such a broad audience. P&P's participation also made sense because visual collections face a specific problem that Web 2.0 can help solve. Most people don't even know that libraries and archives have photographs. Our digitized images have been available online since the early days of the World Wide Web, but a lot more needs to be done to build awareness and connections.

In addition, P&P brings beneficial experience to Web 2.0 projects because we are familiar with receiving help from both researchers and volunteers, who have long assisted libraries, archives, and historical societies by providing caption information for pictures through reading room visits and e-mail conversations. We wanted to learn how this long collaborative tradition for visual materials could expand by opening the special collection vaults to Web 2.0 forums. Finally, by having our own account on a social media site, we could ensure that authentic digitized images and metadata were accurately credited to their repository, along with links to enable discovery of related collections and services.

A number of questions about how Web 2.0 environments might support the Library's strategic goals guided our work. The Library's Flickr Pilot Project team formalized the following objectives for the pilot:

- Increase awareness by sharing photographs with people who enjoy images but might not visit the Library's own website.

- Gain a better understanding of how social tagging and community input could benefit both the Library and users of the collections.

- Gain experience participating in emergent web communities interested in the kinds of materials in the Library's collections.

Setting the Stage

In April 2007, the Library launched its first public blog and then gathered our small team to pilot the next Web 2.0 project. Just nine months later, in January 2008, Flickr used two of the Library's historical photo collections to open a new space called The Commons and invited people to help archives, libraries, and museums describe their images.[3] This rapid development happened because the Web 2.0 spirit brings a freedom to focus on broad goals and let specific plans evolve along the way.

Our team included technical, curatorial, policy, and project management expertise. We also involved stakeholders in the legal, copyright, and communications offices to ensure a successful implementation. No one worked full-time on the project, and resource requirements were minimized because no new staff were available. In addition to outlining goals and steps, we established several measures of success. To gauge increased awareness of collections, we could count views, contacts, referrals to our website, and news media reports. Non-numeric measures included gaining enough experience with Web 2.0 to be able to better evaluate benefits and costs. The most important measure, of course, would be user feedback.

We considered an in-house solution, but that would have been a long-term activity needing more than the available resources. Instead, we decided to use an established social media site. Aside from the obvious need for an environment that supported tagging and photo sharing, the optimal site would provide a connection to a visually focused community.

This pilot was the Library's first project to use a third-party social media site to deliver its content. The Library's ongoing concern is to mitigate the potential issues that arise with user-generated content. As a federal government agency, for example, the Library needs to avoid the appearance of commercial product endorsement from user comments that include links to "dot com" addresses. Nor, for example, can obscene language be accepted. Fortunately, the guidelines developed to moderate the Library's own blog work well with third-party sites.

Flickr quickly emerged as the best fit for the pilot. Since its start in 2004, Flickr became a popular photo-sharing website with free viewing from any browser and more than 36 million members.[4] Anyone with a Yahoo! account (a no-cost service) can sign in and interact with the photographs by adding comments, tags (key words), and notes (annotations placed on the images). They can also easily share the photos electronically, designate photos as favorites, and become contacts to receive automatic feeds of new images.

The availability of open-source and Flickr application programming interfaces (APIs) enabled straightforward technical procedures. We developed an automated method to derive Flickr display titles, dates, and descriptions from existing catalog records; a means to associate images in the Flickr account with the corresponding source photos in the Library's collections; and a repeatable method for ongoing uploads of additional photo batches. We can also download the user-generated content to mitigate the risk of losing the information if Flickr changes its mission.

Only one red flag surfaced. The existing rights statement options in Flickr did not fit our relationship to the photos, because we are not the images' creator or rights holder. Working with the Library's legal and copyright experts, we contacted Flickr management to discuss possible solutions, which ultimately led to the "No known copyright restrictions" statement. Reflecting a "no known copyright" status simplifies the sharing of historical photographs by making an observation based on a good faith effort, rather than an assertion of public domain status.

Our conversations with George Oates at Flickr inspired her to see a larger opportunity and create The Commons. (See Figure 1.) She opened an unanticipated and remarkable opportunity for cultural heritage institutions to share archival photographs without known copyright restrictions. During the first fifteen months of the Flickr Commons existence, twenty-seven small and large archives, libraries, and museums from nine countries

Figure 1: The Commons homepage in Flickr (http://www.flickr.com/commons) represents the site's goals and a sampling of "buddy icons" for participating institutions.

launched accounts to share selected collections and invite the public to contribute information.

By the fall of 2007, we began meeting weekly to draft such documents as an FAQ page and a Flickr profile. We also drew in more P&P staff to be ready to respond to comments. Their knowledge of visual collections has been invaluable, and they can share the workload, so that each person moderates the account for one week every other month. The Library purchased a Flickr Pro account for $24.95 to allow for an unlimited number of photos to be loaded. For the launch, we selected approximately 3,100 photos from two collections that had proved popular on our website. The color views of the Great Depression and World War II homefront were likely to encourage interaction based on personal or family experiences and included several unidentified images. The Bain News Service glass negatives from the 1910s have little subject information beyond abbreviated key words in their titles, making them promising candidates for additional research and description. Each collection became a separate "set," or unit, in Flickr, which made it easy to offer relevant contextual descriptions and links to related resources. Our internal communications plan involved meeting with small groups of senior library managers and also preparing a Library-wide presentation for any interested staff, called "Opening the Photo Vaults: A Web 2.0 Pilot Project to Enhance Discovery and Gather Input for the Library's Photograph Collections."[5]

Results

We evaluated the Flickr pilot project's first nine months in a detailed report, "For the Common Good."[6] We are enjoying the many different ways that users define their own experiences and regularly invent new ways to engage the photographs. Many comments are fan mail, ranging from "Beautiful!" to "I happened across this account tonight. What treasures! Thank you for adding them to Flickr. They are pictures I might not have ever seen otherwise." Flickr members also contribute then-and-now pairings of images, combine photos with maps, make jokes inspired by the images, and suggest new collections they'd like to see. Other comments discuss history in general, recollect personal experience and grandparents' lives, and recreate photo scenes in modern settings.

The wealth of new information added through comments has been beneficial. (See Figure 2.) In addition to a steady core of about twenty "history detectives" who visit the photostream regularly, experts in highly specialized fields also step in to untangle the identification of a labor strike, a type of automobile, a ship's name, and more. Conversations among multiple members can develop over the course of several months. For a photograph of blind weavers, one person identified the photographer, others worked out the type of musical instrument shown in a corner of the room, and another added the photographer's biography to *Wikipedia*.[7]

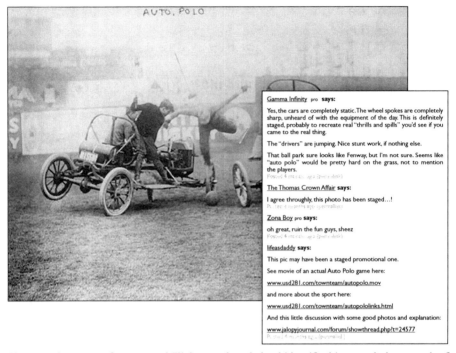

Figure 2: Comments from several Flickr members helped identify this staged photograph of auto polo with links to movies and magazine stories.

The Flickr "history detectives" have provided most of the additional and corrected information, including place names, more precise dates, event names, and fuller names for individuals in photos previously identified only by surname. Without prompting, the new information is generally supported with links to the *New York Times'* online archive, *Wikipedia*, and websites devoted to specific areas of interest, such as military aviation and sports history, which aids in vetting new information. This willingness to expend high levels of effort resulted in updating more than 500 catalog records in 2008. Another thousand records are being updated from 2009.[8]

The Indicommons is another good example of the depth of community engagement. (See Figure 3.) In December 2008, Flickr community members who felt passionately about the value of The Commons created a robust discussion group within Flickr and also opened a blog site to highlight collections. They curate exhibits that gather thematically related photos from across The Commons, interview Commons users as well as archivists, develop applications to help both public users and image contributors, and post news of events at the physical repositories.[9] They inspire closer looking at images and extend the pleasure of exploring old photographs.

Numeric measures also indicate success in raising awareness of photographs in cultural heritage repositories. Flickr's promotion of The Commons draws tremendous attention to the venue. In the first 24 hours after launch, Flickr reported 1.1 million views on the Library's account, with 3.6 million total views a week later. By October 2008, our account was averaging 500,000 views each month. By July 2009, the monthly average for views was 800,000, and total views had exceeded 18 million.

The goal to raise awareness fits well with the preferred activity of most Flickr members—looking at photographs (the viewing statistic). The next

Figure 3: *Indicommons* contributors frequently gather then-and-now pairings of photographs, such as this ca. 1900 view of Wales from the Photochrom Collection with a view from 2008.

most popular activities are marking a photo as a favorite and designating the Library as a contact in order to receive automatic feeds of newly loaded photos. Far fewer people provide tags and comments, but the cumulative result is impressive. By July 2009, Flickr members had submitted more than 17,000 comments (from 6,000 accounts) and more than 104,000 tags on the photos. The crowd-sourcing benefit of user-generated tags and requests for photos to join subject-based Flickr groups has resulted in increased discovery of our photographs. The high level of accuracy in both the additional information we have verified and the spelling of the tags has been reassuring.

One photo can inspire such a wide variety of activity that it can be difficult to tell that the crowd-sourcing goal to gather identifying information has also succeeded. A statistical snapshot from the last week in June 2009 illustrates the range of engagement. The week involved 155,000 views, 1,250 favorites, and 180 comments. Among the comments, 66 (34 percent) added new identification information to photographs, while 114 (59 percent) were personal reactions to the pictures. Most of the reactions were praise for a single photograph or the whole project, but there were also extended conversations and debates among Flickr members about subject matter or technical characteristics of photography. People with interests as varied as parachutes, "fashion at the races," and "why Canada is best" sent us requests to join their thematic group displays that pull together images from across Flickr. The bulk of the comments with additional information (50 out of 66) were for the Bain News Service photographs, which have the least subject identification. Because we add 50 new Bain photographs at a time, the proportions of weekly comments indicate a strong degree of interest in adding new information to make photographs easier to find and understand.

An unexpected outcome is the high visibility the Flickr account images receive on major search engines. When users search with relevant keywords, search engines return results that give images on Flickr greater weight and a higher place on the results list than their counterparts in the Library's Prints & Photographs Online Catalog. A Google search for baseball player Germany Schaefer produces the LC Flickr account photo "Germany

Schaefer, Washington AL (baseball)" as one of the top five results on the first Google page; the catalog version of the same photo does not appear until several pages later in the search results.

The ease with which archives, libraries, and museums can contribute whatever descriptions they have is also satisfying. The language, amount of detail, and elements are up to each Commons contributor as long as there is a title and a date. Each repository can choose which printing, blogging, and tagging features to turn on. Joining a community where metadata already varies widely has simplified the collaboration. The opportunity to explore so many interesting photographs from sister institutions is also a pleasure; we're Commons users, not just contributors.

Challenges

The greatest disappointment is not having the resources to maximize the potential benefits from joining online photo-sharing communities. We can accomplish a lot by spending about fifteen hours each week with the Flickr members. But we have also limited most of our interaction to focus on verifying information and answering questions. We have prioritized the loading of new content over updating the master copies of the descriptive records in our own catalog.

We add new images each week, with more than 6,400 images available in July 2009. In addition to expanding the set of underdescribed Bain Service news photos, we provide sets that emphasize viewing pleasure or encourage exploration of special events at the Library by highlighting such collection treasures as "Migrant Mother" by Dorothea Lange or images related to an Abraham Lincoln exhibition. We have also built sets in collaboration with other Commons members to commemorate a World War I anniversary and International Women's Day, which underscores the benefits of a pooled resource of cultural heritage pictures. Flickr members have welcomed nonphotographic pictures, too, including Illustrated Newspaper Supplements from the "Chronicling America" project.

The greatest challenge is moderating the activity on our account. Relatively few instances of user-generated content have had to be removed as inappropriate spam or obscene language, but the issue of distracting notes remains to be solved. Complaints from Flickr members have increased as notes proliferate to the point of obscuring some images. Flickr members have also objected to name-calling notes that disregard the "do play nice" community guideline. After taking a hands-off approach to notes for almost two years, we are considering deleting noninformational notes for at least the sixty photos that have ten or more notes. We would retain the notes that identify parts of photographs, such as the names of people in a group portrait, or transcribe words on signs.

The issues related to culturally sensitive images continue to be important to discuss among all archives. Flickr members help provide context by linking to websites where the voices of indigenous peoples are represented and by linking to multiple perspectives of controversial events. For example, a view titled "A Lapp family, Norway" was connected to a Saami blog and a Saami-sponsored website. When historical language in captions offends a Flickr member, other members respond with reminders of the context. The primary complaint about the project overall is that the numerous casual interactions diminish serious history or overwhelm the new information provided. Other observers have pointed out that Flickr exists to allow many kinds of activities in the same space, much as people attending an exhibition can react to a picture in different ways.

Lessons Learned

Anyone thinking about offering photographs through Flickr or another photo-sharing site could start by becoming familiar with what institutions have already reported on their experiences.[10] A leap of faith in trying something new may also be needed. Our implementation team had no idea how the community would respond to old photos in a site that is largely contemporary digital camera work. The warmth of the reception from Flickr members and the media was a wonderful surprise.

If an institution already has digitized pictures and descriptions, most of the challenges are not likely to be technical. Things someone new to Flickr should keep in mind include:

- Getting to know the online community and learning how to partic-ipate as a community member rather than a silent observer. Setting up an account is an easy way to become conversant with the many features for organizing, searching, and interacting.

- Being ready to respond to comments and questions and to reach out to new groups and having staff with expertise in the content ready to assist and interact. The level of engagement provided by the archives or library helps shape the amount of involvement from the community.

- Developing criteria for moderating the content, if the community members will be allowed to provide comments, tags, and notes; also, being familiar with any community guidelines. Members referee each other's behavior, but occasionally inappropriate content may need to be deleted.

- Being prepared to cede some control of what happens to the content once it is placed on Web 2.0 sites.

Our primary lesson learned is that Flickr is not a "national union cata-log" for all pictures from all archives; it's one of many places for people to interact with cultural heritage collections. Nor are third-party sites the final solution for interaction. While retaining responsibility for the master digital images and their descriptions, archives and libraries also need to incorporate Web 2.0 tools, such as comments in their own catalogs. That way, all of the pictures, including the rights restricted, can benefit from increased engagement and crowd sourcing.

Next Steps

Interest in this project remains high within and outside the Library, and we expect to continue to add new images each week and to report on our experience in a variety of venues. We are also looking at the costs of the growing Flickr content and the kind of resources needed to expand the benefits of a virtual reading room and virtual volunteer corps. Were more resources available, we would like to respond to more of the fan mail for specific pictures by more often pointing out related images at the Library or elsewhere.

We would also like to recognize the regular volunteers publicly and to invite Flickr members to select photos for new sets and offer on-site tours for Flickr members to view original photographs. We could sponsor groups to gather images around user-defined themes. We would also talk more with other Commons members to support each other in special events and cross-collection discoveries. We would make our individual voices and excitement about discovering new connections among photographs more visible.

Building on the success of the Flickr project, Library staff have begun several other pilots that tap social networking sites. We use Twitter, YouTube, iTunes U, and Facebook to help our collections and programs reach new communities of users. We want to take more kinds of collections, along with many more photographs, to the people.

Notes

[1] "About the Library," Library of Congress, http://www.loc.gov/about/generalinfo.html (accessed July 21, 2009).

[2] See the website for the Library of Congress's Prints & Photographs Reading Room at http://www.loc.gov/rr/print/.

[3] Other cultural repositories used Flickr long before we did, and they continue to be successful outside of The Commons forum. For example, the Eastern Kentucky University Archives uses its account (http://www.flickr.com/photos/ekuarchives) to share collections that attract alumni and local history interest and to document current events.

[4] The Commons, Flickr, http://www.flickr.com/commons (accessed July 21, 2009). The membership figure is from a discussion with Flickr's general manager, Kakul Srivastava, on April 16, 2009.

[5] Library of Congress Flickr account, available at http://www.flickr.com/photos/library_of_congress; Webcast about the project development, http://www.loc.gov/today/cyberlc/feature_wdesc.php?rec=4281.

[6] Michelle Springer et al., "For the Common Good: The Library of Congress Flickr Pilot Project," October 30, 2008, available at http://www.loc.gov/rr/print/flickr_report_final.pdf (accessed July 21, 2009).

[7] Byron, photographer, "Weavers at Work," 1910–1915, available at http://www.flickr.com/photos/library_of_congress/2163450764 (accessed July 21, 2009).

[8] To view the updated records, search for the phrase "Source: Flickr Commons Project," in the Prints & Photographs Online Catalog at http://www.loc.gov/pictures (accessed April 4, 2010).

[9] *Indicommons*, available at http://www.indicommons.org (accessed July 21, 2009); Discussion group, Flickr Commons, http://flickr.com/groups/flickrcommons (accessed July 21, 2009).

[10] See a bibliography of reports at http://www.indicommons.org/about/bibliography (accessed July 21, 2009).

Harnessing User Knowledge: The National Archives' *Your Archives* Wiki

Guy Grannum

Overview of the Repository

The National Archives is a government department and an executive agency of the Ministry of Justice. It was formed in 2003 following the merger of the Public Record Office and Historical Manuscripts Commission; in 2006 it was joined by the Office of Public Sector Information and Her Majesty's Stationery Office. The National Archives is the UK government's official archive and holds the records of government departments and the courts of law for England and Wales and the United Kingdom, containing almost 1,000 years of history from the Domesday Book to digital records and archived websites. In addition, The National Archives provides guidance to government departments and the public sector on information management and the care of historical archives, publishes all UK legislation, and leads on the reuse of public sector information.

There are about 600 staff in two locations in Kew in Surrey and Norwich; the archive is based in Kew. Researchers come from all demographic groups in the United Kingdom and from overseas; most are researching family and local history, looking at such sources as maps, censuses, military, migration, citizenship and court records. In 2009-2010 more than 90,000 researchers visited the archives, more than 600,000 documents were produced, and more than 130 million documents were downloaded from our website and from those of our partners.

Business Drivers

The National Archives often receives feedback from researchers who wish to share their knowledge of our records to improve the catalogue of our holdings and other resources. While there are processes in place to make verifiable amendments to the catalogue, such as changes to the descriptions and dates, until the establishment of our website *Your Archives,* there wasn't a mechanism to store more detailed comments. This information is often extremely useful, but incorporating it into the catalogue and other resources is time-consuming, as there are issues to consider such as accuracy, completeness (for example, does it relate to the complete document or to selective items?), and the need to rewrite it to meet editorial standards. We wanted to develop an online interactive knowledge management system in which researchers could file and share their information. In addition, we wanted a system in which the content could be edited in order to be corrected, expanded, and improved. We investigated a number of websites that allowed user contributions and decided that wiki technology met most of our needs and the needs of our users.

Setting the Stage

The proposal to create the *Your Archives* site was made in The National Archives' Priority Action Plan for 2006–2008. Under the "Bring history to life for everyone" strand, priority 4 states: "Harness the expertise of those using our records, though online subject forums and innovative approaches such as user generated content."[1]

The project started with a requirements-gathering exercise using feedback from users and staff. There were two prerequisites: it had to allow users to add comments to the catalogue of archival holdings, and it had to be an out-of-the-box solution as it was not possible to amend the software and functionality behind the catalogue. The requirements included:

- Comments to be published immediately.

- Contributions to be editable by other users—allowing users to collaborate to correct, improve, and expand content.

- A registration function so that contributions can be attributed to specific users.

- An audit function so that users can see what changes have been made, by whom and when—this enables contributors to identify and reuse their work.

- Ability to include hyperlinks to internal pages and to external websites.

- Ability to tag or categorize pages so that users can find related articles.

- Simplicity of use.

- Ability to be indexed by popular search engines.

- Ability to protect specific pages from being edited.

- Ability to export and reuse the content—this would enable us to migrate the data onto another platform if necessary or reuse the content elsewhere.

- Editable code to enable staff to tailor the software.

After identifying business and operational requirements, we reviewed a number of online services such as e-commerce websites, blogs, forums, and wikis. Most of these did not allow user contributions to be edited by other users or weren't as interactive as we would have liked. Wikis seemed to offer the best solution, meeting most, if not all, of our mandatory requirements; we reviewed four different wikis, and MediaWiki, as used by *Wikipedia,* was the most flexible and manageable of the four, and it possessed a number of other benefits, including:

- It is free to download.

- It is widely used because of *Wikipedia,* and its format and functionality are familiar to researchers.

- It uses wiki-code, which is simplified HTML, to format content and to create templates, making it relatively easy to understand and reuse.

- It has separate tabs for content and notes.

- It back-links (What Links Here) to see other articles that hyperlink to that page.

- Because it is open-source software, it has a large developer community who have created tools (extensions) and enhancements to the software; for example, we have installed the extension to add footnotes, and there are others we may add in the future.

Using MediaWiki also had some risks:

- Because it is free open-source software, there is no support from the developer.

- The program uses PHP and MySQL, which are not used in other National Archives' applications.

- Formatting text can be complex, but the familiarity of MediaWiki means that there is already a large user base—as one contributor noted in his or her blog: "It doesn't matter if people haven't formatted their pages properly or don't know how to insert a link. As long as you put up some relevant information, someone else can sort it out."[2] Third-party applications may not continue to work on later versions of the software.

At the same time we considered the risks of running a user-generated website and wrote policies and procedures to help manage these risks—as a government department and a national archive we had to ensure that we were acting responsibly. In particular, we considered how to manage spam, vandalism, pornography, and so on. For example, would we moderate content, and, if so, at what stage in the process—before or after publishing? What language and words would be unacceptable? Would users be able to upload images or other files? Would users need to register? MediaWiki allows us to manage all these elements; for example, there is a spam filter that we can amend, there is a registration function, we can delete pages and specific versions, we can block users from editing, and, if necessary, we can protect specific pages and even the whole site from further editing. A user needs to register and validate his or her e-mail address before he or she can make any contributions, and the user cannot upload any files. In addition, we have links to feedback and complaint forms on every page.

Probably the most contentious decision we made is to post-moderate content. We did this because pre-moderating might deter users because there wouldn't be the immediacy and interactivity that many users want, and they might make an assumption that we had checked and approved the content. We do not do this but we check all new content and links to ensure that nothing breaches the terms and conditions. To date, we have found very few instances of spam or inappropriate content or links. Post-moderating has also raised concerns from some users and staff about the control of content before publishing, issues surrounding trust and

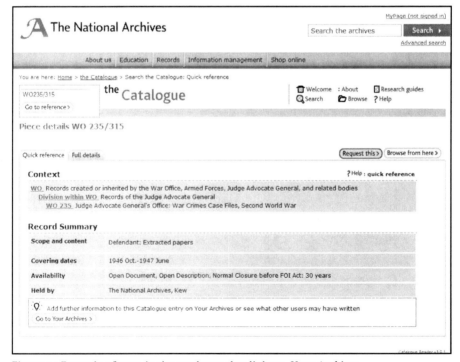

Figure 1: Example of page in the catalogue that links to *Your Archives*.

the accuracy of content, and questions on whether it is appropriate for a government department and trusted archive to more or less relinquish editorial authority to the user. Every page contains a disclaimer, and we hope that researchers will validate statements; at least with a wiki, if someone finds something inaccurate or misleading, they can easily amend it. We have also created a number of housekeeping templates that contributors use to highlight articles that could be improved.

One of the primary aims of *Your Archives* is to enable users to add information about our records. We placed a button on the Document Details page of the catalogue so that researchers can go to *Your Archives* to see if there is any additional information; otherwise, it creates a special catalogue page inviting the user to add content. (See Figure 1 for an example of an online catalogue page with the link to *Your Archives*.) We also developed an extension in MediaWiki that recognizes National Archives' document references in articles and automatically hyperlinks the reference and creates a catalogue page in *Your Archives*. (See Figure 2 for an example of one of these catalogue pages in *Your Archives*.) These catalogue pages have a hyperlink to the relevant document description in the online catalogue, so researchers can browse the catalogue or make a request to see the document. We also embedded the MediaWiki "What Links Here" toolbox function on this catalogue page to show other articles in *Your Archives* that refer to that document reference.

We ran an in-house trial service of *Your Archives* for four months before the site went live on April 24, 2007. In the trial, onsite researchers tested the concept and refined the functionality and improved the site. During this time, we created more than 500 pages to show users how they can use the site and the sort of information they can contribute. Most of these pages were created from unpublished finding aids and notes kept in the reading rooms; putting them into *Your Archives* has made them fully searchable and accessible for the first time. In addition, we put up some transcriptions of wills and a number of miscellaneous items of information from e-mails and our in-house discussion forum.

Your Archives is managed by staff in the Knowledge Transfer Team in the Advice and Records Knowledge Department—all staff in the department

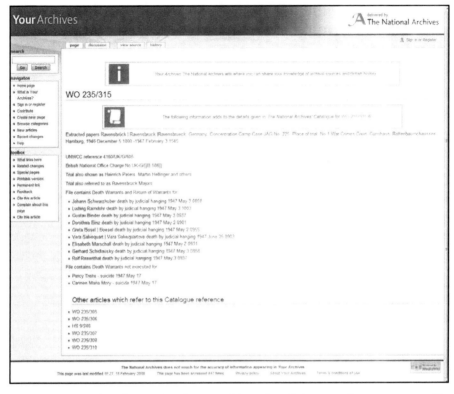

Figure 2: Example of page in *Your Archives* that links to references to specific documents.

spend a proportion of their day giving advice and assistance to researchers who visit, telephone, or write and therefore have a good understanding of the archives and sources for historical research. The Knowledge Transfer Team is responsible for developing tools and processes to capture, share, and reuse information about the records and research advice.

Results

We have been pleased by the response from researchers and staff and the nature and quality of contributions. This was an innovative project, and we couldn't compare the service with other archives to see how it would be received or used. From the time we went live in April 2007 until the time of this writing (November 2010), more than 20,400 articles have been written—about half of the articles were created by the *Your Archives* team from finding aids and the remainder have been created by researchers wanting to share their knowledge. There have been more than 254,400 edits, which vary from amending a typo, adding a category, or correcting format to adding significant new information. There are more than 29,600 registered users, of whom there are about 50 regular contributors who add content or tidy up articles. Since we went live, there have been more than 29 million page views and more than 4 million visits, which is the equivalent to 7 pages per visit—about 30 percent of these visits come from Google searches.

On the whole, feedback has been very positive, with researchers and staff happy that there is a space where they can store information or collaborate with others. It has been considered innovative and was recommended as the *Guardian*'s education website of the month in June 2007, received a special mention in the 2008 *ArchivesNext* Best Total Web Experience category, and was commended in the 2008 Good Communications Award in the IT and E-government category. There have also been negative responses, relating mostly to trust and reliability of the information and the appropriateness of a national archive allowing user contributions to enhance the catalogue. The feeling is that many researchers will trust all information presented by The National Archives, so we should ensure that only accurate and validated information is published. There have also been comments about the terms and conditions—unlike other wikis, the content is not covered by Creative Commons; instead, when adding content, authors are assigning us nonexclusive rights to their contributions. Because much of the information relates to our archives, we wanted the flexibility to repurpose and reuse the information in the catalogue and in other TNA resources; also, contributions by staff made during the course of their work is subject to Crown Copyright.

The user community has been using *Your Archives* in ways we hadn't considered: researchers have been writing transcripts, abstracts, and indexes of digitized sources, opening up the archives in a way that wasn't possible before. One researcher has created indexes to documents he uploaded to Flickr; others have been indexing the content of Digital

Microfilm they downloaded from our DocumentsOnline service (Digital Microfilm has been uploaded with only the catalogue description and no additional metadata); another researcher has written information on war memorials and sculptures and has uploaded many of his photographs to complement his articles; and yet another has been opening up the history of the security services. Internally, staff have used *Your Archives* to share information previously held in personal notebooks, files, and e-mails, and on the records management system; and, while preserving collections of artwork, the Collection Care Department is using *Your Archives* to provide a technical description of the media used with brief biographies of the artists. We are also learning from other "Wikipedians," who have taught us, for example, to use code to create sortable tables, sort articles in categories, and create templates, as well as other tips for enhancing the service.

Challenges

Some issues and challenges have already been discussed. Others include the following:

- We have put in processes to help manage spam and inappropriate content, and to date we haven't seen too much spam. We have a spam filter, but we have heavily amended it because it stopped many valid historical terms and even surnames. We have created several templates for users and moderators to use—such as warning users that the content contains historical terms that may be considered offensive, inviting users to translate articles, or suggesting that a page should be deleted.

- *Your Archives* is not the best place to ask for general research advice, although questions and discussions relating to interpretation, arrangement, structure, and content of subjects or documents is appropriate under the Notes tab.

- MediaWiki comes with a very basic editor with which users can do some simple formatting, but to create a table, indent text, or insert links, footnotes, or images, users need to know a bit of wikicode or HTML. This could be a barrier for some users.

- An ongoing challenge is educating the user. First, to encourage more contributions, users need to know that *Your Archives* is a website on which researchers can share their knowledge and editors (those who amend text) can become contributors and occasional contributors can become regular contributors. Second, to improve the quality of contributions—for example, by asking users to include sources and to expand their stories to bring out the evidence for their statements and to give contributors confidence to format text.

Lessons Learned

For institutions thinking of developing their own user-generated service, there are a number of things to consider:

- Define what you are aiming to achieve and why and who the audience is.

- Obtain senior management support and find a champion—this is particularly important if you need resources to maintain the service.

- Discuss real and perceived risks and get agreement on how these will be managed and mitigated.

- Have a clear exit strategy on what you will do with the site should you need to close it.

- Make extensive use of existing knowledge and guidance. Look at other sites that are using the same software or have a similar audience and at technical and user groups. Join in discussions and don't be afraid to ask for help—you are part of the user community.

- Have plenty of Help pages explaining what people can contribute and how, and work with your community to agree on standards and guidance.

- Review existing content to refine or develop standards, guidance, and templates to help users.

- Seed the site with content that will help users understand what types of contributions you would like and how you would like them.

- Have regular dialogue with contributors; they are using your service and understand its strengths and weaknesses.

- Carry out regular user surveys to find out what users think of the service and to identify barriers to its use.

- Don't be too heavy-handed when moderating as you might put people off from contributing. It's not always obvious what is acceptable or where to post contributions. People need direction on what to do or how to do things differently. In particular, work with new users to build their skills and confidence.

- Consider what technical support you will need to maintain and develop the site; will this be in-house or through a managed service?

Next Steps

A business review of *Your Archives* was carried out in July 2010 and it was decided that user contributions should be more visible and integrated with our other online services and moved onto a common platform. As a major part of The National Archives' Rediscovering the Record project, we will build on our experience of managing *Your Archives* and from user feedback to improve the user experience and to develop new resources and functionality. For example, under the redevelopment of the online catalogues, user contributions will be embedded on the catalogue details screen and will be findable via an improved catalogue search. We aim to include a rich text editor and structured templates to help users write contributions, enabling user tags, and to develop further the ideas instigated by contributors, such as supporting researchers who have accessed or uploaded digitized content and work with them to index or catalogue these records by providing guidance, standards, and templates.

The nature and variety of contributions and user feedback demonstrates that researchers consider *Your Archives* to be a versatile and valuable resource that complements The National Archives' catalogue and finding aids. We have to continue to be proactive by promoting the site widely and to continue to work with the research community and contributors to increase the quantity and quality of contributions and the direction in which the service should develop.

Notes

¹ The National Archives, "The National Archives Priority Action Plan," October 18, 2006, available at http://www.nationalarchives.gov.uk/documents/priority-action-plan.pdf (accessed January 6, 2011).

² Gavin Robinson, "Google Base and Great War Soldiers," *Investigations of a Dog*, December 27, 2007, http://www.investigations.4-lom.com/2007/12/27/google-base-and-great-war-soldiers/ (accessed January 6, 2011).)

Bringing Life to Records: Mapping Our Anzacs at the National Archives of Australia

Tim Sherratt

Overview of Repository

The National Archives of Australia is responsible for preserving and making accessible the records of the Commonwealth of Australia. It employs more than 400 staff, with offices in Canberra and every state capital. Its holdings include more than 360 shelf kilometers of records—around 69 million items. Through its digitization program more than 1.6 million items have been fully digitized, making nearly 20 million digital images available online. The National Archives' website now provides the main point of access for researchers, with more than 2 million images viewed through the online database RecordSearch in the year 2007–2008.

Business Drivers

Most people now experience the collections of the National Archives of Australia online. With an obligation to provide "an accessible, and interpreted, national archival collection," the Archives is looking to new technologies to enhance access and improve efficiency.

The idea for Mapping Our Anzacs arose during planning for a travelling exhibition on the impact of World War I, timed to coincide with the ninetieth anniversary of the war's end. Public interest in commemorating

Australia's war effort was as strong as ever, so a website that encouraged local participation seemed a useful way of extending the exhibition and its accompanying education program.

The major focus of both the exhibition and the website was the National Archives' holdings of 376,000 service records documenting the experiences of Australian men and women during World War I. These records had been fully digitized and described as part of a major project entitled "A Gift to the Nation" but were still somewhat buried within our collection database.

Mapping Our Anzacs was intended to highlight these records and open them up to local communities. First, a map interface would allow users to discover service records by place of birth or enlistment. Second, users would be able to add tributes—online versions of the war memorials that remain a feature of just about every town, large or small.

While the exhibition and the records themselves provided the main drivers for the project, there was also a growing desire within the institution to explore some of the possibilities of Web 2.0 technologies. This desire was tempered somewhat by a range of familiar concerns centered on issues of authority and control. Would user contributions detract from the reliability of the records? Who would take responsibility for any errors in user-created content? Would the potential for abuse demand vigilant moderation? Mapping Our Anzacs gave us a chance to start working through such issues.

Setting the Stage

We had an idea, a budget and a launch date; what we needed was a plan. While in theory we had around six months to play with, the project had to fit in around the ongoing work of our small web team. On the content side we had one person cleaning up the data. At the technical end we had someone connecting the various components and making it all work within the Archives' web environment. In the middle there were two of us trying to marry content and technology and create a usable resource. While we had a range of useful skills, none of us had tackled a project quite like this. We all had to learn on the job.

With few models or examples to work from, we began to experiment—researching available technologies, throwing around possibilities. Our first efforts were largely focused on the map interface, and before long we had a working prototype using Javascript and Google Maps. But what we also needed was a better understanding of how users might interact with the site.

We started from the idea of the online memorial—a list of names compiled by users that would be linked through to service records. Our example was a local historical society creating a site to commemorate their community's war effort. But what if they had more information—photographs or family histories—how could this sort of material be incorporated? Further inspiration came from a visit to the local historical museum in the small Victorian town of Chiltern. On one wall

Figure 1: World War I Honour Roll at the Chiltern Athenaeum Museum.

was a typical roll of honor, listing the names of those who had served in the war. But underneath were framed portraits of many of those listed. (See Figure 1.) They were people, not just records. Could we create something like this online?

There were some exciting possibilities emerging, but concerns remained. Would anybody actually want to contribute? Strong interest in family history and a growing community desire to commemorate the experience of World War I offered anecdotal support. We just had to ensure that this interest could be translated into engagement—that the barriers of participation were low enough to encourage visitors to become collaborators.

But what of concerns that such material might detract from the authority of the records or open our institution up to liability? We needed to make it clear where public contributions began and archival data ended.

Welcoming, but separate; open, but managed—a tricky balancing act was required. The answer, we decided, was to create a separate "scrapbook" using the blogging service Tumblr. The "scrapbook" label was intended to be encouraging—this was not a database, or formal register, it was a place to leave your thoughts, comments, information, or memorabilia. This was reinforced by our terms of service, which simply required contributions to be relevant and respectful.

A "scrapbook" was also something quite different to a finding aid. The informality helped to make the boundary clear between record and response. The separation was physical as well as intellectual. While the scrapbook shared many of the design elements of the main site, it was hosted by Tumblr, not the National Archives. By using the Tumblr application programming interface (API), however, it was easy to pass information between the two sites. We could also use the API to provide a basic moderation facility.

But this meant that an important part of the site's functionality would be dependent on an outside service. To make sure we considered all of the implications of this, we developed a risk analysis and contacted Tumblr staff to inform them of our plans. Our major concern was simply the continuity of the service. While there could be no guarantees, we judged that this risk was manageable. Tumblr staff were interested in the project and offered their assistance, if necessary.

Results

On April 25 each year, Anzac Day, Australians remember the sacrifices
made in war. Over the Anzac Day weekend in 2009, we were astonished
to receive more than 200 scrapbook posts. Of course we had expected an
increase in use, particularly after the site was featured on the Australian
version of the *Today* show, but this remarkable response certainly confirmed
the site's success. In the six months since its launch, there had been almost
94,000 visitors to Mapping Our Anzacs. More than 1,000 scrapbook posts
had been contributed and 280 tributes created.

The greatest success was in the type of posts being contributed rather
than their sheer volume. Our scrapbook had proved to be just that—as well
as photographs of service people and their families, there were pictures of
medals, headstones, letters, newspaper clippings, pay books, identity disks,
diaries, postcards, and certificates. (See Figures 2 and 3.) Some people
simply commented "my grandfather," while others wrote detailed accounts
of family history. Perhaps most moving were those who took the opportunity to leave a message for their loved one: "You were the best dad."

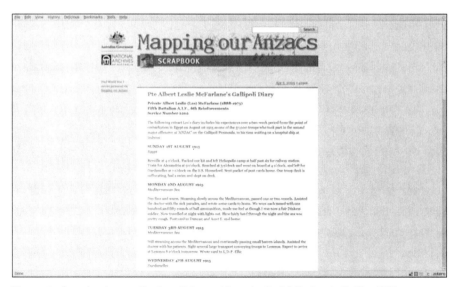

Figure 2: Scrapbook contribution: Private Albert Leslie McFarlane's Gallipoli Diary.

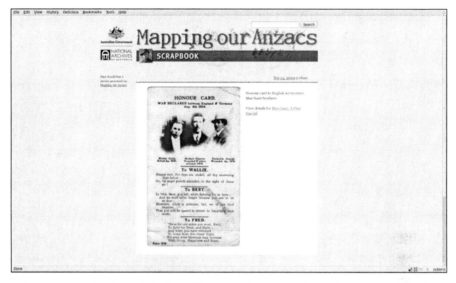

Figure 3: Scrapbook contribution: Honor card to English servicemen, the Marchant brothers.

Some have taken a systematic approach. Our most frequent contributor is gradually attaching photographs of headstones and memorial plaques that she has gathered from local cemeteries. (See Figure 4.) Others are posting their own contact details in the hope of linking up with family. Perhaps most interesting are the notes that provide links to other people or documents—to family members, for example, or to a later service record. These are helping to build a rich web of contextual data. Equally valuable are the corrections and additions that are being offered by eagle-eyed users, pointing out transcription errors or helping us track down elusive locations.

The success of the scrapbook has somewhat overshadowed the tributes, or online memorials, that really provided our starting point. Many tributes have been created and, as we had hoped, schools and other groups are using them to document the impact of war on their local communities. However, some compromises at the implementation stage have meant that it is not as easy to build them as we had hoped. There has also been some confusion by users between the tributes and the scrapbook. This is one area of the site we certainly hope to improve.

Even though the digitized service records had been available online for some time though our collection database, it's clear that many people are discovering them for the first time through Mapping Our Anzacs. It was "a stunning find for me and my siblings" wrote one grateful user. The scrapbook has aided discovery, providing another way into the records. Indeed, with the addition of a MediaRSS feed for CoolIris, the scrapbook provides two new entry points—one of them a three-dimensional wall of faces and families. (See Figure 5.) By embedding the records in these new contexts and making them easier to find, Mapping Our Anzacs has successfully garnered extra value from an existing asset.

The site has also been recognized by others for its successful use of Web 2.0 technologies. We were pleased to be joint winners of the Best Archives on the Web Award and surprised to be cited by the federal minister for finance in a speech launching a Gov 2.0 task-force. Recognition such as this has helped strengthen the case for future innovation in the Web 2.0 sphere.

Figure 4: Photograph of a headstone added to scrapbook.

Figure 5: Photos from the Mapping Our Anzacs scrapbook displayed using CoolIris.

Challenges

Success brings its own problems. One of the main challenges has been simply managing the sheer volume of posts and feedback. This was particularly acute, of course, after the Anzac Day deluge. As a result, we have had to consider ways of streamlining our processes.

The Tumblr API allows us to set the status of a new post as "private." We can then examine the post using the Tumblr dashboard before making it public. This works well enough as a basic form of moderation; however, the dashboard is not really designed for this purpose and it takes several clicks to release each post to the world.

But while moderation takes considerable time, it requires little intellectual effort. Despite concerns about abuse, our contributors have caused us few dilemmas. The only significant questions that have arisen concern the reuse of materials from other sources. This has made us consider whether preemptive moderation is necessary or appropriate.

While the site includes detailed help information, it's clear from the feedback that there are certain aspects that continue to cause difficulty. This provides useful data on how the site might be improved, but it has also made us think about how we communicate with our users. At the moment the content we provide is fairly static—there is no way of informing visitors of recent updates or developing quick guides to common problems. If we took a more active approach to communication, we might be able to decrease the number of help requests while building a greater sense of community.

Similarly, while we have been excited by the number of corrections submitted by users, we can now see ways in which we might have structured the feedback process to capture their corrections more easily and efficiently. For example, a "submit a correction" link on each individual's page could automatically capture the person's details, saving both us and our contributors from potential confusion.

We have suffered through the expected number of software glitches and have a growing list of things we'd like to improve or develop, but overall the experience has been much more rewarding than painful.

Lessons Learned

Perhaps the most valuable lessons revolve around trust. Having entered into the project uncertain of what to expect from public participation, we have found ourselves in an evolving, creative partnership. Our users have defined what the scrapbook is and have taken an active role in improving and developing the resource. Our trust has been repaid many times over, helping us build something that in many ways has exceeded our expectations.

Trust is also necessary in the support of new ideas. Mapping Our Anzacs was a very different type of project for the National Archives, challenging ideas both of access and user engagement. By taking the risk, we have not only gained valuable publicity and user support, we have opened up the realm of possibilities for future development.

In terms of technology, the project demonstrated the power of the mashup and the efficiencies that can be gained by using existing web services. Tumblr and Google Maps and their associated APIs gave us a kickstart that enabled us to do a lot with a little.

Next Steps

There are so many exciting possibilities! Obviously, our first priority is to improve those areas of the site that continue to cause our users grief. There are a number of navigation and usability tweaks that should improve the overall experience. Similarly, we can now see ways in which we might streamline moderation and management processes.

We hope to build on the success of the scrapbook and tributes by enhancing and extending their functionality. Improved editing and creation tools could assist contributors while also enriching the connections they build. We might, for example, provide widgets that make it easier to link the records of family members or friends. Over time this could develop into a complex network of relationships, providing new means of finding and visualizing the records. Similarly, there are ways in which we might reuse the existing content of the scrapbook posts to develop new modes of discovery.

We could also do more to feature the labors and passions of our contributors. We could give them the option of exposing a public profile that lists all of their scrapbook posts. This would help foster a sense of community while providing yet another means of exploring connections between records.

Recent developments in geospatial technology and mobile devices perhaps offer the most exciting possibilities. Our original aim was to give the World War I service records back to local communities to imbue the records with a greater sense of context, locality, and belonging. Perhaps we will have succeeded when tourists exploring a small country town can press a button on their mobile phones to retrieve a list of service people born near their current location. Perhaps they will take a photo of a name on the local war memorial and use it to automatically retrieve that service person's record or create an online tribute. Perhaps they will come across a headstone in the local cemetery and immediately upload a geocoded photograph to the Mapping Our Anzacs scrapbook.

Instead of merely being markers on a map, the records will start to overlay and inform the very spaces in which we move. The stories they contain will become part of our journeys; the people they document will have found their way home.

Wikipedia as an Access Point for Manuscript Collections

Michele Combs

Overview of Repository

The Special Collections Research Center (SCRC) at Syracuse University (SU) originated with the purchase of the personal library of German historian Leopold von Ranke in 1892. Since then SCRC has grown to more than 100,000 printed works and 2,000 archival collections (more than 30,000 linear feet), including important editions, manuscripts, documents, letters, diaries, drawings, photographs, and memorabilia. SCRC currently has nine full-time staff, with three of those being manuscript processors (two grant-funded and one permanent). Patrons include SU students, faculty, and staff; genealogists, researchers, and middle and high school teachers and students from the surrounding community; and out-of-town researchers from the United States and internationally.

Business Drivers

More than 13 percent of the world's Internet users visit *Wikipedia* in a given day.[1] Worldwide, it is the seventh most-visited site and the number one reference site.[2] As of 2009, the *Wikipedias* for all languages have a combined total of more than 1.74 billion words in 9.25 million articles in approximately 250 languages; by word count, the English *Wikipedia* is twenty-five times the size of the next largest English-language encyclopedia (*Encyclopaedia Britannica*).[3]

Since July 2008 we have systematically sought out *Wikipedia* articles about individuals or organizations whose papers we hold in our Special Collections Research Center manuscript collections. If the articles exist, we review and edit them for accuracy based on our research and holdings; if not, and if the person or organization is sufficiently notable, we create a new *Wikipedia* article. At the bottom of the article in the "External links" section, we add a link to our finding aid for that collection.

Our motivation appears at first blush to be a selfish one: exposure. As many studies have demonstrated, we must go where our users are, and more and more often they are online. However, our actions also align with Point VI in the Society of American Archivists Code of Ethics: "Archivists strive to promote open and equitable access to their services and the records in their care without discrimination or preferential treatment. . . . Archivists recognize their responsibility to promote the use of records as a fundamental purpose of the keeping of archives."[4] We are thus ethically bound to increase knowledge and use of not just our own holdings, but of archives and special collections material as a whole. Because so many of those who start their search for information with *Wikipedia* articles are students or other inexperienced researchers, we believe it is critical for special collections repositories to establish and maintain a presence there, to make these "information novices" aware of the infinite store of rich primary source materials available to them—letters, journals, photographs, diaries, sketches, clippings, unpublished writings, and so on—and to help them realize that *Wikipedia* is only the beginning of their information quest, not the end.

In some ways, *Wikipedia* is the best thing to happen to manuscript collections in years, as it affords a simple, convenient, centralized, targeted way to connect with people who are looking for what we have, even if they don't know it, and to educate novice information seekers on the existence of sources they might otherwise never encounter.

Setting the Stage

Because anyone can edit *Wikipedia* from any computer connected to the Internet, no infrastructure, hardware, or software is required. I had been editing *Wikipedia* on my own since 2006, so when we began, I had more than 1,000 edits to my name; as a result of this experience and based on *Wikipedia*'s extensive editing guidelines, we set the following criteria: (1) In accordance with *Wikipedia*'s policy on spam,[5] we would not link to our finding aids from every single possible related article; we would link only from those for which we have *unusual or significant* related material; (2) In accordance with "*Wikipedia* is not just a collection of links"[6] and "*Wikipedia* is an Encyclopedia,"[7] we would also edit to improve the *content* of the articles. The determination of "unusual or significant" is somewhat subjective; factors include the size of our collection, the quality of it (original material vs. published material accessible elsewhere), and the significance of it (highly unusual items, or items important for a particular reason).

Our Library IT Services (LITS) already had software installed to monitor and generate server statistics; from this we knew we could assess whether the links generated any traffic to our finding aids.

The project to retroactively convert our existing finding aids to Encoded Archival Description (EAD) and post them on our website had been in progress for two years, so we already had a substantial number of finding aids online. Our first task, therefore, was to bounce our existing EAD finding aids against *Wikipedia* by checking whether there was an article on that person or organization that could be addressed immediately; we found twenty to thirty of them. Now, as part of our regular workflow each week when we upload newly converted EAD finding aids, we check *Wikipedia* for related articles and/or create new ones as applicable. For the retroactive part of the project, only one person was involved. The regular workflow step involves one to three people, depending on how many we have working on finding aids at any given time.

Results

The results have surpassed our expectations. Before beginning this effort, roughly 50 *Wikipedia* articles had links to SCRC collections; we have no way of knowing who added them but assume it was done based on individuals' personal knowledge of the existence of particular collections. In July 2008 we began the review/edit/link process; since then we have created 13 new articles with finding aid links and added finding aid links to 43 others. Server statistics showed a continual increase in finding aid visits (See Figure 1.); for example, in December 2008 we received 624 visits to our finding aids originating from 88 unique *Wikipedia* articles. Five months later, in May 2009, we had 880 visitors to our finding aids originating from 113 unique *Wikipedia* articles.

On average, between August 2007 and July 2008 we had 270 visits to our finding aids each month originating from 42 unique *Wikipedia* articles. The average for the first five months of 2009 was 780 visits from 103 unique *Wikipedia* articles. By roughly doubling the number of articles, we have tripled the number of people who found our finding aids.

An unexpected side benefit involves foreign-language users. Although we edit only the English-language site, because the *Wikipedia* project as a whole supports 250 languages and actively encourages the translation

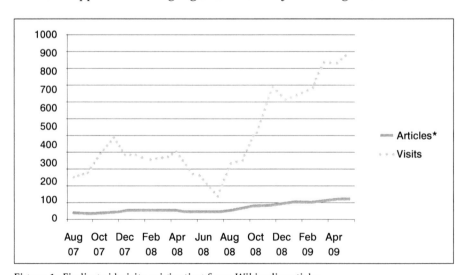

Figure 1: Finding aid visits originating from *Wikipedia* articles.

of articles into other-language *Wikipedia*s, our links are often transferred to other-language editions. Thus far we have seen visitors from articles in (among others) the French, German, Polish, Russian, Portuguese, Spanish, Italian, and Dutch *Wikipedia*s.

Recently an SU undergraduate student came into our reading room to ask about one of our collections; in conversation, she mentioned that she had started her research on *Wikipedia* and thereby discovered our material.

Challenges

The first challenge involved the nature of *Wikipedia* and the definition of spam. *Wikipedia* has a core of alert editors who monitor regularly for "spam" (the adding of links intended to drive traffic to one's website). In July 2007, WikiProject Spam initiated a discussion of whether links added by librarians to primary source material qualified as spam; because I was an active *Wikipedia* editor and self-identified as a librarian, another user alerted me to the discussion.[8] The discussion opened with this, from user Katr67:

> [User] Mdazey . . . has been adding links to various collections at the University of [X] library to numerous articles (129 at last count). I was somewhat concerned that this was spam (the user has made little effort to create content except for direct copy and paste and slightly changed but still copyvio biographies), but was hesistant to have y'all check it out, until today. . . . Apparently this is a spam effort sanctioned by the U[X] library.

Other users chimed in with similar observations. Mdazey defended the links, citing "discussion lately in library university circles on how to enhance *Wikipedia,* and to provide more sourced materials to *Wikipedia* pages." User Nposs then brought up the question of conflict of interest: "being associated with the website, you are not in the best position whether it is a good addition or not. Best to propose the link on the talk page of the article and let other editors decide." Nposs also proposed that a better approach would be to "add some of the content (in a non-copyvio[9] way) and link the reference. That is how *Wikipedia* gets better—through the addition of well-referenced content (not linking to external websites)."

The fact that most libraries are nonprofit was deemed irrelevant, as "non-profit organisations often receive funding from government, from a larger part of an organisation . . . the more links to your website, the more people know you. . . . So the (number of) weblinks are a measure of your efficiency, and hence you do get more money, or only, a better recognition)" (Dirk Beetstra).

The discussion continued for a little more than three weeks. Many participants were librarians or archivists (mention of the discussion was also posted to the SAA list); topics included whether a link to a description of an archival collection was useful, whether it was appropriate to link only to unique items/collections (e.g., multiple universities have first editions of *Tom Sawyer*; linking to only one of them would be inappropriate), whether a good article needed external links at all, and "an unfortunately ignorant tendency among some denizens of the internet to believe that what cannot be digitized must have no value (Eclecticology)." More than one person referred to the article "Using Wikipedia to Extend Digital Collections," which appeared in *D-Lib Magazine* in May/June 2007.

Defenders of the links included the following:

> The links are useful contributions and in no way spam. Hinting to quality (noncommercial) sources is always a welcome enrichment. (Historiograf)

> I welcome the efforts of the Librarians . . . making knowledge broadly available to as many people as possible matters far more than bureaucratic trivia about where to put external links or about citation formats. (Eclecticology)

> . . . quite a few users, especially students, are using Wikipedia as the first step in their research process. Students often go to Wikipedia to get a good overview of a topic, as well as to get ideas of where they can find additional sources. History students especially need to base their research papers on primary sources (like archival material), going beyond secondary sources like encyclopedias. Given this fact, it seems helpful to these users to let them know where they may find related sources to aid their research. (SMA Archivist)

At the end of the day, the consensus was that such links should not automatically be considered spam (as would, for example, a link to Coca Cola's website), but that editors wishing to add such links would do well to respect the spirit of *Wikipedia* by contributing substantively to its content as well. This discussion gave me the idea for our project and also led directly to our two guidelines: add content whenever possible, not just a link; and only link if our collection (as represented by our finding aid) has something unusual or significant to offer.

A second challenge (which has not yet arisen but well may in the future) is what to do if the URLs to our finding aids change. If we were to move them into a database, for example, all the links we have placed in *Wikipedia* would be dead. The best solution here would probably be to put redirect files on our server to send users from old URLs to new ones.

Finally, there is no reliable way to ensure that the links we add are not removed; however, that's true of any and all edits made to *Wikipedia* and simply must be accepted.

Lessons Learned

The first and best piece of advice is to get to know *Wikipedia*—its policies, best practices, writing style, and common courtesies. The best place to start is with *Wikipedia's* "Help" section at http://en.wikipedia.org/wiki/Wikipedia:HELP, which includes the Five Pillars, WP Manual of Style, copyright information, procedures for setting up and updating your account, and much more. Respect the spirit of the project by contributing content, not just links (editors are remarkably quick to spot those who don't care about improving *Wikipedia*, just about boosting their visibility). Rather than using a single account for all editors from your institution, set up individual *Wikipedia* accounts so that each editor is responsible for all edits done on his or her account. Become part of the *Wikipedia* community: identify yourself as a librarian or archivist on your *Wikipedia* user page, contribute to articles unrelated to your collections, take part in library- or archives-related projects and discussions, and, if time permits, assist with routine tasks like New Page Patrol or disambiguation.

Building this kind of "street cred" on *Wikipedia* may or may not need to be done on one's own time. Publishing on *Wikipedia* is not, in essence, that much different from publishing in many other professional venues, such as contributing to an encyclopedia or anthology (or collection of case studies!); consultation with management can best determine whether and how much work time staff can or should spend on these indirectly related, but professionally and institutionally beneficial, activities.

Second, don't be intimidated! *Wikipedia* encourages users to "Be bold when updating pages!"[10]—it is, after all, a collaborative project with more than 9 million users and 158,000 active editors. Your finding aids don't have to be perfect, or in a particular format, before you link to them; although we undertook this as part of a larger process of converting all our finding aids to EAD, it would work equally well with finding aids in HTML, PDF, or even Word format.

Next Steps

As we move forward, we would like to improve our tracking of how often a visit from a *Wikipedia* article turns into a reference question or a site visit; options include adding a single question when users who came from *Wikipedia* leave one of our finding aids ("Did you find what you were looking for?") or asking researchers who contact us how they originally found our collection. At this point we are looking only at articles about specific people or organizations whose papers we have; we would like to explore whether there are articles on concepts, events, or other larger topics to which we might usefully contribute.

In addition, we have a number of collections that include extensive correspondence and/or diaries, so we're also interested in undertaking a day-by-day blogging project, similar to *Papa's Diary* (http://papasdiary. blogspot.com/) or *WWI: Experiences of an English Soldier* (http://wwar1. blogspot.com/).

Notes

[1] "Wikipedia.org," *Alexa.com*, http://www.alexa.com/siteinfo/wikipedia.org (accessed December 9, 2010).

[2] "Wikipedia is more popular than . . . ," *Wikimedia*, http://meta.wikimedia.org/wiki/Wikipedia.org_is_more_popular_than . . . (accessed June 7, 2009).

[3] "Wikipedia: Size comparisons," *Wikipedia*, http://en.wikipedia.org/wiki/Wikipedia:Size_comparisons (accessed June 7, 2009).

[4] Society of American Archivists, "Code of Ethics for Archivists," http://www.archivists.org/governance/handbook/app_ethics.asp (accessed June 7, 2009).

[5] "Wikipedia: Spam," Wikipedia, http://en.wikipedia.org/wiki/Wikipedia:Spam#External_link_spamming (accessed June 7, 2009).

[6] "Wikipedia: What Wikipedia is not," Wikipedia, http://en.wikipedia.org/wiki/Wikipedia:NOTLINK (accessed June 7, 2009).

[7] "Wikipedia: Wikipedia is an encyclopedia," Wikipedia, http://en.wikipedia.org/wiki/Wikipedia:ENC.

[8] For the full discussion, see http://en.wikipedia.org/wiki/Wikipedia_talk:WikiProject_Spam/2007_Archive_Jul#Library_links_discussions.

[9] *Copyvio* is *Wikipedia* shorthand for "copyright violation."

[10] "Wikipedia: Be bold," *Wikipedia*, http://en.wikipedia.org/wiki/Wikipedia:Be_bold (accessed June 7, 2009).

Liberating Archival Images:
The PhotosNormandie Project on Flickr

Patrick Peccatte, translated by Lynne M. Thomas

Background of the Project

My name is Patrick Peccatte. I have a background in mathematics and informatics as well as in information science. I am a computer scientist, and I have worked in libraries and in newspapers. My actual work concerns different applications of XML and metadata, essentially for printing, editing, and the web, but also for photography libraries, archives, and museums. I am also interested in the semantic web, as well as history and philosophy.

The PhotosNormandie project in which I am involved with Michel Le Querrec is designed to create better descriptions for a collection of historic photos of the Battle of Normandy, which occurred during World War II, from June 6, 1944, through the end of August of that year. The 2,763 photos in this collection come from the National Archives of the United States and Library and Archives Canada. Five years ago these images were made available on the Archives Normandie 1939–1945 website (http://www.archivesnormandie39-45.org) by the Conseil Régional de Basse-Normandie (Regional Council of Lower Normandy) on the occasion of the sixtieth anniversary of the liberation of Normandy. For our project we use the Flickr platform to redistribute these images via our own photostream (http://www.flickr.com/photos/photosnormandie). Our photostream has been active on Flickr since January 2007—a year before the Library of Congress began its Flickr Commons initiative. Our project is about collaborative work toward cultural heritage goals. Any visitor to our Flickr collection can search, display, and download high-resolution photos. To comment on the photos, the user must open a free Flickr account and propose their corrections and additions to improve the existing captions. Discussion threads between project participants are used to validate proposed modifications. It is a process of *redocumentarisation*, as we use Roger T. Pédauque's French neologism—that is to say, a collective enterprise that aims to treat anew a collection of documents; it is about describing an iconographic corpus using the numerous possibilities opened by Internet technologies.[1] This is a true process to rethink fully the photos as documents or parts of documents (in French, *redocumentariser*). This is not a folksonomy that is a typical feature of the social web. It is a collective work with a well-defined objective to produce thousands of better captions for photographs.

Business Drivers

The images provided on the Archives Normandie 1939–1945 website are of good quality, but the captions had many inaccuracies and inconsistencies. Some of the errors were very significant from a historical point of view, and we also found obvious mistakes concerning descriptions, which greatly diminished the value of this publicly available collection. At the end of 2006, Michel Le Querrec—a serious amateur historian of the Battle of Normandy—and I decided to improve the descriptions of the photos using the collaborative possibilities of Flickr. We had two principal, intertwined objectives: make these photos better known by exposing them on a popular platform and, thanks to the newfound visibility, obtain better information by allowing viewers to augment the captions. Flickr was attractive as a platform because it was not onerous for us to set up what we wanted, and it was both cost-free and easy to use. The project would be attractive both to visitors who were curious about the historical period but who would not have particular comments to add to the photos and to the impassioned amateurs who could bring accurate information to the project. (See Figure 1.)

Setting the Stage

The photos we used are in the public domain, according to the terms of use on the Archives Normandie 1939–1945 site (http://www. archivesnormandie39-45.org/conditions.html). They are also available on a

Figure 1: An example image (Image p013447) from the PhotosNormandie Flickr project showing French citizens celebrating their liberation.

French commercial site called Archives de Guerres (http://www.archives-de-guerres.fr/) and on several other sites. After trying unsuccessfully to interest the Conseil Régional de Basse-Normandie in our project, we decided to strike out on our own. The first task consisted of downloading all of the public domain photos available on the Archives Normandie site along with their captions. Then we had to put the captions into image files using the International Press Telecommunications Council Information Exchange Model (IPTC/IEM) metadata format and a program I wrote.[2] Our technical approach rested on utilizing the information associated with an image—the IPTC metadata. This meant that metadata fields were saved and stored in the image file under the control of the IPTC/IIM standard. It used textual fields (Title, Caption, Keywords, City, Country, etc.) stored in the image file. When we uploaded a photo containing the IPTC metadata to Flickr, metadata were automatically decoded and used to add information to Flickr fields. This technique of metadata encapsulation allowed the textual description to always be available with the image and easily reusable; there was no risk of information loss, and we remained relatively independent of the technology used to expose and exploit this resource. The editorial work always remained in our control because it was stored in the image files. We were not captive to Flickr, which we could easily replace, if necessary, with another platform that supports IPTC metadata.

To facilitate discussion, we created a Flickr group, "Discussions sur PhotosNormandie" (http://www.flickr.com/groups/discussionphotosnormandie), which provided a way to see and comment on multiple images at the same time (as opposed to having discussion take place in comment threads that are attached to one specific photo).[3] Now, whenever a comment is added to a photo, we add the photo to this group's pool, making it easy for people to see which photos have had comments added recently. This group has been augmented automatically by a program that uses RSS feeds supporting subscriptions to comments posted by users, although using the Flickr group web interface may be easier for those users that have not yet learned to use RSS feeds. Recently, we also implemented a Yahoo pipe for the comments on the photos, because we are trying to provide multiple ways for people to keep track of the conversation.[4]

The validation of information received during a discussion is done collectively by the group of participants who are all greatly knowledgeable about the Battle of Normandy. We have observed very little disagreement in the discussions, and when a disagreement surfaces, generally over the choice of one term over another, the group reaches a consensus relatively quickly.

Results

The project has been very well received by the public. Since its launch on Flickr in January 2007, we have counted a total of 5 million visits on the photos, our photostream, sets, and collections—an average of more than 3,000 per day—and the 2,763 photos have been viewed more than 1 million times. The number of really active contributors remains relatively modest. We have obtained information from about 41 users of Flickr and a dozen or so of these participate regularly in the project. In total, we have completed, corrected, and put in place more than 5,000 descriptions. This number is much higher than that of the photos, because some captions have been corrected numerous times.

Most of the improvements concern the following:

- The identification of localities, people, and military units.
- Precise dates.
- Better descriptions of images.
- References to books, articles, and websites.
- The identification of censored photos, color photos, doubled photos, and photos in series.
- Historical context, such as precise information on a movement of a military unit, a military action, and so on, in relation to the image.
- Iconographic context that helps using other photos and films.

We have also used the TinEye reverse image search engine.[5] This application helped us to find some images in the collection that have been already used in other web pages, allowing us to improve some captions. For example, using TinEye, we found another publication of our photo p013390, which identified a female U.S. Army officer whose name we had spent a long time researching.

We have added new information to the descriptions for numerous photos with incomplete information. For example:

- The identity of actor Edward G. Robinson in photo p013391.

- The son of the mayor of Sainte-Mère-Église in 1944 gave us information about photo p012405.

- The identity of famous photographer Robert Capa changing the film in his camera in photo p013283. (See Figure 2.)

Figure 2: Image p013283 in which photographer Robert Capa is now identified.

Our photos have also been reused by other Flickr users. A group called "D'hier à aujourd'hui" ("From Yesterday to Today") (http://www.flickr.com/groups/hier-aujourdhui) put together photos from the PhotosNormandie collection with recent photos taken from the same areas.

Challenges

We have not encountered serious problems in the course of this project. The most difficult aspect is maintaining the interest of the participants, bringing in new corrections or identifications, asking questions, or proposing new hypotheses about problematic photos or those about which we know very little. My greatest disappointment is that we have obtained very little information from direct witnesses to this period, because, unfortunately, there are fewer and fewer of them and they are generally unfamiliar with the web. Nonetheless, there remains much to learn about these photos and about certain details of these historic events. The majority of information is provided by secondary sources and indirect witnesses, often from users in Normandy who have good local and familial knowledge of these events.

We also have a challenge caused by our method of updating the edited captions. We do not preserve the comments written by various users on individual photos because we update captions by removing one photo and replacing it with a new one with the new caption, which means that we lose the discussion that led to the creation of the new description. We have considered this a minor inconvenience in the majority of cases, but for certain photos we would have liked to preserve the discussion that resulted in the new caption. However, this is the price we pay for embedding the IPTC metadata in the image file, keeping our data totally independent of the platform for collaboration provided by Flickr.[6]

Lessons Learned

One must make a distinction between the technical production side of the work (the managing of the image and metadata files) and a second level for the organization of the conversations about the caption information. Indirect contributions given by the users of different specialized forums form in fact a supplementary network, which is absolutely necessary to activate in this type of project. This is because passionate amateurs have often already developed methods and places on the web for disseminating their information, and they can be reticent about using something new (because it is necessary to create an account, learn how the site works, etc.). It is important to search for those who are already experts capable of participating and to collect information using the preexisting forums or mailing lists—in our case, those devoted to D-Day, the Battle of Normandy, the Atlantic Wall, and other specific topics. With time, the project succeeds in creating a small community that entices the regular users of other forums to join in.

The success of the project is based on the simplicity and flexibility of the collaborative tool that is Flickr and on the quality of the comments but also on the important work of the leaders. We have defined two indispensable functions for our project:

- A chief editor, Michel, who is able to synthesize information collected in a discussion or from other sources and write a precise and coherent caption. According to our process, anyone may propose new descriptions to the group, but it is the editor alone who decides the final text based on the collected information.

- A technical administrator, myself, who must carry out some functions despite the automation already in place.

We must also not forget that the PhotosNormandie project got results because the online photos were relevant to a local historic heritage and were relatively recent.

To summarize, when such a collaborative description project is developed, before the launch of that project it is important to identify a community that is likely to be interested, to give yourself the means to convince this community to work with you, and, in the end, to assume the responsibility for the real work that the project will generate.

Next Steps

Following is a list of improvements that we are planning for PhotosNormandie, from simplest to most complicated:

- We hope to add geotagging to the photos, that is, to write into the image files the coordinates (latitude and longitude) of the place where they were taken, with a view to facilitating their positioning on maps such as Google Maps.

- We would like to locate more of the related materials that we suspect exist. For example, American photographers of the Signal Corps were usually accompanied by cameramen. We are searching for these films that were created at the same time the photos were taken. We have found several films on YouTube, Dailymotion, and the site for the National Institute for Audiovisuals, but there are certainly many more, and there are probably other photos related to those of the project, not only in military archives but also in newspaper archives and maybe in private collections.

- We actually describe the photos in French. We have often been asked to provide descriptions in English. We would like to do so, but we need someone who is not only capable of translating the actual descriptions (which is already a huge job) but who will also develop the project and build and maintain an English-speaking community. We would like to do this, and we also hope to broaden our group of regular participants to other users outside of Normandy.

- The site Archives Normandie 1939–1945 has more than 14,000 photos. We have only used those that are in the public domain. The other photos, which are not in the public domain and are not available in high resolution, have captions that are just as erroneous and sparsely detailed as those images with which we are working. We hope that it will be possible one day to make all of these images available to the public, perhaps in a more restrictive form (without high resolution, for example) in order to improve their descriptions as well.

Otherwise, the experience acquired in the course of this project is very positive and certainly applicable to numerous domains that need the participation of specialists scattered across the world. I would like to personally participate in other collaborative indexing projects with sufficiently motivated communities to work collectively on the web.

Finally, it seems desirable to move beyond the limits imposed by Flickr and begin to define a real collaborative platform that facilitates the work of experts associated with the *redocumentarisation* of image collections (i.e., the "reprocessing" of images as web-based documents or parts of documents) and which gives the collaborators control of the editorial process. Such a new platform must also support more specialized metadata schemas. I would like to participate in the development of such a future platform that would be more effective than Flickr in supporting the needs of professional historians, archivists, and other information specialists, as well as our passionate amateur collaborators.

Notes

[1] Roger T. Pédauque, *La redocumentarisation du monde* (Toulouse: Cépaduès éditions, 2007). See the abstract on http://bbf.enssib.fr/consulter/bbf-2007-04-0122-012 [in French] (accessed January 17, 2011).

[2] "International Press Telecommunications Council," *Wikipedia*, http://en.wikipedia.org/wiki/IPTC (accessed January 17, 2011): "The International Press Telecommunications Council, based in London, United Kingdom, is a consortium of the world's major news agencies and news industry vendors. It develops and maintains technical standards for improved news exchange that are used by virtually every major news organization in the world. . . . The IPTC defined a set of metadata properties that can be applied to images, part of a broader standard developed in the early 1990s and known as the IPTC Information Interchange Model (IIM). Embedded IIM image information is often referred to as an 'IPTC header.' . . . Because of its nearly universal acceptance among photographers—even amateurs—this is by far IPTC's most widely used standard."

[3] Note that this original discussion group contains primarily French-speaking participants. We have started another group, "Discussions in English on PhotosNormandie," http://www.flickr.com/groups/discussionsinenglishonphotosnormandie, for the convenience of English-speaking participants.

[4] The Yahoo pipe can be found at:
http://pipes.yahoo.com/pipes/pipe.info?_id=KhPOVRD32xGivg9nYEsBXw.

[5] This tool can find images using digital signatures technique; it finds exact matches, including those that have been cropped, edited, or resized (http://tineye.com/).

[6] Note that the discussions that take place in our Flickr groups are preserved in accordance with Flickr's standard policies.

New Tools Equal New Opportunities: Using Social Media to Achieve Archival Management Goals

James Gerencser

An old proverb tells us that opportunity knocks but once. A variation on that theme instructs us that an opportunity missed is an opportunity lost. The clear message of these statements is that one should be bold rather than hesitant because there will be no second chance. Delay will only lead to loss and, in time, regret.

Thankfully, opportunities are not always as impatient as these sayings would have us believe. Some opportunities may wait for us to make up our minds, allowing us to consider our options carefully. They may also present themselves to us again, offering a second chance, or even a third, a fourth, or more. In the end, time is often not so great an enemy as we might be led to believe.

As archivists, we are also managers, charged to make effective and appropriate use of our finite resources. We are responsible for the rare and unique materials in our care, for the space in which we work, for our coworkers as well as the people we serve, for the tools and equipment we need to perform our jobs, and for the funds that are provided in support of our operations. We then balance these responsibilities in light of the competing needs of our parent organization, our particular department or office, and our patrons.

In striking a balance, the archival manager is constantly seeking opportunities that will allow more effective use of resources. This requires searching for the highest-quality products at the lowest costs. It involves examining the ways we do our jobs in an effort to improve efficiencies. It means exploring new services to meet changing user expectations. And it involves maintaining an awareness of the environment—by staying abreast of developments within the field and within the parent organization, by paying attention to peers, and by listening to patrons.

The World Wide Web presented archivists with an opportunity to make the collections in their care more visible and discoverable to a global public, to make their range of services apparent to interested users, and to make their own role in the information enterprise understandable to whole new audiences. We responded by mounting finding aids online, by creating virtual exhibits, by digitizing our holdings, and by meeting new expectations from our patrons.

Within a few years, another opportunity presented itself. As the web continued to evolve, new applications were created. The interactive nature of these social media, or Web 2.0, tools offered enhancements, providing even more ways to make unique information available to users, to reach new audiences, and to highlight the important role of the archivist as facilitator in the research process. Beyond these enhancements, the new tools also provided the chance to learn from and interact with our users, as well as to work collaboratively with our colleagues. Finally, these tools offered the possibility to reduce costs, as many of the social media applications operate under business models that require less direct financial investment by the user.

This essay seeks to examine, from a management perspective, the opportunities afforded the archival profession by Web 2.0 tools. As archival managers, we need to evaluate their capabilities and consider the potential they offer to help us work more efficiently in achieving our particular mission and goals. We need to think creatively about how social media applications may be repurposed to meet our unique business requirements, and we need to be open to the new ideas that emerge from our colleagues.

We need to understand the challenges that Web 2.0 tools present, and we need to be aware of the impact their use may have on our other activities.

Fortunately, because the tools themselves are constantly evolving, the passage of time does not necessarily diminish the opportunities we are afforded, but instead may serve to increase them. That being said, the profession will still be served best by action. As Richard Pearce-Moses observed, "We need more than knowledge and skills to thrive in the digital world. We need new attitudes. . . . We need archivists who are early adopters. . . . We need risk takers. . . . We need creativity. . . . Opportunities abound for innovation in every aspect of our profession."[1] Opportunity is knocking, and we ought to respond.

Archival Management and Social Media

In his presidential address to the Society of American Archivists in 2000, Tom Hickerson identified ten challenges for the archival profession. A number of these challenges reflected how changes in technology were driving changes in archival practice. As he argued, "everyone must have an underlying understanding of information technology and a flexible approach to learning new skills and devising new methods. Career-long continuing education is required, and we should assume that there will be constant change in both our organizations and our practices."[2] To be successful, archival managers need to maintain an awareness of new developments in technology and consider how these developments may impact their archival operations.

Besides arguing that archivists must stay abreast of ever-changing technologies, Hickerson also suggested that archivists must employ technology effectively in serving their patrons: "Focusing on our users implies that we acknowledge the primacy of their needs and respond by utilizing methods that address those needs."[3] In an increasingly digital world, those needs include more than mere access to content, but a whole range of services, from accurate full-text searching and effective filtering to personal commenting and tagging, from print- and digitize-on-demand to downloadable content that can be remixed and repurposed. For the archival manager, the importance of using technology well is directly linked to serving well the users of archives.

This important link is noted by Michael Kurtz in his contribution to the Archival Fundamentals Series II: "The information technology revolution, with its profound implications in the communications and knowledge arena, has reshaped the focus of the contemporary manager."[4] For archival managers attention has, of necessity, shifted outward to the users as the web has become the dominant means of sharing unique resources with a global public, of reaching new audiences and building communities of users, of collaborating across institutions and across continents, of exploring creative ways to repurpose available tools, and of developing new tools specifically designed to support the archival enterprise.

In this environment of almost constant technological change, opportunities abound for archival managers to apply new methods and approaches to traditional tasks. Managers look for business efficiencies by streamlining processes and by repurposing data that is generated through a particular activity. They look for cost savings by acquiring less expensive hardware and software and by utilizing programs that offer greater flexibility and transportability. They seek useful partnerships, with both colleagues and researcher communities, to spread the work and expenses. They gather information to understand better the needs of their users, and then they develop appropriate responses to those needs. In a climate of seemingly ever-shrinking resources, the necessity of seeking such efficiencies becomes all the more critical.

This heightened sense of resource scarcity, combined with a stronger focus on users of archives, has led archival managers to move well beyond the mere presentation of finding aids and digitized materials on the web. The relative low cost and resource commitment of many of these Web 2.0 tools, combined with their flexibility and general ease of use, has made them a source of regular consideration and exploration. As social media tools have become ever more widely used by the general public, it makes sense that they have also become more widely employed by archival managers for their potential to build new audiences and strengthen user communities while at the same time communicating more effectively with traditional users. Even further, these tools have begun to be used by archivists in ways that serve internal needs and processes in addition to the services they provide to the public.

Recognizing the Potential

As new social media tools were being developed and popularized, there were those who recognized quite early the potential that these tools had for the archival community. The success of crowdsourcing initiatives like *Wikipedia* and image-sharing services like Flickr led some archival managers to consider the value of the open and interactive nature of Web 2.0 applications. How might those applications aid the archival process? What functions would prove particularly useful in an archival context? How could those tools and functions be incorporated into existing workflow models, or how could new workflow models be developed that would better leverage the unique strengths of these tools? Asking these kinds of questions led to valuable speculation about how the opportunities presented by social media would benefit the archival enterprise.

One of the earlier ideas for consideration was presented in a 2002 article by Michelle Light and Tom Hyry, "Colophons and Annotations: New Directions for the Finding Aid."[5] Light and Hyry argue first for greater transparency by providing to researchers, through the finding aid, important information about the archivist's role in processing a collection of records—a role that may, whether intentionally or unintentionally, affect the way users interpret the records being described.

Light and Hyry go on from there to posit that future users of a collection might be able to offer more detailed descriptive information about the collection and suggest new interpretations of the records that would prove beneficial to later researchers.

> Reference archivists and researchers carry on many of the same processes of discovery, interpretation, explanation, valuation, and understanding as those archivists who initially undertook arrangement and description. Each may gain new insight into the context and content of the collection, the significance of certain records, and the relationships among the records within the collection and their relationships

to other collections. Furthermore, each may have radically different perspectives and interpretations.[6]

By providing users with a way to annotate online finding aids, whether through comments, reviews and ratings, or citations, information about the collection could grow over time with each new use. Researchers would be able to highlight individual items that might otherwise go overlooked, they could describe materials by employing different terms and language that are more understandable to particular audiences, they could provide links to related materials found elsewhere, and they could correct and continually update biographies and administrative histories, as well as scope and content notes.[7] In this way the finding aid, which was initially created by the processing archivist, would serve merely as a foundation upon which future archivists and researchers would continue to build, adding value by providing ever more context and interpretation and making the collection more widely and easily discoverable.

Among the goals of any archival manager is to make collections more accessible to patrons. At the same time, the interactivity and ongoing "communal" development described by this finding aid annotation scenario are hallmarks of social media technologies. One can easily see the value in pursuing the model of a finding aid whereby new information could continually be added to enhance the original product. By harnessing and sharing over time, in an open online environment, the knowledge of those archivists and researchers who delve more deeply into particular aspects of a collection and learn perhaps more about the materials than the processing archivist, the archival manager can make collections more discoverable, more understandable, and more valuable to future potential users.

In 2002 Elizabeth Yakel echoed this potential and suggested that archivists should, with the aid of interactive web-based technologies, make records more accessible or more readily useful and useable. For Yakel, accessibility is defined not merely by physical or virtual access to a collection, but also by the descriptive information, systems, and tools that facilitate the user being able to make effective use of that collection. Recognizing that users have a potential role to play in description, Yakel recommended "rethinking the reference process and adding functionalities and services that facilitate use and enhance the researcher's interaction in both the virtual and the physical archives."[8]

Building on these ideas about the opportunities for user input made possible by Web 2.0 technologies, Elizabeth Yakel and her students at the University of Michigan School of Information formed the Finding Aids Next Generation Research Group early in 2005. The group's goals included considering the transformative possibilities that social media offered for the presentation of finding aids online as well as to develop and experiment with one possible model that would allow interaction among archivists and users. The model finding aid that was created utilized wiki software to present online several collections related to the Polar Bear Expedition, an American military intervention into northern Russia following World War I.[9]

Yakel and co-author Magia Ghetu Krause shared the preliminary findings of the research group based on a six-month evaluation of the experimental wiki-based finding aid. The results of the Polar Bear study suggested that "archivists can employ social interaction tools productively in finding aids to add to both the depth and accuracy of descriptions."[10] The clear implication for archival managers was that users could, in fact, be helpful in the descriptive process, that they could add value and meaning to collections that would extend well beyond the scope and content notes prepared by a processing archivist.

In his 2007 article "Archives of the People, by the People, for the People," Max Evans built on these same ideas, suggesting how archival managers could take advantage of both the available technologies and user knowledge to enhance the products of the archivist's work: "The archives of the future depend upon redesigned systems that incorporate lean and effective methods of processing and describing archival holdings, eliminate backlogs, and create high-level, but still useful, discovery tools for customers."[11] Though the ideas he presented involved a variety of work processes and online tools, here I will just address those that directly relate to social media capabilities.

Given the large backlogs many archives face and the challenge of determining what materials would be of the greatest interest to the general public, Evans argued that it would be helpful to consider the input of users when determining processing priorities. This input could come both from the direct requests and comments made by interested patrons, as well as from the usage data gathered and appropriately analyzed by the archival manager. And with Web 2.0 tools, the former would be particularly easy to solicit and gather.[12]

Even further, Evans suggested that users could themselves take part in the processing function. Collections may be minimally processed and described by archivists but still digitized and mounted on the web. Doing so "places these images before thousands of potential volunteers who will use new tools for online metadata collection. It is not just minimum metadata; it is *extensible* metadata."[13] By making the actual contents of collections fully available online to a global public, users would be afforded the opportunity to transcribe, index, describe, and otherwise comment on these materials, to the benefit of both the archives and future patrons. What little descriptive information was available when the documents were first digitized would be enhanced over time through the interactive efforts of a worldwide community of users.

In his scenario Evans essentially re-imagines much of the archival process. Archivists first utilize available technologies to digitize and provide full access to minimally described collections, selected and prioritized through user input. Archivists then invite users to share in the responsibility to more fully describe the materials by taking advantage of the crowdsourcing capabilities of social media. For the archival manager, Evans presents an opportunity to respond to the desire of patrons to have convenient access to collections sooner rather than later, coupled with the potential resource savings by having volunteers contribute to the descriptive process.

Interestingly, all three of these ideas and experiments with social media revolve around the notion that users can be helpful, valuable resources in the archival process. The people we serve are recognized for the information they can add to collection descriptions, for the transcription and indexing services they can provide, and even for the priorities they can help us set through selection. The common thread of these scenarios is that by making the archives a more open space in the virtual environment, archivists may be able to enjoy the assistance and support of our patrons in making the collections in our care ever more interesting and useful to a widening public.

Trying Something New

Today archivists are providing increased access to their unique materials through various social media applications. They are sharing more information about their work processes and products through blogging and microblogging. They are communicating with one another through microblogging and social networking. They are reaching out to users through a wide variety of tools. And they are experimenting with Web 2.0 applications to perform archival tasks, provide access, and deliver services in new ways. The positive results reported by archival managers using social media have encouraged others to enter the fray. The past five years have witnessed a virtual explosion in the use of Web 2.0 tools by archives and archivists, and that trend is likely to continue for the foreseeable future. A look at a number of these implementations of social media by archivists will suggest why they have become so popular and why archival managers increasingly wish to explore the opportunities they offer.

In the pre-digital world, archival work processes were largely invisible to the general public. Collections were accessioned, arranged, described, and then opened to patrons. Once the collection was open, information about it might be shared through press releases, through articles and announcements in scholarly journals, through inclusion in appropriate professional and hobbyist newsletters, and through addition to union catalogs and published resource directories. Until the collection was fully processed, however, information about the collection was generally not made available to potential users.

Now archival managers are utilizing blogs as a way to share information about a collection *while* it is being processed. These processing blogs provide archivists with a way to highlight particularly interesting parts of a collection, they invite user assistance through identification of materials and added context, and they generate interest in a collection, interest that may help to ensure its later use by the public. Stephen J. Fletcher, responsible for the *A View to Hugh*[14] processing blog at the University of North Carolina at Chapel Hill, mentioned among his goals the desire to educate the general public about an archivist's work, making the process itself more understandable and making more apparent to potential users what kind of progress could be reasonably expected from such a large collection.[15] And so long as the processing blog site is maintained, it can serve as an additional access point whereby the collection may be discovered by potential users.

Though not as popular a tool for processing projects, a wiki may also be used to share information about a collection during arrangement and description. The *Coroner Case File Documentation Wiki*, initiated at the University of Pittsburgh by Kate Colligan, is a notable example.[16] Wiki software helped to facilitate the collaborative processing of a single collection of county coroner case files by a group of student interns. Through the wiki, the processors could share information with one another about the materials they were handling, helping each of them to envision the whole and better understand the context of the files with which they worked individually. As director of the collaborative process, Colligan could also use the wiki to better follow and monitor the progress of the individual interns and coordinate the work of the entire team. As with processing blogs, by opening the wiki to public view and by maintaining the wiki site even after the completion of the project, the wiki can continue to serve as an access point by which potential users may discover and explore the collection. And of course, the information on the site can provide additional context that may not be available in as much detail on the completed finding aid.

For the archival manager, the application of Web 2.0 tools to the archival process offers a number of opportunities. An interested user public may be able to offer contextual information that will provide the processors with a fuller understanding of the collection. A group of processors may be able to work more effectively as a team, particularly when there is limited time available to meet in person. The collection being processed will be more visible to potential users, and there is even the chance that particularly interested individuals may donate time or financial resources toward the processing. The investment of time and energy into such a project is also generally minimal as it is merely a form of tracking project progress, something that is probably already being done in another way for purposes of internal reporting and measurement.

Besides information on processing, blog software has also been used as an alternative to standard catalogs. Again, the traditional model of disseminating information about collections, whether through a MARC record, a published finding aid, a publicly accessible catalog or database, or any other means, suggested that collections needed to be fully processed first. But when faced with uneven descriptions and mixed levels of access to collections, the archivist manager needs to seek effective means for improving, in a timely fashion, the discoverability and use of materials. One solution to this challenge has been the "catablog," a tool designed to offer descriptive information through an easily accessible Web 2.0 application.

As they describe in their case study, Robert Cox and Danielle Kovacs at UMass Amherst designed the *UMarmot* catablog to meet two specific goals.[17] Having inconsistent information on collections presented in differing formats and locations (and all due to the natural changes in both personnel and professional standards over time), Cox and Kovacs developed the *UMarmot* catablog to share collection-level information about archival holdings through a dynamic web interface. Being conscious of their own limited resources and those of many of their peers, they also desired to develop a tool that could be easily adopted and adapted by others facing similar challenges and similar resource limitations. A handful of archival repositories have since developed their own catablogs, seeing the value in this particular model for their own operations.[18]

While the catablog may have been conceived as a very basic access tool, its simplicity disguises the many opportunities it presents for the archival manager. Because the catablog is exposed to web search engines, it is fully discoverable by users around the globe. The format of the tool is one familiar to the general public and therefore is very accessible to all range of users. The ability of the archivist to tag entries in a number of different ways allows patrons a variety of options to search, sort, and browse the materials. Individual entries are easily corrected and updated as new information is learned, and basic descriptive information for newly acquired collections can be added quickly, thus making even the most recently accessioned collections available for potential use. Because all of the collections are now at least minimally described and exposed, the usage of those collections can help staff to set priorities for more detailed processing and possible digitization. In the end, the catablog requires relatively minimal resources and yet offers a multifaceted and expandable means to increase discoverability, searchability, and use of collections.

The reference blog discussed in the case study by Malinda Triller is another tool that was designed primarily to aid discoverability but also serves other valuable functions that benefit patrons and archives staff members alike. At the Dickinson College Archives and Special Collections, reference requests received from off-site patrons were traditionally recorded on paper forms that included patron contact information as well as the results of the reference transaction. Now the general subject of the reference query is entered as a publicly viewable blog post,[19] and the patron contact information associated with that query is maintained "behind" the post, hidden from the public and available only to the archives staff. And as the paper form is merely replaced by an online form, the change in reference workflow has a negligible impact on staff time.

Like the catablog, the reference blog creates many opportunities for the archival manager. The primary function is to share basic information about the topic of reference questions, and as the blog is exposed to search engines, future users interested in similar topics and materials may discover the same information that benefited earlier patrons. Each blog post thus serves as an additional access point to collections and content available in the archives. As a history of reference queries, the blog can prove invaluable to archives staff when questions similar to those answered previously are asked. Because the blog posts are tagged, the archival manager can also sort and search the posts to determine which collections receive the heaviest use and may warrant further processing or digitization. Blog posts also include relevant links out to other useful resources (e.g., related web content, finding aids, digitized materials, etc.) so that future visitors to the blog may be able to "self-serve" their research needs.

The "behind-the-scenes" tracking function of the reference blog also creates opportunities for understanding users. Besides the convenience of being able to recall with a few keystrokes the contact information for a particular patron, the archival manager can generate useful statistical data based on the kinds of information collected about the users. If statistics show that genealogical inquiries make up a majority of the requests, perhaps developing appropriate pathfinders or other research tools would be a worthwhile undertaking. If particular categories of patrons are not well represented despite collections that would be of use, perhaps targeted outreach efforts are in order. Are users able to discover and then successfully navigate the various web-accessible resources of the archives, or do the questions make plain that some improvements are in order? If patrons are often referred from or to other repositories that have related collections, perhaps appropriate collaborations with those repositories could be investigated. The reference blog can ultimately be tailored so that archives staff members can record any type of patron information that may be helpful for the archival manager in understanding the organization's users.

While the reference blog is designed primarily to make potential patrons aware of what resources may be available based on previous researcher requests, the reference wiki is designed to provide direct answers to popular researcher questions. Frequently asked questions are a staple of any reference environment, and as a result archives generally maintain ready reference files that contain basic information on important names, dates, and places associated with the archives' parent organization, related organizations, or the local community. These files are routinely used by reference archivists to answer simple queries from both within and outside the organization, and because of their heavy use the files themselves are often well kept and updated regularly. In cases in which staff members have enjoyed a long tenure with an organization, they themselves (and their memories) may become, for many users, a de facto reference file.

The case study contributed by Amy Schindler explores the potential wikis provide for sharing the kinds of information typically found in ready reference files. If certain topics generate routine questions, then providing the answers to those questions in an online environment means less duplication of effort over time among the reference archivists. And if retirements may lead to a loss of readily available institutional knowledge, as was the case at the Special Collections Resource Center at the College of William and Mary, then there may even be a sense of urgency to implement a reference wiki. Once a reference wiki is in place, answers to new queries can be added as a matter of course, allowing the wiki to grow into an encyclopedic resource over time with minimal added effort. Finally, by linking out to other related and relevant resources, the wiki can become a useful tool for an ever-widening audience by making information available that goes well beyond the unique contents of the archives itself.

Besides the efficiencies from reduced duplication of research and the leveraging of local resources by linking to related information, the reference wiki offers other opportunities to the archival manager. As with many other web-based tools, the discoverability of the information on the wiki by potential users through basic web searches may lead to more detailed reference queries and greater usage of locally held archival materials. The possibility also exists that outside users may be able to share additional information with the archives, offering updates and corrections to the wiki. If a crowdsourcing model is applied to the wiki, allowing those outside the archives to comment and update information directly, it is possible that a dedicated and interested user community may develop around the topics and issues that the reference wiki addresses. Members of that user community may then come to serve as advocates for the organization, potentially offering volunteer services, providing public support when needed, or even becoming a source of external funding.

The Web 2.0 efforts described here reflect the idea that increased discoverability and accessibility of informational resources can be achieved while at the same time meeting other managerial goals. Stages in the archival process need not be separated from one another, with social media serving only the reference and outreach processes at the end. Archivists can use blog software to gain greater intellectual control over collections or to manage information about their reference transactions. They can also use wiki software to manage the arrangement and description processes or to build an informational resource that serves both the archivists and patrons.

For archival managers, the idea that web-based tools may be repurposed to do more than they were originally designed to do is an important one. The creative application of a familiar tool in an unconventional way, besides achieving efficiencies, can inspire the development of completely new tools that will combine the most desirable features and functionalities. These early forays into the Web 2.0 world will aid archivists in the process of re-envisioning what may be possible in the future.

Imagining the Possibilities

In 2002 Elizabeth Yakel offered a vision of the future for the user experience. Her vision revolved around ease of access to descriptive information about collections through databases and online finding aids. This descriptive information would be enhanced by bibliographies that reveal the scholars who have used and cited the collections in earlier research. The descriptive information would be further enhanced by finding aid annotations, which will have been authored by the scholars themselves. This wealth of descriptive information would prove invaluable to researchers in deciding what materials would be of greatest interest and use. The researcher would then be able to make appointments to visit the archives, submit patron visitation forms and call slips, and make arrangements for a personal consultation with appropriate knowledgeable staff.[20]

Revisiting this vision after nearly a decade reveals that the imagined enhancements to description are still largely unrealized. That being said, the opportunity to develop and implement this type of user-centered descriptive program is not lost. This kind of functionality might yet be built as a component part of an interactive archival catalog. Computer technologies continue to evolve over time. While particular hardware and software may become obsolete, the core functionalities of these products remain, generally performing better and proving more useful to their audiences.

In the same way, certain approaches to archival practice may become obsolete over time. The professional goals and objectives of archivists may remain fundamentally unchanged, but concepts may continue to be explored and improvements in practice may be developed on an ongoing basis. Opportunities for effective change are always possible amid such an atmosphere of continuous exploration. In this spirit of exploration, it is well worth imagining how social media might further enhance the archival process to the mutual satisfaction of users and archival managers alike.

As mentioned earlier, Max Evans suggested that user input should be taken into consideration when setting processing priorities. If one accepts that such input can be helpful and instructive, then why not solicit the opinion of others in making appraisal decisions as well? One could easily imagine social media providing a means whereby user input could be obtained on the perceived relative value of archival resources. This is not to say that archival managers would necessarily ignore their policies and their professional responsibilities and merely bow to the wishes of others, or that user input should even be taken into account for all potential accessions. It is merely to suggest that among the many different pieces of information weighed—needs of the parent organization, legal regulations, potential research value, etc.—the thoughts of the user community may be worth taking into consideration. Perhaps the backlogs that plague most archives would have been somewhat reduced if other voices were brought to bear on the appraisal process.

Moving beyond appraisal, what about the process of arrangement? Typically this function is performed by one person, or maybe by a small group of people working together if the collection is of a larger size. But what if all the items in a collection are available electronically, whether they be digitized surrogates of paper records or born-digital materials? If the collection exhibits no discernable order on acquisition, would it be possible (or desirable) to crowdsource its arrangement? Users of the collection might be prompted to suggest relationships among individual items or folders of items. Over time, these suggested relationships might reveal an arrangement that appropriately reflects the way the majority of users perceive the materials in the collection and thus may make the collection more intuitively useable by the greatest percentage of patrons.

Alternatively, perhaps no formal arrangement would even be necessary under these circumstances. If the complete contents of the collection are available electronically, and all fully searchable and discoverable in various ways, then an imposed hierarchical arrangement may not be warranted. In such a situation, perhaps all that is needed is an appropriate Web 2.0 tool that provides the ability for individual users to develop an arrangement suitable for themselves. Each personal arrangement schema could be preserved and made available for the use of future patrons. Imagine someone stumbling upon a collection and being provided several distinct perspectives on how to view its contents. Think how differently that person might see the collection than if he or she were shown a single finding aid.

On description, the many ideas mentioned earlier in this essay, as presented in the archival literature by Elizabeth Yakel, Max Evans, and Michelle Light and Tom Hyry, need not be further explained. Suffice it to say that all of them center on the notion that users of archival materials may, if provided the chance, offer translations of, comments on, or other descriptions of resources that they have examined—that users may share what they know and what they have learned to the benefit of others. All of these ideas also derive from the view that information about the contents of a collection, routinely captured and preserved over time, will serve to continually enhance the research value of the materials well beyond the value that the original finding aid by itself could provide.

In the area of reference, it might be interesting to return to the idea of collections being fully available online. As more and more information becomes accessible to a worldwide audience, patrons may very well seek reference assistance from within their own familiar user communities instead of from archivists, whom users may perceive as an unnecessary intermediary. If they wish to continue contributing to the conversation, archivists may need to utilize social media to become active participants with external groups whose interests align with the content of the archives' collections.

Alternatively, archival managers may choose to host virtual communities as a way to facilitate the online research interactions of particular groups of users. Imagine if archives would be thought of not merely as the place that houses and makes available records of the past, but also as the place where individuals meet to discuss the content of those records, the research those records support, and the ideas that they inspire. Through the application of social media, archives could move from being the refuge of the solitary researcher to being the gathering place for those who wish to consider and discuss topics of mutual interest.

Of course, while it is interesting to imagine some of the possibilities that Web 2.0 technologies offer, it is somewhat less helpful for the archival manager to consider these possibilities with a limited focus on a particular archival process, because the impact on other process areas may be overlooked. Indeed, much of the workflow of the modern archives is already somewhat disjointed. Processors may use certain tools during arrangement and description, but then reference and outreach archivists will likely use very different tools to display and make available the collections that have been processed. The systems used to aid discoverability and searchability of resources are typically not so well integrated with those that present and exhibit or otherwise encourage usage and interaction. What archival managers ultimately need are more holistic archives technologies and process models, where the functionalities required at each stage of archival work are integrated into the same tool, or where information is at least easily distributed and communicated among different tools.

The numerous resource limitations and technical challenges may make a fully integrated archival system—one that would satisfy all the requirements and needs of archival managers and users alike (and perhaps even records creators)—hard to imagine at this time. Nevertheless, archivists are continuing to develop approaches to preserving and repurposing data and metadata, and their ongoing exploration of social media tools will likely reveal more and more opportunities to improve and enhance the archival process. There seems little doubt that archival management systems of the future, where the needs and desires of both archivists and users are met more effectively and where the archival processes themselves take place more fluidly and continually, will involve interactive functionalities that are the hallmark of social media tools.

Conclusion

Although many social media tools have been available for a decade, the use of these tools by archives and archivists is still relatively limited. For the most part, archivists are using Web 2.0 technologies for outreach and sharing content. They communicate with their audiences by pushing information out to them in ways both convenient and effective, by blogging, tweeting, and posting on Facebook information about their collections, exhibits, and public programming events. They also provide images, audio, and video through sites like Flickr, iTunes, and YouTube. By capitalizing on the strengths of these tools, archivists are building new audiences and user communities while raising the visibility of their collections and themselves.

While archivists avail themselves of these basic functionalities, they are also exploring the additional opportunities that these technologies offer. Archivists are asking new questions, testing limitations, examining applicabilities, setting and re-setting priorities, and re-envisioning activities. In the coming years, these questions and activities will lead to the creation of new tools and the development of new process models that will help archivists meet their goals and objectives in more efficient ways.

For the archival manager the focus of attention of our goals in more recent years seems to have shifted, to a greater degree than ever before, to our patrons. As Michael Kurtz suggests, "customer expectations are a major 'driver' influencing all business and every organization. Customer needs influence services provided, the way such services are made available, quality requirements, and staff and unit performance standards."[21] Under these circumstances, the value of social media toward the archival enterprise seems all the more critical.

In the early days of the use of the web by archives and archivists, Bill Landis surveyed the virtual landscape and commented on the opportunities available to the profession. He saw the potential of reaching new audiences, of opening the archives virtually, and of making the role of the archivist more apparent. At the same time, he added a note of caution: "Taking traditional paper guides and inventories, research protocols, and ideas about how collections ought to be used and simply translating them into a digital environment seems like a tragic mistake. Such strategies may offer a place to begin, but it is crucial for this profession that archivists remain alive to the possibilities that this new environment offers."[22]

In many ways, the archival profession seems to have heeded this advice. Archivists did, as expected, largely rely on the ideas and practices of a physical world when first approaching the web, but they are now more exploratory in their endeavors. The case studies throughout this book are indicative of this fact. Today's archivists pay close attention to trends and emerging technologies, they imagine how they may make the best use of available tools, and they work collaboratively to build new programs specifically designed to facilitate archival processes. The opportunities to advance the archival mission have been greatly enhanced by social media, providing archival managers with ways to better serve patrons while at the same time effectively managing limited resources. There seems little doubt that archivists will continue to take advantage of these opportunities as they place an increasingly greater value on the varied needs and interests of a global user community.

Notes

[1] Richard Pearce-Moses, "Janus in Cyberspace: Archives on the Threshold of the Digital Era," *American Archivist* 70 (Spring/Summer 2007): 19.

[2] H. Thomas Hickerson, "Ten Challenges for the Archival Profession," *American Archivist* 64 (Spring/Summer 2001): 14–15.

[3] Ibid., 11.

[4] Michael J. Kurtz, *Managing Archival & Manuscript Repositories* (Chicago: Society of American Archivists, 2004), 4.

[5] Michelle Light and Tom Hyry, "Colophons and Annotations: New Directions for the Finding Aid," *American Archivist* 65 (Fall/Winter 2002): 216–230.

[6] Ibid., 226.

[7] Ibid., 228.

[8] Elizabeth Yakel, "Impact of Internet-Based Discovery Tools on Use and Users of Archives," *Comma* 2 (2003): 199.

[9] Magia Ghetu Krause and Elizabeth Yakel, "Interaction in Virtual Archives: The Polar Bear Expedition Digital Collections Next Generation Finding Aid," *American Archivist* 70 (Fall/Winter 2007): 283.

[10] Ibid., 312.

[11] Max J. Evans, "Archives of the People, by the People, for the People," *American Archivist* 70 (Fall/Winter 2007): 389.

[12] Ibid., 390.

[13] Ibid., 395.

[14] University of North Carolina at Chapel Hill, Chapel Hill Library, *A View to Hugh*, http://www.lib.unc.edu/blogs/morton/ (accessed March 15, 2010).

[15] Kate Theimer, *Web 2.0 Tools and Strategies for Archives and Local History Collections* (New York: Neal-Schuman Publishers, Inc., 2010), 42; see also Stephen J. Fletcher's case study in this book, pp. 22–32.

[16] *Coroner Case File Documentation Wiki*, http://coronercasefile.pbworks.com/ (accessed March 15, 2010).

[17] University of Massachusetts at Amherst W.E.B. Du Bois Library, *UMarmot*, http://www.library.umass.edu/spcoll/umarmot/ (accessed March 15, 2010).

[18] Other catablogs include those by Drexel University Archives and Special Collections at http://www.library.drexel.edu/blogs/collections/; *Emma*, the Catablog of Archives, Manuscripts & Special Collections at the Brooklyn Historical Society at http://brooklynhistory.org/library/wp/; Lawrence Public Library Special Collections at http://queencityma.wordpress.com/; and Norwich University Archives & Special Collections at http://library2.norwich.edu/catablog/ (all accessed March 31, 2010).

[19] *Dickinson College Archives Reference Blog*, http://itech.dickinson.edu/archives/ (accessed March 15, 2010).

[20] Yakel, "Impact," 200.

[21] Kurtz, *Managing Archival & Manuscript Repositories*, 4.

[22] William Landis, "Archival Outreach on the World Wide Web," *Archival Issues* 20 (1995): 146.

Alice in the Archives:
The Evolution of the Catablog

Robert S. Cox and Danielle Kovacs

Overview of the Repository

The Department of Special Collections and University Archives (SCUA) of the W.E.B. Du Bois Library is the sole archival and manuscript repository at the University of Massachusetts–Amherst (UMass Amherst), a large public, land-grant university. A staff of three professionals and two paraprofessionals, assisted by students and interns, oversee collections that document the history and experience of social change (such as the papers of W.E.B. Du Bois) and the history of New England. While archival collections are a significant part of its charge, SCUA is resolutely a special collections repository, its 22,000 linear feet of manuscripts and archival collections joined by more than 35,000 printed volumes, tens of thousands of photographs and maps, and rapidly growing electronic collections.

Business Drivers

When we joined the SCUA staff in 2004, we discovered a problem that is all too familiar to archivists: radically uneven access. Like many of our peers, SCUA's collection descriptions bore the vestiges of now extinct standards and reflected varied descriptive philosophies. While about a third of the finding aids were properly marked up in Encoded Archival Description

(EAD), the remainder ranged from idiosyncratic inventories to barely there at all. Although the problem was pervasive, the solution was clear, if labor intensive: a collection survey. Adapting a methodology developed at the Historical Society of Pennsylvania, one of us, Danielle Kovacs, reviewed every collection in the department, recording summary data for each, adding abstracts and search terms as needed, and making assessments of priorities for future work.[1] After eighteen months of hard labor, she had generated a suite of standardized, minimum-level descriptions that for the first time offered not only comprehensive intellectual control, but a meaningful basis for prioritizing processing, preservation, and digitization.

Confirming that no good deed goes unpunished, however, the higher-quality descriptive data from the survey only highlighted how badly we made these data public. The static lists of collection names on our website and the MAchine-Readable Cataloging (MARC) records buried in the library's Online Public Access Catalog (OPAC) but never exposed to web browsers seemed increasingly inadequate. Worse, although user studies have begun to illuminate the issues surrounding the online display of finding aids and to define the varieties of information-seeking behaviors, they provide little guidance on crafting models for organizing online collection-level information.[2]

Leigh Van Valen once theorized that the evolutionary process bears a peculiar resemblance to the Red Queen in *Alice in Wonderland*: organisms are always running just to stay in place. For the better part of a generation, archivists have been proving Van Valen right.[3] Under the selective pressure of the networked world, archivists have been kept running as small pipe yielded to broadband, as systems and software, standards, and even fundamental philosophies have come and gone. More profoundly, we have become caught in a co-evolutionary spiral with the evolving expectations of end users, technology, and desire outstripping the ability of all but a handful of institutions to remain ahead.

Coming from an institution lacking deep pockets, and having worked closely with several smaller institutions with even sparser financial and technological resources, we were keenly aware of what it is to run in place. Shortly after completing the collections survey, we therefore undertook an experiment to satisfy two seemingly contradictory demands: to develop a dynamic interface for serving collection-level information over the web but one that could be adopted even by our peers with the most modest resources. Perhaps because of all of the running that we archival Alices have done for the past generation, it is sometimes easy to forget that not all of us run equally fast. The aging adage that an archive doesn't exist if it is not on the Internet is truer now than ever, yet even as a web presence has become common, hundreds of institutions are held back from full participation in the Internet for cultural, financial, or technological reasons. In seeking to solve our access problems, we hoped to solve theirs.

Our solution was to employ blogging software—cheap, efficient, and nearly ubiquitous—to create the "catablog" we now call *UMarmot* (http://www.library.umass.edu/spcoll/umarmot). Blogs have certain advantages for this purpose: they are familiar, flexible, and easily adaptable; they have strong indexing capabilities; they are easily set up and maintained; their content is fully exposed to Internet search engines; and Web 2.0 technologies are built into their very fiber. The catablog was designed as a piece of "appropriate technology"—technology that fits the technical and financial capacities and cultural predilections of the communities in which they are applied. Rather than reach for the most advanced, complex, powerful, or expensive tools, we sought a solution with a low barrier for entry that made maximal use of limited resources (technological, financial, and human), while permitting future growth and innovation. The result, we hope, is not a discount version of a designer label, but a product crafted to meet current demands with current resources, while remaining flexible, extensible, and, above all, sustainable.

Setting the Stage

Although *UMarmot* began as an experiment in straightforward blogging—a simple effort to update researchers about departmental activities and solicit public comments—we sensed an opportunity to twist the indexing capabilities and presentational plasticity of a blog to new ends. After testing several blogging platforms, we selected WordPress for its low cost and ease of use and administration. To make the leap from blogging to

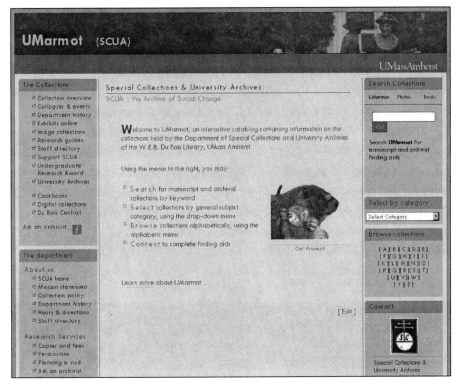

Figure 1: Front page of *UMarmot*.

catablogging, we began by exploiting two pairs of distinctions endemic to WordPress. First, "posts" and "pages" serve different purposes. In a typical blog, posts are daily entries, the most recent of which are (usually) displayed first, followed by successively older posts. In contrast, pages represent more-or-less stable content, informational, analytical, or otherwise. Each collection description in *UMarmot* is issued as a post, while pages are reserved for basic departmental information, including policies, services, our mission statement, and collection policy. (See Figure 1.)

Second, WordPress distinguishes "tags" from the "categories" applied to posts. The former are keywords describing the content of a post; the latter refer to "subjects" under which posts are indexed. As a collection is entered into the catablog, our archivists categorize it under one or more "natural languages," hierarchically organized categories roughly corresponding to areas within our collection policy, and these categories are automatically indexed and displayed as a menu on the sidebar. With the click of a mouse, researchers may select, for example, a list of collections relating specifically to the antinuclear movements or to communism or environmentalism, or they may select the overarching category, social change, and see them all. Tags are used primarily to collocate archival collections according to the history, organization, and functions of the university.

Records in *UMarmot* conform to relevant archival standards, particularly EAD and Describing Archives: A Content Standard (DACS). When a full EAD finding aid is available, the *UMarmot* record is extracted directly from it: the top-level <origination> is used as the title of the post, with the body of the record drawn from <unittitle>, <unitdate>, <physdesc>, , <unitid>, and <controlaccess>. (See Figure 2.) When relevant, we add links to other online resources, including exhibits, digital corpora, and finding aids, and, for visual interest, we often decorate the record with

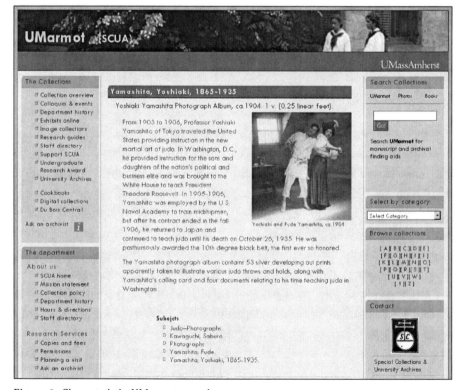

Figure 2: Characteristic *UMarmot* record.

an image drawn from the collection. In 2008 we began to ingest entire finding aids into the catablog. While browsing, researchers see only brief summary information, but "below the fold" (visible only when viewing the full post) we display the remainder of the description, down to and including the inventory. Consequently, *UMarmot* permits researchers to perform a single search encompassing the full content of all of SCUA's holdings, processed and unprocessed alike.

Having set out to create a model that could be adopted by less well-supported repositories, we opted explicitly for technological austerity, selecting a prefabricated "theme" that set the basic appearance for the site and limiting customization primarily to matters of appearance (the stylesheets and page templates), while eschewing anything that required substantial technical skills. Our decision to invest resources in site aesthetics might be viewed by some as a barrier to adoption, but we consider aesthetics too important to ignore: marketing and branding and a desire for a coherent visual identity are critical concerns, but so too is our belief that aesthetics are central to the end user experience.[4] It is important to note, however, that the aesthetic decisions made in building *UMarmot* are not required to make a catablog work: many WordPress themes can be used essentially as is, barely requiring an understanding of html.

The theme we selected for *UMarmot* organizes each page into three columns: two navigational sidebars flanking a content-rich center column. From the left sidebar, we offer links to pages containing narrative overviews of collecting areas and basic information about our repository. Each page may in turn link to individual collection descriptions: the University Archives page, for instance, includes links organized by academic departments, occupations, and functions in the university. In addition to providing contact information, the righthand sidebar provides the major features for navigating our collection descriptions, including a search box, a dropdown menu of collection categories, and a menu permitting researchers to browse collections alphabetically. Our goal in this profusion of points of entry is to provide what we call "layered access": highly structured, richly textured, but variable paths into a thicket of information, suiting varied research styles.

Results

UMarmot was launched as an experiment on the Wordpress.com site in April 2007 and was populated by hand over the course of a few days, one record at a time, from data culled from the collections survey. Because the data for the survey were entered into a database, it was a fairly simple task to export the records with the necessary markup, and as we entered the data, we fine-tuned the records for appearance. *UMarmot* currently contains nearly 800 entries, including all manuscript, photographic, and archival collections (although a few of the latter are provided only at a rudimentary level), as well as collection-level summaries of most major book and digital collections. Although we do not have a sufficient basis for quantifying the impact of *UMarmot* on collection use, lacking both the long-term statistics necessary for longitudinal comparison and any mechanism for distinguishing the effects of *UMarmot* from the fact of simple web presence, we do have strong anecdotal evidence that the catablog has begun to meet its goal, ranging from an increase in use of relatively obscure collections and an increased number of international queries to the adoption of the catablog model by a handful of other institutions. Our staff and student assistants believe *UMarmot* has reduced the time required to answer reference queries and made it easier both for us to assist researchers and for researchers to help themselves. The layering of access and categorization has been singled out by researchers for specific comment. One commenter, reflecting a sentiment expressed by others, called *UMarmot* "one of the best conceived collections I have ever encountered," waxing enthusiastic about the indexing that collocated our diverse collections for social change in one easy-to-use package. It may not be coincidental that since launching, *UMarmot* has ranked behind only the main library homepage and information about library hours in terms of website hits.

The impact has had a profound impact on workflow as well. New collections are accessioned on arrival as they were before, but we now add a stage in which we formally assess the collection's intellectual content and physical arrangement, write an abstract, compile the *UMarmot* record, and post the results, generally within two or three days of the collection's arrival. In other words, collections no longer wait. In this regard, *UMarmot* might be seen as a framework for minimal processing, but our approach is not minimal processing as typically practiced, nor is it "accessioning as processing," or at least not *just* accessioning as processing.[5] Instead, we view the *UMarmot* record as merely the first stage in the life cycle of processing. During this first stage, we seek to minimize the time between arrival and availability, but we maintain a long-term focus on maximizing the intellectual apparatus, however constrained we may be by the realities of resource availability. Our goal is the long term, when the preliminary record will be enhanced by fuller processing and the development of derivative products. Before Greene and Meissner, user studies often suggested that researchers were interested in better and thicker description, yet more recent interventions in the literature suggest that researchers simply want things quicker. To us, this is a false dichotomy: speed of access and depth of description are two stages of a single continuum, and to compromise either compromises the whole. In the spirit of Greene and Meissner, *UMarmot* has become a collection management tool for setting priorities and making decisions about allocating scarce resources to meet the varied demands of our research publics and administrators while minimizing the less productive activities that hinder us. Highly requested collections receive a higher priority for processing (or *re*processing), even as we recognize that for some other collections, the *UMarmot* record may have to suffice for the foreseeable future.

Challenges

From the outset, *UMarmot* was conceived of as an opportunity to exploit Web 2.0 technologies, but while these technologies hold promise, they also raise some fundamental questions. Really Simple Syndication (RSS) feeds stand out for their potential in updating researchers about departmental activities and the arrival of new collections, and it was a trivial exercise to port the RSS feed from *UMarmot* directly into our departmental Facebook page (http://www.facebook.com/pages/Amherst-MA/Special-Collections-and-University-Archives-Du-Bois-Library-UMass-Amherst/66958862119?ref=ts).

Theoretically, commenting by researchers holds even greater potential. Indeed, in their millennial moments, some archivists have enthused about the potential for patron- or donor-generated content, not only to augment traditional collection descriptions but perhaps one day to replace them.[6] Yet our experience with *UMarmot* has tempered our enthusiasm. While we do occasionally obtain valuable (usually genealogical) information regarding individuals represented in our collections, most comments are either basic reference questions, pats on the back, or offers of new material. Each of these is, of course, important in their own right, but as a mechanism for harvesting information from the world at large, they raise the question of whether catablog-based commenting can ever become an efficient means of generating coherent collection descriptions. The comments focus on a relatively small fraction of the whole, and the information is usually focused on a fraction of that fraction, but it comes largely in the form of disconnected facts, leavened with little in the way of meaningful historical context.

Lessons Learned

Based on this experience, we see several hurdles that will need to be overcome before blog-based Web 2.0 technologies can reach their full potential for the collaborative production of finding aids. On one hand, archivists might choose simply to allow comments to stand as received, with some collections accruing content and others not. The cost of this strategy, however, is not just incomplete coverage: genealogical discussion boards provide a glimpse of a dystopic future of inconsistency, dubious accuracy, chaotic organization, internal contradiction, omission, and commission. Alternatively, archivists might elect to organize and integrate useful content directly into a finding aid, editing out the bad and emending the good, but if so, the exercise becomes only trivially different from our current practice of editing finding aids based on comments received by more traditional means.

Several archivists have speculated that wiki-based finding aids might therefore be preferable, enabling true collaboration on the model of *Wikipedia*. Here too, of course, questions of efficiency and coverage rear their heads, but at a more profound level, we may wish to consider whether (or in what ways) finding aids and wiki articles are comparable. For us, a proper finding aid provides an exploration not only of the creator of the collection, but of the context and content of intellectual production, and this exploration is tied resolutely to the material objects that constitute that collection, requiring not only layers of interpretation but an exploration of the materials themselves. The sort of granular commentary received from catablog patrons is surely not unimportant, but thus far there is little to indicate that even an aggregate of such comments would produce a well-conceived, well-articulated, firmly grounded, comprehensive finding aid. Because we continue to view finding aids as our most significant intellectual product and the primary means by which researchers locate information about our holdings, and because they are key elements in crafting our institutional identity, we continue to regard our investment in their production as worthwhile.

Instead of using new technologies to supplant finding aids, then, we have begun to explore ways of leveraging Web 2.0 technologies to supplement and recast them. Late in 2008, for example, we launched *DuBoisopedia,* a wiki in which users of all levels are encouraged to collaborate on articles treating topics, people, and publications related to W.E.B. Du Bois and his life and times. Our goal for this site is not simply to provide a forum for the exchange of ideas about the Du Bois Papers but to create an alternative avenue for mining the digital Du Bois collection (currently under production) as well as to capture more general essays and curricular materials on the life and legacy of one of the twentieth century's great activist intellectuals. Similarly, our *YouMass* wiki builds a collaborative history of UMass Amherst that provides avenues into the archives as well as a means for departments and groups to self-document. In both wikis, we hope to capture and share the rich details discovered by researchers during active use of our collections, information for which there is no place in a traditional finding aid, but while such details can supplement an archival description, they cannot replace it.

Next Steps

Whatever calculus we use in developing the next-generation catablog, we plan to adhere to the same principles used for *UMarmot:* appropriate technology, layered access, standards compliance, flexibility, and extensibility. More than that, we look forward to incorporating new ideas from our peers as they extend the model to suit their cultures and preferences. Where necessity meets paucity, as it often does in the archival world, the greatest creativity can result.

Notes

[1] Philadelphia Area Consortium of Special Collections Libraries, Consortial Survey Initiative (2009), http://www.pacsclsurvey.org/ (accessed September 9, 2009).

[2] See, for example, Barbara Craig, Wendy M. Duff, and Joan Cherry, "Historians' Uses of Archival Sources: Promises and Pitfalls of the Digital Age," *Public Historian* 26 (2004): 7–22; Wendy M. Duff and Catherine A. Johnson, "Where Is the List with All the Names? Information-seeking Behavior of Genealogists," *American Archivist* 66 (Spring/Summer 2003): 79–95; Catherine A. Johnson and Wendy M. Duff, "Chatting Up the Archivist: Social Capital and the Archival Researcher," *American Archivist* 68 (Spring/Summer 2005): 113–129; Christopher Prom, "User Interactions with Electronic Finding Aids in a Controlled Setting," *American Archivist* 67 (Fall/Winter 2004): 234–268; and Helen R. Tibbo, "Primarily History in America: How U.S. Historians Search for Primary Materials at the Dawn of the Digital Age," *American Archivist* 66 (Spring/Summer 2003): 9–49.

[3] Leigh Van Valen, "A New Evolutionary Law," *Evolutionary Theory* 1 (1973): 1–30.

[4] Stephen P. Anderson, "In Defence of Eye Candy," *A List Apart* (April 21, 2009), http://www.alistapart.com/articles/indefenseofeyecandy (accessed September 9, 2009).

[5] Mark A. Greene and Dennis Meissner, "More Product, Less Process: Revamping Traditional Archival Processing," *American Archivist* 68 (Fall/Winter 2005): 208–263; Christine Weideman, "Accessioning as Processing," *American Archivist* 69 (Fall/Winter 2006): 274–284.

[6] See Weideman, "Accessioning as Processing," and Donna E. McCrea, "Getting More for Less: Testing a New Processing Model at the University of Montana," *American Archivist* 69 (Fall/Winter 2006): 284–290.

A New Look for Old Information: Creating a Wiki to Share Campus History

Amy Schindler

Overview of Repository

The Special Collections Research Center (SCRC) in the Earl Gregg Swem Library is located at the second oldest university in the United States, the College of William and Mary in Williamsburg, Virginia. The College of William and Mary is a public liberal arts university attended by 5,700 undergraduate students across 36 programs and 1,925 graduate students across 12 academic and professional degree programs.

The Special Collections Research Center (SCRC) is home to more than 1,000 collections in four areas: manuscripts collections, university archives, the Warren E. Burger Collection, and rare books and periodicals. Focused on Virginia history, but with national significance, the unique manuscripts collection includes letters from presidents and slaves; account books of colonial merchants and twentieth-century funeral homes; and other items providing evidence of events and people great and small from the seventeenth to the twenty-first centuries. The university archives collects material documenting the history of the College of William and Mary from eighteenth-century bursar's records and other official records to twenty-first century YouTube videos. The Warren E. Burger Collection consists of the lifetime professional and personal papers and memorabilia of the late chief justice. The rare books collection is a growing collection that provides research opportunities in areas of Western thought and experience focusing primarily on Virginia history but including collections covering many other areas and interests from the fifteenth through the twenty-first centuries.

The SCRC annually serves more than 50 university classes and 2,000 researchers, including students, faculty, administrators, and the general public, with approximately half visiting the department in person. The collections are cared for by 4 full-time equivalent (FTE) professional staff, 2 FTE paraprofessionals, 1.5 FTE support hourly staff, 15 volunteers, 10 undergraduate student employees, and 3 to 6 graduate student interns and fellows.

Business Drivers

In early 2007, the SCRC had a minimal presence via the library's website, with a basic description of the department and its collecting areas, brief descriptions for a few collections, a handful of older online exhibits, and lists of the university's honorary degree recipients and commencement speakers. Like many institutions of a certain size, Swem Library's website has over time had several design templates, which did not always allow for a great deal of flexibility, and staff were constrained in what was allowed outside of the templates. In 2007 the SCRC was redesigning its website to conform to the then-current template as well as pursuing means to share as much information from and about the department's collections as possible.

Meanwhile, the university archives staff had over the years assembled useful and frequently-referred-to information known within the department as the Buildings File and Vital Facts. The Buildings File was a 150-page Word document providing information about more than 50 past and present university buildings and campus landmarks. The Vital Facts included information on frequently requested topics from students, administrators, and the curious public, including the first women and African American students at the university, the coat of arms, regalia, and traditions. This was a great deal of information conscientiously assembled by years of staff research and rekeying, but it was tucked away on shelves in the department's lobby in binders, making it for all intents and purposes inaccessible to the public except for those relative few who visited in person or were interested enough to contact staff.

In recent years, both the rare books librarian and manuscripts curator had retired from the library after decades of service. Further, with the departure of the previous university archivist in 2006 and a longtime University Archives assistant expected to depart soon after my arrival in 2007, the loss of institutional knowledge gained from answering internal and external inquiries over several years was quite obvious. It is fair to state that the University Archives assistant's departure was anticipated with some trepidation by staff members, including myself.

As of early 2007, the SCRC did not have a collections database in which staff and the public could search for basic biographical and administrative information about the individuals and organizations making up the SCRC's collections. While this was less of a concern for well-known individuals or organizations—such as alumnus Thomas Jefferson or Phi Beta Kappa, which was founded at William and Mary—it did mean that information was not necessarily as accessible as it could have been to staff and the public alike. The SCRC was interested in a tool that would provide the opportunity to capture the information that might be in paper finding aids, binders, or files in the department. It would also provide an opportunity to gather at least a portion of the information already known to staff yet not necessarily documented in writing as well as information staff continued to unearth in the course of their processing and reference work. Especially with the continuing growth of inquiries received via e-mail, staff were sharing a great deal of information, but it was not necessarily being captured and made available to share the next time a similar question was raised (and they always are raised again).

In addition to the need to share information about the collections with the public and each other, staff also needed a way to share lists of material pulled for specific classes and tour groups with each other and users both before and after on-site visits. Finally, while the SCRC did not yet have a collections database, plans were under way, which would create the need for project documentation, both for staff and for other operations in the department.

Setting the Stage

In recent years the SCRC has reorganized itself to streamline operations across collecting areas and to bring the department into the current century. Department staff discussed establishing a wiki to share information with each other and users. The library's information technology (IT) staff were using an installation of MediaWiki for internal uses such as project documentation. When contacted about establishing a wiki for the SCRC, the library's IT staff assured the SCRC that it could be set up in "about an hour" without any problems (and it was).

The *SCRC Wiki* (http://scrc.swem.wm.edu/wiki) was established on March 15, 2007, with no formal policies in place. The nearest approximation of a mission statement was the need and desire to share the collections of the SCRC and the information amassed from those collections with the university community and the general public while also meeting the administrative needs of the department. I was the de facto administrator of the wiki with library IT handling all installation and maintenance issues. Initially, in an attempt to encourage as many staff, students, and members of the public to edit the wiki as possible, we allowed anyone to edit wiki pages without registering a username. Due to spamming, in August 2007 those wishing to add or edit content were required to register with a valid e-mail address.

Now the primary need presented itself: content. An obvious place to start was the Buildings File. An undergraduate student was assigned the task of copying and pasting the 150-page document into a simple template in the wiki with minimal immediate editing and additions by staff. Basic best practices were established at the time with rough directions for required sections, source citations, and categories. Since its launch, the template for pages has been revised and expanded, disclaimers have been incorporated, and mandatory use of categories has been established. (See Figure 1.)

A part-time support staff member and I organized the former Vital Facts documents—some of which were already available to staff as Word

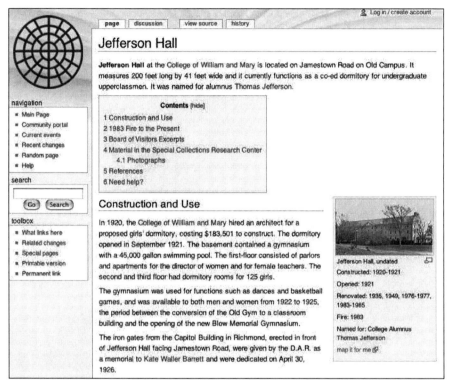

Figure 1: Jefferson Hall Wiki Page–A typical William & Mary buildings wiki page created from content formerly found in the paper-only Buildings File.

documents–into logical wiki pages as quickly as possible. Later, SCRC support staff and graduate students took on specific projects, including creating pages for the dozens of campus buildings and properties not already available electronically, writing brief biographies for all of the university's presidents, department histories, and so on. For the first eighteen months of the wiki's existence, University Archives staff also began adding–on an irregular basis–information that they had gathered to respond to inquiries from offsite researchers. The most well-developed wiki pages were often those tied to in-depth questions from internal users. For instance, when the university was planning a new logo, the *SCRC Wiki* became the place for gathering information related to historical branding, including school colors, nicknames, and mascots. (See Figure 2.) It was also expected that responses to reference and research questions using manuscripts and the rare book collection would be added to the wiki. Adoption in those collecting areas has been sporadic to date, with training and other efforts ongoing to increase participation by all staff.

The immediate measures of success for the *SCRC Wiki* at the time it was established were seemingly straightforward, yet not necessarily easily documented: would the wiki be used by and useful to department staff? The first researcher was directed to the *SCRC Wiki* for information about three weeks after its launch.

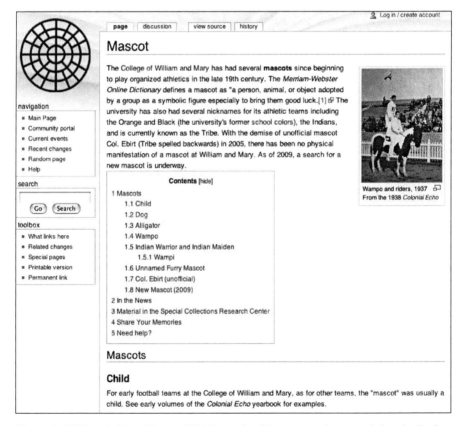

Figure 2: William & Mary Mascot Wiki Page—A wiki page greatly expanded and edited to respond to queries from internal university users.

Results

The Swem Library uses Google Analytics on its web pages, but this tool has not been running on the *SCRC Wiki*. Presently, the statistics provided within MediaWiki are the only measures being gathered on a monthly basis. The statistics gathered by MediaWiki include the most linked to categories, files, and pages, as well as the most viewed pages. As of November 2010, the wiki included 3,998 pages, 160 files uploaded, 965,923 page views, 13,131 page edits, and 341 registered users (most of whom are not active).

As part of a larger strategic planning effort, the department is reviewing the statistics it gathers and how they are analyzed, which may include further measures related to the wiki. One change—due in large part to staff's and researchers' increasing reliance on the wiki—is that the department's front desk now tallies the number of people who visit the SCRC whose information needs are met by staff going to the wiki or another online resource using the public computer terminals in the lobby. In the past, onsite users were only counted if they used material in the reading room.

All reference e-mail and telephone questions answered by University Archives staff are now added to the wiki, either through editing existing pages or creating new pages. While the binder formerly known as the Buildings File went online within weeks, additions continue, including creating pages for overlooked and new buildings, adding current and historical images, including Google Maps Street Views of current locations, adding links to recent news stories, and posting general revisions that were unheard of with the former document. On a campus as old as and as historically aware as the College of William and Mary, there are many individuals with an administrative need for this information who regularly use the wiki, including the Office of the Historic Campus, Alumni Association, University Relations, Web and Communication Services, and Facilities Management. Undergraduate students are frequently in search of information about campus buildings and landmarks for personal research, projects for classes, stories for student newspapers, and a variety of other areas. These offices and individuals will follow up with staff for further information and often express their appreciation for the information already found in the wiki.

Each instance of an *SCRC Wiki* page being cited on a web page, in a university news story, in a blog post, or by another avenue is a sign of success. When the president of the Asian Student Council, a student group on campus, began investigating the history of Asian American students on campus, he shared his findings with the University Archives and asked that they be added to the wiki page. As staff have come across additional information related to the topic, it has also been added to the page. The first time another student shared a link to the Asian American Students wiki page on Facebook with her classmates was a moment worthy of a small victory dance in our offices. During the university's search for a new mascot, the mascot search committee linked to several relevant pages in the wiki in news stories and blog posts—and that was before I was a guest blogger and did the same. It is a simple matter to find information about the relationship of alumni such as Presidents James Monroe and John Tyler with William and Mary, but bringing the results of inquiries regarding lesser-known and even anonymous alumni to the world via the wiki is a sea change for the department.

It is progress when we can, in a very simple way, save a university staff member or other researcher a wait while we return his or her phone call or reply to an e-mail. The instances of people mentioning that they found information on the wiki and are contacting or visiting the department for further information is evidence of the wiki functioning in the manner we had hoped. The department has also received at least one donation for which the donor specifically mentioned the wiki when making the gift.

Challenges

While the launch and use of the wiki is viewed as a success, the limited participation in creating and editing pages outside of those who are required to do so or those who have witnessed its benefit to their own area of interest remains a struggle. As challenges go, it does appear to be one remediable by ongoing outreach and training. First, we must continue to make the case about the wiki's usefulness to department and library staff not currently using or adding content to the wiki, as well as researchers. While there are university staff who are frequent consumers of the wiki, there is a significantly smaller number who are producers of content. Faculty, staff, students, alumni, and other users have specifically shared information with department staff, directing that it be added to the wiki, but the tool is not one with which they are familiar or are interested in editing themselves, presumably because it is unlike other online information sharing, such as discussion boards, forums, and the like. The SCRC—and the university—should do a better job of relating how this and other tools can be of use to students, faculty, and staff for class work, research, and administrative needs. Both the SCRC and the library include links to the wiki from their main pages, indicating that it is an important information source for users. Considering that the SCRC has not yet widely publicized the wiki with a feature story in a campus or alumni publication or even on the library's own website, the relatively limited participation to date is not entirely surprising.

The installation of MediaWiki has proven to be problem-free and supported by Swem Library IT without significant incident. While the wiki does find itself dealing with some spammers, the amount of spam was drastically reduced after we required users who wished to edit pages to create usernames with a valid e-mail address. The need to eventually separate the rapidly growing number of administrative pages (material pulled for classes, manuals for the collection management database and institutional repository, or a greatly expanded accessioning and processing manual) from the content pages (people, places, events, etc.) in the wiki was of mild concern to staff. In 2009 this issue was dealt with when all SCRC administrative pages were moved to a new SCRC staff wiki hosted by university IT in Wikispaces. While still visible to the public, this wiki is only edited by staff. (See Figure 3.) These administrative pages were often created and edited by staff who have not been regular contributors to the other pages created for users, and so maintaining their interest in the non-staff wiki and increasing their content contributions will be useful going forward, as they are well versed in using the wiki software.

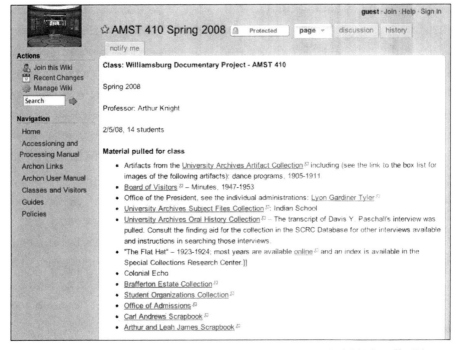

Figure 3: Material Pulled for AMST 410 Class Spring 2008—A typical SCRC staff wiki page tracking material pulled for individual classes for use by staff and students.

Lessons Learned

It proved valuable in the case of the wiki to begin creating content around specific topics: campus buildings and landmarks, honors and awards bestowed by the university, presidents of William and Mary, and so on. Creating a core group of pages ensured the creation of related content and allowed for the population in phases. The organizing of pages into these categories was a simple matter, but the importance of maintaining the flexibility of the tool by remaining open to changes and new opportunities, whether in the case of subject matter or organization, is important. For instance, when the university was going through its logo redesign followed by a search for a new mascot, pages related to university mascots, nicknames, school colors, and related topics were created and enhanced. While a certain amount of planning is ideal, if not required, implementers should strive to remain open to new content as it is suggested by others or as it suggests itself.

As with any implementation, staff and users may express interest and their intention to use the new (fill in the blank), but sometimes it simply must be mandated. Ongoing training and outreach to staff who are required or just "encouraged" to use the wiki is necessary. While the SCRC hoped that non-staff who know a great deal about the SCRC's collections and campus-related topics would participate, our experience has shown that the majority of those who saw a demonstration but were not specifically invited to contribute have remained passive.

Next Steps

Some of the next steps will be administrative in nature. The department and library are undertaking an effort to improve metrics in general but having a clearer vision of what should—and could—be collected from the wiki would be helpful. However, the case could also be made that during the wiki's soft launch—from 2007 through early 2008—any data collected would have been inconclusive. The department expects to begin regular and ongoing surveys of its users in 2009–2010. This data will provide measurable comment, criticism, and evaluation for the first time.

The next steps for continuing to increase the population and popularity of the wiki could go in a variety of directions. There has been discussion of more actively soliciting content from current students, alumni, faculty, and staff by posing questions via e-mail newsletters and blogs as well as direct communication with individuals whose memories we know could and should be captured. These questions would take the form of asking people to share their memories in the way that formal oral history interviews and college and university alumni association magazines often do, such as: What was Barrett Hall like when you lived there as a student? What stories do you recall about ghosts on campus?

While neither the SCRC nor the Swem Library has a marketing plan per se, a feature story about the wiki in the library's news feed would be a first step to wider media placement to include the many small, local newspapers especially hungry for publication-ready stories, as well as the university's news stories and the alumni magazine. The wiki has proven itself to be a valuable resource to staff and users and the need to ensure it is available and shared continues just as the need to ensure the public is aware of the SCRC's collections or even the SCRC itself.

Double-duty Blogging: A Reference Blog for Management and Outreach

Malinda Triller

Overview of Repository

Dickinson College is a private, liberal arts college located in rural central Pennsylvania with an enrollment of 2,300 students. The Archives and Special Collections unit is housed within the library, which is one of five departments constituting the Library and Information Services (LIS) division of the college.

The Archives and Special Collections unit's primary responsibility is to preserve and provide access to the institution's official records, dating back to its establishment in 1783. These materials encompass approximately 1,600 linear feet of documents, photographs, artifacts, and video and audio recordings. Dickinson's Special Collections includes roughly 800 linear feet of manuscript collections documenting the lives of individuals associated with the college, as well as various aspects of local history. These manuscripts include the papers of the fifteenth president of the United States, James Buchanan (Class of 1809), and noted eighteenth-century scientist and theologian Joseph Priestley, along with the records of several of Carlisle's oldest churches and items related to the 1979 accident at the Three Mile Island (TMI) nuclear reactor, which is nearby. This unit also cares for approximately 20,000 rare books and periodicals, with particular strengths in religion, travel accounts, literature, and history.

The college archivist, a Special Collections librarian, one support staff member, and a revolving crew of approximately a half-dozen students and interns maintain the collections and respond to an average of 100 on-campus and 250 off-campus reference requests annually. The repository's primary users are Dickinson students, faculty, and staff, although the unit also serves members of the local community, as well as genealogists, students, and scholars from around the globe.

Business Drivers

Historically, researchers have discovered archival resources, such as those at Dickinson, through finding aids, catalog records, citations, personal referrals, or the direct mediation of an archivist. Since the proliferation of the web, however, it has become apparent that a simple Google search is now the general research method of choice. Consequently, more and more individuals are contacting Dickinson as a result of stumbling on the institution's electronic finding aids or digital collections within their keyword search results. As with all repositories, however, only a small percentage of the college's collections are described online, and even fewer have been inventoried to the item level. As a result, staff invest large amounts of time hunting for the golden nugget of information that lies buried in a voluminous report or the particular photograph that an off-campus researcher requires.

It has been a practice at Dickinson to keep detailed records of all such distance reference requests. Traditionally, staff have recorded these transactions on paper forms that capture each researcher's contact information and method of contact, the nature of his or her request, and the response provided. However, these forms historically have been filed in a drawer by date and are only accessible internally. According to this system, then, the knowledge gained from any particular reference interaction could not benefit future researchers unless they contacted Dickinson directly and had the good fortune to reach a staff member who not only remembered the earlier inquiry but could recall roughly when it occurred so as to locate the relevant paper form.

For example, imagine that a family member is seeking genealogical information about Anna Elizabeth Low (Class of 1891), one of Dickinson's earliest female graduates. The college does, in fact, possess some information about Low in drop files and college publications, including a detailed memoir and some correspondence. However, the items do not represent a cohesive collection, and there is currently no online finding aid or catalog record available to make them visible to the public. If the family genealogist in question were fortunate enough to discover Low's connection to Dickinson and subsequently contact the institution, staff would provide that individual with the information or photocopies requested. Then, according to the traditional paper tracking system, the staff member would file a handwritten record of the transaction. Any additional future researchers with an interest in Low would need to rely on their own detective skills to discover her relationship to Dickinson and contact the archives directly. On receiving such repeat requests, archives personnel would then either need to re-create the initial search from scratch or locate the record of the earlier transaction among many years' worth of forms.

Imagine, however, that the record of the initial reference transaction about Low were available on the web, rather than solely in paper form, so that anyone with Internet access could search for her name on Google and discover that Dickinson holds resources relevant to the search. A tool such as that would not only serve to document past reference inquiries for the internal benefit of the institution's employees, it would also facilitate the quick and easy discovery of Dickinson's holdings and even help to generate new requests. In essence, such a tool would allow archivists to catalog their collections on the fly in response to user demand, often to the item level. By leveraging technology in this way, it would be possible to provide new public access points to materials that would otherwise remain hidden in the ubiquitous archival processing backlog or lie buried within unwieldy collections lacking item-level description.

Setting the Stage

To streamline the reference process and provide new access points to Dickinson's collections, in early 2007 the college archivist approached a member of the Academic and Technology Services (ATS) Department, another unit within the LIS division, to discuss the possibility of implementing blog software to meet the archives' reference tracking needs. This small working team identified a number of functional requirements for this endeavor. The primary necessity was that the selected tool be simple to use and maintain, while at the same time offering a high level of flexibility and customization. It was also particularly important that the software provide staff with the ability to restrict access to confidential data, such as researchers' names and addresses, to internal users only, while making a summary of each research question and the subsequent response freely available and discoverable on the web. The team ultimately chose to use Drupal, an open-source content management platform. This product was chosen for its simplicity and flexibility, as well as the fact that ATS staff had utilized that tool successfully for other unrelated projects and were therefore already familiar with its architecture and functionality.

Using the paper tracking document as a model, the ATS representative created a simple data entry form within Drupal that included all of the fields of information routinely captured during a reference transaction. A number of new fields were also included in the electronic form, so that staff could easily document who uses the Archives (e.g., alumni, scholars, students, etc.), how researchers discover Dickinson (e.g., search engine, referral, citation, etc.), which online tools they visit before making contact (e.g., electronic finding aids, digital collections), and the purpose of their requests (e.g., publication, school project, genealogy, etc.). The ATS representative then applied the permissions feature offered by Drupal to identify each field as either public (available freely on the web) or private (accessible to selected internal staff only) to protect the privacy of individual researchers.

The information captured by this new electronic form automatically generates a blog post available at http://itech.dickinson.edu/archives. (See Figure 1.) Both the general public and staff are able to view a brief summary of each reference transaction, including what specific information each researcher sought and what, if anything, archives personnel were able to provide. This public portion of the blog is discoverable using

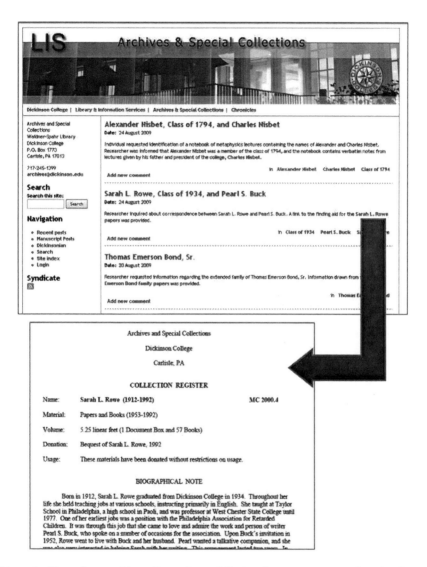

Figure 1: The reference blog allows the public to view a summary of past reference transactions. Hyperlinks in the blog entries connect to finding aids and other digital resources maintained by Archives and Special Collections.

Google, so that a simple keyword search has the potential to lead someone to Dickinson's resources. Once on the blog, both researchers and staff can navigate through the tool using a free-text search box, as well as tags, which staff apply to each entry, placing particular emphasis on proper

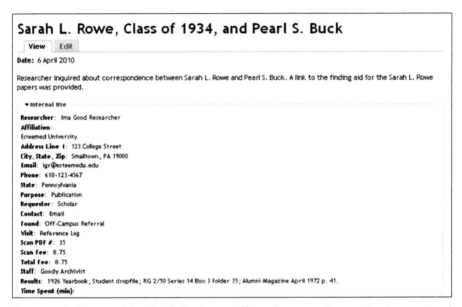

Sarah L. Rowe, Class of 1934, and Pearl S. Buck

| View | Edit |

Date: 6 April 2010

Researcher inquired about correspondence between Sarah L. Rowe and Pearl S. Buck. A link to the finding aid for the Sarah L. Rowe papers was provided.

▼ Internal Use

Researcher: Ima Good Researcher
Affiliation:
Esteemed University
Address Line 1: 123 College Street
City, State, Zip: Smalltown, PA 19000
Email: igr@esteemedu.edu
Phone: 610-123-4567
State: Pennsylvania
Purpose: Publication
Requestor: Scholar
Contact: Email
Found: Off-Campus Referral
Visit: Reference Log
Scan PDF #: 35
Scan Fee: 8.75
Total Fee: 8.75
Staff: Goody Archivist
Results: 1926 Yearbook; Student dropfile; RG 2/50 Series 14 Box 3 Folder 35; Alumni Magazine April 1972 p. 41.
Time Spent (min):

Figure 2: Archives and Special Collections staff members record researchers' contact and other demographic information, as well as details about any resources found and copy services provided for each reference transaction.

nouns, such as the names of specific individuals, organizations, places, and events. Drupal also allows staff to embed hyperlinks within each transaction summary, providing the ability to make connections between blog posts and other relevant electronic resources, such as finding aids and digital collections. In addition, members of the public themselves can share their knowledge and provide leads to additional resources by submitting comments to an approval queue, granting staff the opportunity to approve and respond to appropriate remarks and questions from researchers.

Internally, selected personnel are also able to use the blog to view who made each request and other confidential data about individual interactions. (See Figure 2.) In addition, the Archives and Special Collections unit takes advantage of Drupal's reporting capabilities to monitor usage efficiently. In the past, an individual had to hand-calculate reference statistics from the paper tracking forms. Now Drupal generates monthly or annual reports automatically using a feature readily available from the internal interface, saving personnel time and eliminating the possibility of human error. If desired, staff can export the blog's statistics into word process-ing or spreadsheet software to create and distribute attractive reports and charts, although the archives team at Dickinson does not currently take advantage of that particular feature.

Results

Dickinson's reference tracking blog officially went live in April 2007. At present, staff still use the legacy paper forms to capture initial notes for each request, as paper's portable nature makes it convenient to keep by the telephone and to carry to the stacks while consulting the collections. Once each transaction is completed, the archivist or special collections librarian transfers the information from the paper form to the blog. To optimize access points to the college's resources, the two professional staff members have also begun inputting data from past transactions, dating back to January 2007, so that as of December 2010, the blog contained 820 posts. Each post provides a new access point to Dickinson's collections, increas-ing the potential that users will discover material that would otherwise have remained hidden.

Although the blog currently documents only four years' worth of reference interactions, it has clearly proven its effectiveness. In November 2007, six months after the blog's creation, the Dickinson team became aware that Google had indexed the site, and three months later the team began receiving inquiries resulting from researchers' discovery of the new tool. In several instances one blog post has generated a number of additional requests. For example, in January 2008 a researcher inquired about an obscure report regarding the aftermath of the 1979 accident at the Three Mile Island nuclear reactor. The document was not itemized in any published finding aids, but the college archivist did succeed in locat-ing it within the voluminous records of a Pennsylvania nuclear energy watchdog group. The archivist subsequently provided the researcher with a copy of the report and posted a summary of the transaction to the Drupal blog. Across the next eighteen months, five other researchers contacted Dickinson requesting the same report, at least three of them specifically mentioning that they had seen reference to it on the archives blog. One of those researchers ultimately travelled to the archives after discovering the extent of Dickinson's TMI resources and has since written an article based on those materials, which has been accepted for publication.

Researchers have also begun to take advantage of the comments feature the blog offers. More than a dozen individuals have utilized this function to share information or to pose new questions. Members of the staff check the approval queue regularly to publish and respond to legitimate submissions and to delete spam messages, of which there are relatively few. Archives personnel hope that this interactive feature will grow in popularity with researchers.

Challenges

In the three-and-a-half years of its existence, the reference blog has proven in large part to be simple to populate and easy to maintain. Data entry takes moments, and necessary updates, such as the addition of new fields, are handled by a member of ATS or, in some cases, by archives staff themselves and are straightforward and essentially trouble-free. One minor challenge presented by all databases of this nature is the need to apply consistent metadata. To prevent inconsistencies in tags and other critical fields, the ATS representative who built the blog incorporated drop-down menus and auto-complete fields into the electronic data entry form that generates all posts. In addition, only the archivist and Special Collections librarian populate the blog, which also contributes toward greater consistency.

Lessons Learned

The Dickinson Archives and Special Collections staff have encountered few obstacles in implementing the reference blog. Admittedly, they have, however, benefited from the ongoing support of readily available in-house technical staff. Repositories and lone arrangers without access to such resources will likely find it necessary to devote additional time to researching and learning to customize blog software that is appropriate to their needs.

What Dickinson's personnel have gained from their experience with the blog is an appreciation for the benefits of careful planning and testing during the creation of a new tool of this type. Since the initial implementation of the reference blog, it has become necessary to alter the data entry form to capture additional pieces of information deemed useful by the staff. While it is quite easy to add, delete, or modify fields within Drupal, frequent changes result in incomplete and inconsistent data over time, making the blog less useful for purposes of gathering meaningful longitudinal statistics. It is possible to minimize the need for regular tinkering and adjustments by investing a significant amount of time up front to carefully identifying what types of information need to be captured and how that data can best be structured for the sake of efficient data entry and accurate reporting.

The Dickinson team also learned the value of thoroughly testing a resource before implementation through an issue that arose with the comments feature of the reference blog. During the development phase, staff experimented with data entry and keyword searches to evaluate the tool's efficiency and effectiveness. No such trials were conducted with the comments feature of the blog, however, as the archivist and Special Collections librarian simply assumed that they would receive automatic e-mail notifications each time a user submitted a comment. After implementing the blog for more than twenty months, however, they were surprised that they had not received any comments. They mentioned their concerns to the ATS representative, who corrected their misunderstanding about the e-mail notifications and instructed them in checking Drupal's comment approval queue to approve and respond to legitimate comments, as well as to delete spam. In doing so, the team discovered several comments users had submitted months earlier and have since made it a habit to check the comment queue regularly.

Next Steps

The reference blog has greatly improved staff's ability to connect users with Dickinson's collections. With this tool in place, every exchange with a distance researcher creates a new access point to the institution's resources.

The comments feature, as well, allows members of the public to contribute their own knowledge about Dickinson's collections or related materials held by other repositories. In essence, the blog facilitates on-demand, collective cataloging generated at the point-of-need. And it requires only a minimal investment of time, compared to that required to generate a formal catalog record, to compose or update a finding aid, or to encode a finding aid in Encoded Archival Description (EAD).

Having experienced the benefits that the reference blog provides in fulfilling and documenting distance reference requests, the archives team is currently in the process of developing a similar tool to record on-campus requests. This tool would essentially mirror that used for off-campus inquiries but would be accessible strictly internally, as many on-campus requests are of a sensitive or confidential nature and often of interest to a more limited audience. Archives staff expect that this internal blog will greatly streamline the process for responding to repeat and follow-up requests from administrators, faculty, and staff.

There is also interest in creating a supplemental resource that would include digital surrogates of archival materials, so that researchers could not only discover the existence of a particular document but access an electronic version of that item at the point of need. Such a feature would, in many cases, more quickly satisfy user demand, while also reducing the amount of personnel time spent fulfilling repeat requests for popular or commonly requested items.

All archives possess hidden treasures that have yet to be fully described or perhaps described at even a minimal level. A tool such as the reference blog not only helps to make those resources easily visible on the web; the information it captures about the types of materials requested most frequently can also help archivists understand which resources are in highest demand. The Dickinson team plans to use the data it gathers through the blog to assist in short- and long-range planning, specifically when prioritizing collections for future processing and when compiling evidence in support of grant applications, thereby allowing the staff to be highly responsive to users' needs and to focus their energies where they will have the greatest impact.

Old Divisions, New Opportunities: Historians and Other Users Working with and in Archives

Robert B. Townsend

As discussed in Kate Theimer's preface to this volume, the shift to Archives 2.0 is built in part on a user-centered approach, taking advantage of Web 2.0 technologies that rely heavily on user input and engagement. The changes brought about by the use of Web 2.0 tools present a sea change for all of us whose perceptions have been shaped by a century of professional expectations and ideals about what it means to practice our respective crafts, including archivists, historians, educators, genealogists, and other kinds of researchers. They confront us with choices that are not simple or easy. Historians are certainly no more comfortable with some aspects of Web 2.0 than many archivists—mere mention of *Wikipedia* can still incite an intellectual riot at a conference of historians. But as the contributions in this section demonstrate, teachers, students, and genealogists are eager to engage with archives in new ways. To fully embrace Web 2.0, archivists need to look to this diverse community of users as potential collaborators, whose interests and engagement with your materials can be harnessed to serve archives and their staff.

As we all adjust to these new realities, it may help to know that the problems confronting both archives and their users are not entirely new. Early archivists faced similar challenges at the turn of the twentieth century, including the problems of balancing limited resources against the rising needs and shifting interests of researchers. Of course, the challenges were significantly greater back then, given the lack of a strong and vital network of archival institutions and professional archivists. But then, as now, archivists had to develop new sets of skills, new canons of practice, and new forms of engagement with their user communities. Drawing on recent research into the development of the archival and history professions, my own experience as director of research at the American Historical Association (AHA), and the three essays that follow, this section casts an eye in two directions—looking backward, to note examples where archives and users confronted similar problems in the past, and looking forward, to cast a rather hazy glimpse into where some of these technologies seem to be taking us. Web 2.0 opens at least three areas where the relationship between archives and users can be transformed—in the process of discovery, dissemination, and advocacy.

This essay, and the three that follow, highlight the diversity of audiences and users wrestling with these issues, including academic historians, genealogists, and student researchers. All of the authors in this section acknowledge that regardless of whether a particular user is looking for specific information about an ancestor or trying to vacuum through an entire series of records, they look to archivists for leadership to help them on that journey. With Web 2.0, that relationship becomes more dynamic, however, and implies rethinking the traditional notion (first proffered at the dawn of the archival profession in 1935) that "The historian is the man in front of the desk, seeking expeditious service. The archivist or custodian is the man behind the desk."[1] Historians, genealogists, and students are no longer sitting patiently—or impatiently—on the other side of that desk. They are now becoming actively involved with primary source materials through linking, tagging, and, in some cases, posting archival materials on the web. Genealogists, teachers, and a host of others are engaging with documents and records online in innovative ways, creating an opportunity for the archival profession to engage with users in new and creative ways and to draw their efforts back in to your benefit as well.

Regardless of their research agendas—whether conducting individual research as genealogists or historians or assisting research work by students—archives users confront similar issues. We all grapple with emerging ways to discover and access materials, trying to sort through the often overwhelming abundance of material online and also needing to work through the new challenge of determining authority and provenance of online materials. I recognize that archivists face similar problems and also need to balance some users' unrealistic expectations with the larger necessity of managing and preserving the materials. As the following essays demonstrate, the Internet creates a variety of challenges (but also fresh opportunities) for archivists in their roles as intermediaries between users and materials.[2]

Despite their complexity, the need to carefully work through these issues is becoming increasingly urgent to many users. As one colleague recently observed, over the past fifteen years we have moved from a situation of information scarcity (in which finding and gaining access to materials was the greatest challenge to use) to a situation of information abundance (where the greatest challenge seems to be trying to avoid drowning).[3] This creates new opportunities and problems for different user communities. For those trying to acquire specific types of archival information, it can be a terrific benefit. As the interviews with genealogists in this section demonstrate, the availability of digitized census record data in proprietary online databases opens a type of research activity that was previously unimaginable. Information that has been converted from paper to electronic files, tagged with useful metadata, and made available electronically allows researchers to find remarkably useful and highly specific pieces of information—and then link them in a much richer tapestry of information in collaboration with others. But that represents only one type of use. For others, such as historians who want to trawl through a larger set of records to develop a sense of relationships and changes over time, the online medium is still an unsatisfactory substitute for traditional methods of archival research. This is due in part to the more solitary habits of many historians but also because the types of materials of interest to them have not been scanned and made available in sufficient quantity. (This is not intended as a criticism, by any means. The problems of large-scale scanning projects such as Google Books demonstrate the results of moving ahead too quickly and without paying sufficient attention to problems of scanning quality and metadata.)[4] As a result, there are significant differences in the needs and interests of the different user communities, depending on the research habits, materials, and support structures on which they draw.

Web 2.0 technologies promise to recast the relationship between archives and their user communities. But the breadth of the changes and the diversity of potential users means that for the next stage of archives using the web to be effective, archivists will need to draw heavily on input from users. One essential element involves harnessing the knowledge and expertise of those who may lack the professional skills of archivists but can be helpful participants in the archival endeavor. This means leveraging the knowledge and interests of particular user communities in a way that benefits your institution—by promoting your materials, encouraging greater use, and assisting with tagging, cataloguing, and dissemination.

As a framework for thinking about these issues, it may help to look back a century ago, when the line between archival practice and use was less distinct. Back then, academics, local historians, and genealogists could serve in multiple roles—using, collecting, organizing, and teaching historical records. Looking back at how this multiplicity of roles played out during the transition to the professionalized and institutionalized archives of the present highlights some of the potential issues and opportunities now presented by the Web 2.0 environment. More than that, it suggests ways that the archives can develop a more mutually beneficial relationship with their users.

New Opportunities to Share Information

Discussion of the changing relationship between opportunity and expectation online appears in all of the essays in this part of the book. Each of the authors and participants celebrate the way new media simplifies access, makes new discoveries possible, and increases the opportunities for collaborative work around a particular set of sources. At the same time, the authors and participants demonstrate a heightened awareness of and interest in the work of the archives.

In many ways, this heightened level of user engagement with the work of the archives is similar to the pioneering period of the late nineteenth and early twentieth century—though at that time there was a more fundamental problem of establishing institutions and professional practices for gathering, cataloging, and storing historical materials. The Web 2.0 environment represents a similar challenge for the archives, calling for large-scale strategic thinking, rebuilding of institutions, and the establishment of new sets of relationships. Looking back to the late nineteenth and early twentieth century, it is easy to identify a similar sort of transitional relationship where users were actively involved in the work of archives and collecting. For instance, "preservation" of the content in significant documents, such as it was, often occurred only through publication in document collections. As you might expect, the dissemination of such representations of primary documents was done in a fairly haphazard way and often in an unprofessional fashion (rather like many of the web "archives" we see today).[5] Where institutional repositories did exist, they often relied on outside researchers to come in and develop the finding aids for their materials—somewhat comparable to the often limited finding aids one finds online today and the tendency to lock them in discrete institutional silos.[6] More generally, it was often incumbent on users to gather personal manuscript collections and pressure local, state, and federal governments to be responsible stewards of their own materials.

From a user's perspective, one of the most obvious benefits of the Internet is that it lowers the threshold for interaction and contact with archives. All of the authors and participants in this section observe how online source materials are fundamentally changing the way users work, in both their research practices and their pedagogy.

At the most fundamental level, the Internet allows users to reach out and easily contact archivists for information about their archives, while search engines allow users to discover online resource guides, finding aids, and digitized collections. The opportunity to search online catalogs, ask questions of archives staff, and prepare an entire research trip in one sitting is still a wonder. All of these changes help to lower the anxieties of users as they approach the archives.[7] It is somewhat surprising, however, that archives do not seem to be doing more to build on these changes and take greater advantage of the opportunity to share information on the web. In many of the grant applications we receive at the AHA, historians still often observe that they have consulted the available online catalog but "won't really know what the archives have until I get there." An ideal goal would be to develop more detailed finding aids for users, which would lower that threshold worry. The quality of most online finding aids remains fairly primitive and often provides only minimal information for potential users, and the often terse responses about materials from overworked staff members that echo the perceptions of many correspondents ("you will find out what we have when you get here") offer little comfort. Even the information about how to use the archives tends to be fairly limited.[8]

In an effort to harness Web 2.0 technologies to address this user need, the AHA recently developed an *Archives Wiki* (available at http://archiveswiki. historians.org; See Figure 1). It was our perception and experience that researchers needed a better tool to assist them in their preparations for diving into a new archives, which is invariably fraught with an array of unique problems and choices, many of which have to be assessed and determined from afar (ranging from basic questions about who to contact and where to stay, to more specific questions, such as how many boxes a user can access at a time and the archives' photocopying policies).

Using wiki technology, we tried to harness the working knowledge of the tens of thousands of historians, researchers, and archivists working on and in collections. Our goals were fairly typical of most Web 2.0 projects—to leverage the interests of a specialized community to aid each other. For a small organization such as the AHA, it would be impossible to try to gather that information and keep it up to date, especially because our interests encompass archives around the world. While the scale of the project already seemed large enough, we recognized that the information a particular researcher would want to know is much more specific—something that can only be obtained at the ground level.

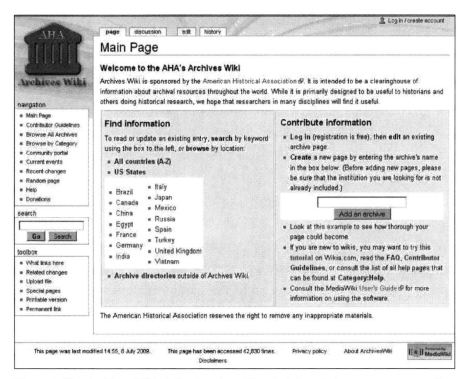

Figure 1: The *Archives Wiki* of the American Historical Association represents one effort to harness Web 2.0 technology to fill in gaps of information about how to use particular archives.

Given that, the wiki's Web 2.0 technology seemed ideal. So we established the site largely based on user input and tried to suggest a taxonomy of questions to answer (including categories such as location, contact information, collection summaries, photocopy policies, and the like). The response thus far has been quite positive, as 71 users have already come in and added information on 230 archives in 16 countries. It is a modest start, but it reflects the possibilities of the medium, and, as of January 2010, the site had already been accessed almost 60,000 times.

We drew our inspiration for this from efforts by the AHA a century ago, when the organization and quite a few private historians spent a great deal of their own time and resources to develop finding aids and catalogs for historical materials that would otherwise not be visible or available to research. At the time, researchers largely had to rely on the informal knowledge of other users, so the AHA spent considerable effort trying to systematize that information—ranging from large centralized efforts to construct card catalogs for distribution, to smaller amateur efforts that resulted in summary essays about particular archives in AHA publications. But looking back on those efforts decades later, one can see that the fundamental problem with these projects was that they could only capture a moment in time and quickly became obsolete. Relying on a more dynamic medium such as the wiki offers the hope that this information can evolve over time.

There are numerous other cases in which drawing in users to participate in the development of metadata and the process of tagging can potentially extend your staffing resources while leveraging their interest and specific knowledge.[9] Ideally, this can extend to information about the fresh availability of new materials in your collection. As recently as thirty years ago, the newsletter of the AHA provided page after page of information about the newest acquisitions from various archives around the country and the world. That ended in the 1970s, largely as a result of the rapid growth in new materials acquisitions and the rising costs of printing. While the AHA is not in a position to provide that sort of service today, archives can effectively do a significant amount of work themselves simply by setting up blogs for announcements.

From a user's perspective, blogs can provide one of the best vehicles for making new acquisitions and the availability of new materials known to potential users. When a new collection is added only to the listings in a database catalog, it is usually buried in the "deep web" and rarely indexed by Google. As a result, it is effectively lost to most users because a Google search is becoming increasingly important to researchers trying to sort through the massive sea of online information.[10] By posting such items on a blog, you can quickly and easily make these materials more discoverable by those who might use them.

Making Materials Available in New Ways

Simply knowing about the materials in the collection and knowing how to access them are not sufficient for many users. As the essays in this section demonstrate, the most enthusiastic users want to make copies of materials and share them either with a wide audience (through publication on the web) or to a more discrete group (such as students or members of an extended family). The "collections" created by many of these interested users are often poor substitutes for the quantity and quality of the original materials, but they can provide a useful entrée into the larger body of materials available on a given subject in archival collections.

This again is not without precedent in the relations between users and archives. A century ago many antiquarians, genealogists, and historians were actively taking documents and other source materials and "preserving" them the only way they knew how—by publishing their content in source readers, journals, and, in some cases, academic histories that were little more than strings of documents.[11] In most cases they were doing this simply as private citizens relying on their own personal resources to gather and purchase these materials (some were even wealthy enough to create institutions to store them, as in the Bancroft and Huntington libraries). In other areas of the country, modest collecting was done by state libraries and historical societies but not in a systematic or particularly consistent way. They often broke up record groups and dispensed with certain documents that did not fit in the narrow state or local framework of their institutions and the preconceptions of those doing the gathering about what was significant in their past.[12] It was only with the rise of scientific historians and their attitude toward source materials that historians began an active program to promote and support the collection, preservation, and dissemination of documents in professionally run institutional repositories.[13] While the academics became increasingly interested in promoting the development of a separate archival profession, many in the discipline shared the "DIY" ethic of many amateur researchers well into the 1920s, emphasizing the collective responsibility of all researchers to preserve and disseminate historical material.[14] In one of the earliest guides to good historical practice in the United States, for instance, two Harvard professors admonished authors to "append the text of rare and important documents, exactly transcribed."[15]

While there have been signs of interest from the archival community, we seem to be at a stage that is more akin to the practices of the early twentieth century, when amateur users often took the lead in the publication of documents and records. Members of the archival community often seem too settled in their conservation function to engage in active publication efforts. This seems to have deep roots in the professional ethos of the archival profession. Shortly after it was established, the Society of American Archivists decided that new (at the time) copying technologies meant the profession no longer needed to worry about the publication of historical work. As one committee chair noted, "recent progress of microcopying, near-printing, and other cheap methods of reproduction" changed the game for the archival profession. "Formerly it was printing or nothing. Now, however, these cheaper methods make it unnecessary to print many documentary materials which nevertheless ought to be reproduced."[16] Today archives are able to take advantage of the low entry costs for putting materials on the Internet, which is analogous to the printed collections of documents in the early twentieth century made possible by improved cost efficiencies in the printing industry. This kind of publication is now possible for almost anyone with a scanner, some relatively inexpensive software, and a great deal of enthusiasm for a particular subject. This is evident in the proliferation of source materials published online by historians and genealogists who seem to be reviving the sharing ethic of a century ago. Ideally, the web creates an opportunity for archives to harness this enthusiasm of their users.

The work of a number of the authors in the AHA's Gutenberg-e program (a series of electronic monographs that often included digital archives of source material) offers a useful example of how this could work. The digital archives attached to Helena Pohlandt-McCormick's *"I Saw a Nightmare . . .": Doing Violence to Memory: The Soweto Uprising, June 16, 1976* is a case in point. (See Figure 2.) (http://www.gutenberg-e. org/pohlandt-mccormick/pmh02w.html.) In the course of her research in

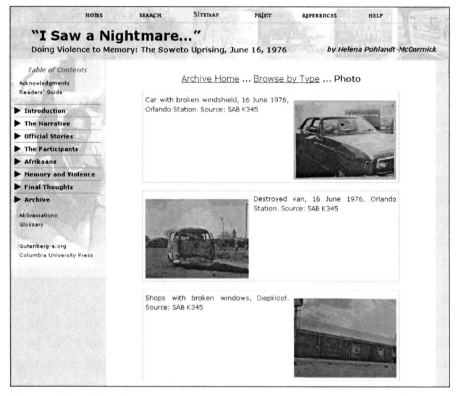

Figure 2: The archive of more than 1,300 images gathered for Helena Pohlandt-McCormick's monograph *"I Saw a Nightmare . . .": Doing Violence to Memory: The Soweto Uprising, June 16, 1976,* have been deposited with the National Archives and Records Service of South Africa and made available for its use.

the archives of the South African Truth and Reconciliation Commission, she was given access to an enormous wealth of "placards, posters and hand-written letters, as well as historical police documents and black and white police photographs produced at the time of uprising."[17] In the course of her research she made digital copies of more than 1,300 images. When she published these materials in her own book, she also deposited copies with the archives that held the original materials (the National Archives and Records Service of South Africa in Pretoria) and, with their permission, at a local archives in Soweto established specifically on the subject (the Hector Pieterson Memorial Museum). This suggests the type of synergy that can be cultivated between archivists and users in the digital age.[18]

However, capitalizing on existing user scanning efforts like this one will require more openness from archives and users alike. Archives will need to be willing to allow users to make digital copies of their holdings and develop an institutional structure that can take those digital materials back in a way that can serve both the archives and other users. For the Gutenberg-e project, staff at the Columbia University libraries constructed a sophisticated database that could store such digital images and assure that they were properly described and tagged. In the process, many of the authors had to participate in the practices of the archival community, constructing metadata that could demonstrate both source and provenance.

The good example of the Gutenberg-e authors notwithstanding, many academic users would need to be convinced about the long-term value of giving back to the archives. A number of authors I have worked with on digital projects were reluctant to make the "raw materials" of their research easily available to those who might want to "second-guess" their readings. That may just be a habit of mind that is peculiar to some scholars (and a most unfortunate one at that). In comparison, as Kate Theimer's conversation with genealogists in this section demonstrates, other researchers are much more eager to share the materials they have collected with a larger community of extended family through their chosen networks. This sort of collaborative work can be a highly engaging pursuit for users who care enough about their subject and are willing to share. And for the purposes of many other researchers, the fruits of such amateur gathering and posting can be quite sufficient. Unfortunately, from a scholarly perspective and the interests of long-term use, this practice tends to be quite deficient. The materials posted generally lack many of the essential hallmarks of professional archival practice, such as metadata allowing us to assess the provenance of particular materials. And the materials are generally posted without the necessary institutional framework to assure the long-term viability of those materials, making their availability temporary at best. As Jeffrey McClurken notes in his essay, this problem extends even to the online resources of many archives, as regular shifting of web addresses and the disappearance of materials make it difficult to rely too heavily on online source materials for research or classroom use. In this respect, most of these new projects are like the primary source collections published a century ago with standards that were little better than the digitizers of the present. Then, as now, such works are viewed with quite reasonable caution by teachers and researchers alike. The issue, then, is how to preserve the advances of decades of archival professionalization while moving forward with the new media.[19]

This highlights a number of tensions between the professional stamp of authority and the cultural norms of the different user communities involved. There is considerable discussion in the history community about the disparities in use between the few scholars who pride themselves as being cutting edge in their use of technology and the much larger number of scholars who are still working to integrate their research into the online medium.[20] Like many archivists, academic historians are deeply suspicious of participating in a space with the general public. This is evident in the general response to *Wikipedia*, which has been formally banned from some college history classrooms for its lack of quality and accuracy.[21] In contrast, the discussion among genealogists demonstrates the benefits of the more collaborative work environment in a common field of research. Based on a long-term practice of collaboration, they are quite comfortable with sharing information and discussing best practices.

For most users, the opportunities of the new media in the archives remain more prospective than real, though we can already see the outlines of some of the possibilities. For the genealogical community there is already ample evidence in the large-scale digitization of census records. These clearly rely on well-funded projects catering to a particular set of interests, but the genealogy sites have generated a new engagement and enthusiasm for genealogical research among those previously shut out by the expense of traveling to the archives and painstakingly searching for these types of materials. And judging from some of the interest communities developing within sites such as Ancestry.com and Footnote.com, they can clearly create secondary opportunities for those seeking to develop networks around digitized archival materials.

Whether something similar for scholars and teachers might emerge remains to be seen. For scholars, the availability of digitized archival materials creates significant new opportunities for the classroom, allowing us to connect students with the "real stuff" of history in exciting new ways. The essays by Tobi Voight and Jeffrey McClurken reflect similar evidence from my surveys of dozens of online course syllabi over the past decade, which shows a significant increase in the number of archive-based student assignments at schools, colleges, and universities. These projects encourage students to dig into primary source materials and think deeply about how they fit together. While the use of primary source materials is nothing new in the history classroom, the availability of a much larger corpus of materials significantly expands the amount of creativity and effort they can be asked to apply to these materials. I have seen this more tangibly in responses to a digital archives of materials from World War II that the AHA published online five years ago, as I regularly receive letters of thanks and copies of papers from students.

Beyond the interests of the classroom, other scholarly researchers are discovering the benefit of digging into digitized materials in new and more sophisticated ways. Historians such as Dan Cohen, executive director of the Center for History and New Media, are now using sources converted from print to create new types of scholarship.[22] By running sophisticated algorithms on large blocks of primary sources, historians working on these sorts of materials will be able to discover new patterns in historical materials that previously could only be guessed at. But this is an opportunity that can only grow at the same pace as digital versions of the materials.

The obvious analog in the past to this sort of transitional moment is to the way the institutionalization of archives changed the relationship between scholarship and materials. As archives were developed and systematized in the early twentieth century, researchers were able to engage the materials in new and more sophisticated ways. Instead of relying on poorly constructed and widely scattered collections of documents that had often fallen into private hands or were locked away in poorly maintained facilities, the consolidation of materials into professionally run archives opened a wide range of new opportunities for users. Scholars were able to work through much larger sets of related materials, identifying patterns that had not been possible when materials were more widely dispersed. Likewise, the development of genealogy as a truly democratic and popular activity developed in parallel with archival institutions that could serve that audience.[23]

Again, this kind of success can breed new expectations. I have found that making materials available online can in turn create new demands. For one of our online archives, for instance, I get two or three requests a month for additional information about the materials from teachers and students; requests from journalists and publishers seeking permission to use particular images; as well as other requests from researchers asking for permission to link or reuse the material in a different context. This is not an onerous task by any means, but it does draw off a small amount of staff time. Ideally, this can serve as a useful way of measuring the value of your materials and a gauge of user interest in your efforts.

Converting Users into Advocates

Beyond the dissemination of documents, the new level of interaction with users—and ideally contact with a much larger number of users made possible by an online presence—can in turn create new opportunities for improving the health and well-being of your archives. A century ago, when the line between collecting and other sorts of use was less distinct—and researchers did not feel that sitting patiently on one side of the desk was their only role—users were much more engaged advocates for the archives. Ideally, Web 2.0 can help to revitalize the sense that users are real stakeholders in the archives.

Shortly before the turn of the century, the American Historical Association developed a Public Archives Commission to systematize the advocacy efforts of those working in these border areas between preservation and research. The Commission relied on the initiative of researchers to treat these materials not just as objects to serve as the basis of interpretive scholarship but also as a trust to be shared with other users. So historians working with the manuscripts were called on to gather evidence of the often disgraceful situations of governmental archives.[24]

This kind of work was viewed at the time as an essential part of the practice of history, rather than a wholly subordinate service to the work of interpretive research. The most noted exemplars of this ethic were J. Franklin Jameson (whose career extended from being an academic at the University of Chicago to head of the Manuscript Division at the Library of Congress), and Waldo G. Leland (often credited as one of the first leaders of the archival profession). The resulting reports, published as a report to Congress by the U.S. Government Printing Office, described materials wedged away in leaky attics or fire-trap basements of sundry government buildings and cataloged both the holdings and the treatment of those records.[25] This cast a spotlight on the extreme deficiencies in the way governments at every level were treating their own materials and also provided essential finding aids to other researchers subsequently seeking to use those records. By bringing such neglect to light, and giving it national exposure in a federal report to Congress, the commission focused attention on these issues and helped to generate funding for their proper care and management.[26] As a result of their efforts, and local initiatives that brought together genealogists, antiquarians, and scientific historians, by the 1930s half the states and the federal government had developed archival policies and repositories, which relied heavily on the initiative and enthusiasm of the user community. These reports also began to articulate basic models and standards of archival practice in the United States, which helped to generate the essential resources and institutional basis for the archival profession.[27]

At present, the distance between archives and many of their users seems to make similar efforts unlikely. While the AHA regularly calls on its members to support funding for institutions at the national level, I rarely see similar efforts at the state and local level. To the contrary, these efforts often seem to occur too late to do any good.[28] This sort of ongoing alliance between users and archives seems particularly important in tight financial times, promoting a habit of active engagement and advocacy on behalf of public institutions by the user community.

By creating a significant presence on the Internet and attracting a user audience that is national and international in scope, you can create a larger community of interest for your institution—one that can be activated fairly quickly on your behalf, particularly if you collect the e-mail addresses of interested users or utilize Web 2.0 tools such as Facebook, Twitter, or blogs to regularly engage and communicate with them. Digitizing collections and sharing them on the web provides an extension to a larger audience that also serves as its own leverage in discussions with legislators and potential funders. I was recently lobbying on Capitol Hill on humanities issues and found members of Congress particularly enthused about the enhanced value and reach of digital materials. The idea of opening records to wider audiences and new uses seemed quite exciting to them. Perhaps this cannot aid every institution, but it can create a larger constituency of users with a real stake in the health of your archives.

Community (Re)building Online

The users of archival materials represent a broad and diverse constituency with widely disparate interests and needs. As the essays in this part of the book demonstrate, users are united by a common enthusiasm to see more material online and have opportunities to do more with it. Recognizing that most archives are tasked with doing more with very limited resources, I hope they will see the technologies of Web 2.0 as an opportunity to do more with what they have. Identifying core user communities and engaging them as collaborators and advocates for your mission can create new opportunities for expanding the work and materials of the archives to a larger community of researchers, teachers, and students.

For archivists and users alike, it may help to know that while the technologies may be new, the problems and possibilities are not. Recalling the past relationships between archives and users provides a helpful way of seeing beyond both the traditional relationships between archives and their users on one hand and the whizz-bang aspects of Web 2.0 on the other. Digital media create an opportunity to diminish the gap between archivist and user in a way that can revitalize that relationship—making the users participants in the work of the archives and stakeholders in their ongoing vitality and health.

In this regard, the new media can perhaps take us back to the future. As students, teachers, genealogists, and researchers grapple with the way technology is reshaping their own activities, there is an opportunity to create a new set of relations with your users. And in a time of increasing competition for economic resources, engaging the users and making them participants in the work of the archives can significantly aid the archives in achieving their missions.

Notes

1 "Report of the Special Committee to the Executive Council," *AHA Annual Report 1935* (October 15, 1935), 176.

2 As a useful counterpoint, see Roberta Lamb and Rob Kling, "Reconceptualizing Users as Social Actors in Information Systems Research," *MIS Quarterly* 27, no. 2 (June 2003): 197–236.

3 John C. McClymer, *The AHA Guide to Teaching and Learning with New Media* (Washington, DC: American Historical Association), http://www.historians.org/pubs/free/mcclymer/index.cfm (accessed January 3, 2010).

4 See Robert B. Townsend, "Google Books: Is It Good for History?", *Perspectives on History* (September 2007): 45–47, http://www.historians.org/perspectives/issues/2007/0709/0709vie1.cfm (accessed January 3, 2010).

5 Lucile M. Kane, "Manuscript Collecting," and G. Phillip Bauer, "Public Archives in the United States," in *In Support of Clio*, ed. William B. Hesseltine and Donald R. McNeil (Madison: State Historical Society of Wisconsin, 1958), 29–76.

6 See, for instance, Leslie Whittaker Dunlap, *American Historical Societies, 1790–1860* (Philadelphia: Porcupine Press, 1944), 85–89.

7 As a point of comparison, see Laura B. Spencer, "What Price Simplicity: A User-Centered Meditation," in *Creating Web-Accessible Databases: Case Studies for Libraries, Museums, and Other Nonprofits*, ed. Julie M. Still (Medford, NJ: Information Today, Inc., 2001), 135–141.

8 Some of these frustrations are evident in a recent study of users at the University of Illinois Archives, reported in Christopher J. Prom, "User Interaction with Electronic Finding Aids in a Controlled Setting," *American Archivist* 67 (Fall/Winter 2004): 234–268.

9 Kevin Andreano, "The Missing Link: Content Indexing, User-Created Metadata, and Improving Scholarly Access to Moving Image Archives," *Moving Image* 7, no. 2 (Fall 2007): 82–99.

10 While most student and general research currently starts with Google, academic historians appear slightly less likely to use Google due to lingering skepticism about the quality of the information available on the Internet. See Wendy Duff, Barbara Craig, and Joan Cherry, "Historians' Use of Archival Sources: Promises and Pitfalls of the Digital Age," *Public Historian* 26, no. 2 (Spring 2004):

7-22; and Rebecca Griffiths, Michael Dawson, and Matthew Rascoff, *Scholarly Communication in the History Discipline* (New York: Ithaka Strategic Services, 2006).

[11] The first series of the *William and Mary Quarterly* (now available through JSTOR) demonstrates this earlier tradition, as it was largely a collection of genealogical notes and source material. Similarly, the initial mandate of the American Historical Association's Public Archives Commission placed publication first among its goals to develop "methods of publishing, arranging, and preserving official documentary material." "First Report of the Public Archives Commission," in *Annual Report of the American Historical Association, 1900, Vol. II* (Washington, DC: Government Printing Office, 1901), 10.

[12] See Kane, "Historical Manuscripts," 34-35.

[13] For a good summary of this transition, see Peter J. Wosh, "An Archival Anniversary: Waldo G. Leland and the First Conference of Archivists in 1909," *Archival Outlook* (November/December 2009): 10-21.

[14] See, for example, Lester J. Cappon, "The Archival Profession and the Society of American Archivists," in *Lester J. Cappon and the Relationship of History, Archives and Scholarship in the Golden Age of Archival Theory*, Archival Classics Series, ed. Richard J. Cox (Chicago: Society of American Archivists, 2004).

[15] Edward Channing and Albert Bushnell Hart, *Guide to the Study of American History* (Boston: Ginn, 1896), 221.

[16] C. C. Crittenden to members of the Committee on the Publication of Archival Material, Society of American Archivists, July 10, 1939, Society of American Archivists (1939 to 1940), Box 20, Solon Buck Papers.

[17] Helena Pohlandt-McCormick, *I Saw a Nightmare . . .": Doing Violence to Memory: The Soweto Uprising, June 16, 1976* (New York: Columbia University Press, 2007), http://www.gutenberg-e.org/pohlandt-mccormick/archive/ (accessed January 3, 2010).

[18] For other examples of these sorts of projects, see Daniel J. Cohen and Roy Rosenzweig, *Digital History: A Guide to Gathering, Preserving, and Presenting the Past on the Web* (Philadelphia: University of Pennsylvania Press, 2006), 25-35.

[19] Although somewhat dated, see *Preserving Digital Information: Report of the Task Force on Archiving of Digital Information Commissioned by the Commission on Preservation and Access and the Research Libraries Group* (Washington, DC: Commission on Preservation and Access, 1996), http://www.oclc.org/programs/ourwork/past/digpresstudy/final-report.pdf (accessed January 3, 2010).

[20] See, for instance, the observations of the Commission on Cyberinfrastructure for the Humanities and Social Sciences in Our Cultural Commonwealth (New York: American Council of Learned Societies, 2006), 21. The report is available online at http://www.acls.org/cyberinfrastructure/OurCulturalCommonwealth.pdf (accessed January 3, 2010). Despite these differences, a recent survey of more than 4,100 historians in the United States found that almost 80 percent were regular users of "Online archives or other web-based primary sources" for their research. Robert B. Townsend, "How Is New Media Reshaping the Work of Historians?" *Perspectives on History* (October 2010).

[21] These issues and some related myths are discussed in Roy Rosenzweig, "Can History Be Open Source? Wikipedia and the Future of the Past," *Journal of American History* 93 (June 2006): 117-146.

[22] See, for instance, Daniel J. Cohen, "From Babel to Knowledge: Data Mining Large Digital Collections," *D-Lib Magazine* 12, no. 3 (March 2006), http://www.dlib.org/dlib/march06/cohen/03cohen.html. For larger context, see Christine L. Borgman, *Scholarship in the Digital Age: Information, Infrastructure, and the Internet* (Cambridge, MA: MIT Press, 2007), 211-226.

[23] For one example of users in the genealogical and history communities working together to develop proper archives and institutional apparatuses, see Katharina Hering, "'We Are All Makers of

History': People and Publics in the Practice of Pennsylvania German Family History, 1891–1966" (PhD diss., George Mason University, 2009), which details the development of archival institutions in Pennsylvania.

[24] On the general significance of the Public Archives Commission, see Ernst Posner, *American State Archives* (Chicago: University of Chicago Press, 1964), 18–19, and James M. O'Toole and Richard J. Cox, *Understanding Archives & Manuscripts* (Chicago: Society of American Archivists, 2006), 61.

[25] The reports first began with the *Annual Report of the American Historical Association for the Year 1900* (Washington, DC: Government Printing Office, 1901), which constituted the entirety of a 300-page volume with reports on Connecticut, Indiana, Iowa, Massachusetts, Michigan, Nebraska, New York, North Carolina, Pennsylvania, and Wisconsin. The reports were a regular feature in the AHA annual reports until 1912, when the timing of their release became more irregular and slowly tapered off to the last report in 1922.

[26] See, for instance, editorials like "The Safety of Records," *Chicago Daily Tribune*, May 24, 1907; "Association Preserving Archives," *Christian Science Monitor*, October 21, 1911; and "Archives House Is Aim," *Washington Post*, December 29, 1915.

[27] Lester J. Cappon, "Tardy Scholars among the Archivists," in *Lester J. Cappon and the Relationship of History, Archives and Scholarship*, 47. In some instances, the reports of the commission provided a negative example, when critics charged that academics produced inferior reports, prompting calls for more professional surveyors. See for instance, "Review and Notices," *Publications of the Southern History Association* 7 (January 1903): 41–44.

[28] A recent example at the time of this writing was the sharp curtailment in research support at the Oregon Historical Society as described in "Statement Regarding Budget Reductions at OHS—Posted 3/2009" at http://www.ohs.org/research/library/index.cfm (accessed March 18, 2009).

Is National History Day Ready for Web 2.0?

Tobi Voigt

The Internet is rapidly changing, leaving National History Day (NHD) coordinators, teachers, and students struggling to determine its best uses for historical research. Because middle and high school students are among the most avid users of the newest Internet applications, it is important to determine how Web 2.0 tools can help archives connect with the next generation of historical scholars. This case study explores how teachers and students are using Web 2.0 tools to conduct research for the National History Day program and makes recommendations on how archives can best use Internet tools to meet student and teacher needs.

Each year, more than half a million students and thousands of teachers nationwide participate in NHD, one of the oldest and most highly regarded academic history programs in the country. Students in grades 6–12 spend a school year conducting extensive research on a historical topic of their choice through libraries, archives, museums, oral history interviews, and historic sites. They analyze their sources, draw conclusions about their topics' significance in history, and present their work in original papers, websites, exhibits, performances, and documentaries. These final projects can be entered into competitions at local, state, and national levels, where they are evaluated by professional historians and educators.[1]

In addition to introducing teenagers to the world of historical inquiry and scholarship, the NHD program helps students develop critical think-ing, problem-solving, research, reading, written communication, and presentation skills, as well as self-esteem and confidence. Since 1980, more than 5 million former participants have gone on to careers in business, law, medicine, and countless other disciplines where they use skills learned through NHD.[2]

When Dr. David Van Tassel began the program at Case Western Reserve in Cleveland, Ohio, in 1974, students relied on library card catalogs, archival finding aids, and other print tools to conduct their research. Since the late 1990s, National History Day students have increasingly used the Internet to find their sources—both primary and secondary. Online collection databases now make it easier for students to find primary source documents and help to dissolve boundaries imposed by limited access to quality source material.

However, the rapid growth of the Internet as a research tool is leaving NHD program coordinators reeling with basic, but urgent, questions regarding its use and value. One of the key judging criteria states that students must conduct research from a wide array of sources. If this is the case, how much should we hold students accountable for visiting libraries, museums, and historic sites to conduct research, especially when some of the best source material can be found online?

The relatively recent arrival of Web 2.0 technologies further complicates these questions. Web 2.0—as defined by one of its first conceptions, *Wikipedia*—is a "perceived second generation of web development and design that facilitates communication, secure information sharing, interoperability, and collaboration on the World Wide Web."[3] Web 2.0 implies a new degree of interactivity between website content providers and their end users. First-generation Internet sites, commonly known as Web 1.0, were (and still are) composed of one-way communication; visitors to Web 1.0 sites receive information passed down from a person or institution. Web 2.0, in contrast, gives visitors a chance to contribute to and shape the sites they visit.

Web 2.0 use raises a new host of questions for History Day participants, teachers, and coordinators: How reliable is user-generated content? Can it be considered authentic for research purposes? Does Web 2.0 make it easier or more difficult for students to find reputable source material?

Before NHD can answer any of these questions, it must determine how teachers and students use the Internet for historical research. The results of a nationwide survey of History Day teachers and students provide some insight and suggest trends regarding student Internet use. Conducted between January and April 2009, the survey was administered via SurveyMonkey.com and advertised nationally to History Day teachers and students through listservs and e-newsletters. Of the 65 people who completed the survey, 30 (46.2 percent) were History Day teachers. Twenty-four (36.9 percent) were current History Day students, while 4 (6.2 percent) were former contest participants. Seven additional people (10.8 percent of respondents)—mainly museum professionals, historians, librarians, and archivists who work as program coordinators—rounded out the sample. The small number of responses does not present a representative sample, but the results do provide trend data on which further studies may be based.[4]

Table 1

Sources Used for History Day Research	# of Responses	% of Respondents
Internet – search engines (Google, Yahoo)	61	93.8%
Community library	56	86.2%
School library	54	83.1%
Internet – websites of libraries, archives, museums and/or historical associations (Library of Congress, NARA)	51	78.5%
Personal correspondence or interviews	46	70.8%
Internet – online encyclopedias (MS Encarta, etc.)	44	67.7%
Research Library/Archives (NARA, Library of Congress, etc.)	39	60.0%
Internet – library catalogs (WorldCAT, Pathfinder, etc.)	36	55.4%
College or University Library	33	50.8%
Museum or Historical Society	32	49.2%
Internet – Web 2.0 (YouTube, *Wikipedia*, Flickr, etc.)	30	46.2%
Other (please specify)	7	10.8%

The survey began by asking questions related to general research sources, and survey participants indicated that the Internet is a prime tool. Respondents were provided a list of research resources and asked to select the tools they use most often for NHD research. Sixty-one of the 65 respondents said they used Internet search engines, like Google and Yahoo. However, community libraries and school libraries ranked second and third, respectively, above other Internet resources, including archive and museum websites, online encyclopedias, and library catalogs (see Table 1 for the full survey results).[5] Nonetheless, 55.4 percent of the respondents claimed to use the Internet when conducting NHD research, with almost 65 percent of that group indicating that more than 50 percent of their research is done using the Internet. (See Table 2.)[6] When asked the number one reason they or their students use the Internet, the top three responses (picked from a provided list of options) were: it's easy (33.8 percent), it helps me identify which repositories have information on my topic (24.6 percent), and it's fast (21.5 percent). (See Table 3.)[7]

Table 2

Percentage of Research Conducted Using Internet	# of Responses	% of Respondents
0 – 25%	8	12.3%
51 – 75%	32	49.2%
26 – 50%	15	23.1%
76 – 100%	10	15.4%

Table 3

Reasons for Internet Research	# of Responses	% of Respondents
It is easy.	22	33.8%
It helps me identify which archives, libraries, museums, etc., have information on my topic.	16	24.6%
It is fast.	14	21.5%
Other (please specify).	8	12.3%
It helps me find people who have information on my topic.	4	62.0%
It helps me find tips that make my research and project creation better.	1	15.0%

In addition to general Internet usage, survey respondents were given a list of Web 2.0 applications—including wikis, video and image hosting services, social networking sites, and blogs—and asked if they use them to conduct NHD research. Sixty-two percent of respondents use *Wikipedia* or other collaborative online encyclopedias, 47 percent use image-hosting sites like Flickr, and 37 percent admitted to using YouTube. Only 5.1 percent indicated that they use MySpace, Facebook, or other social networking sites, and only 3 percent use blogs. (See Table 4.)[8]

Table 4

Use of Web 2.0 for History Day Research	# of Responses	% of Respondents
Wikipedia (or other collaborative online encyclopedias)	37	62.7%
Flickr/Google Image Search (or other photo-sharing sites)	28	47.5%
YouTube (or other video-hosting sites)	22	37.3%
None/Does not apply	9	15.3%
MySpace/Facebook (or other social networking sites)	3	51.0%
Blogs	2	34.0%

The reasons respondents provided for use of Web 2.0 sites varied, depending on the type of website. Most respondents indicated that they use *Wikipedia* for preliminary research only, with one teacher remarking that his students use *Wikipedia* only "to find basic information which allows them to utilize better search terms when students are first starting their research." Another respondent, a History Day student, uses *Wikipedia* "to get an overview of my topic before I start my research." These comments are in keeping with those of most of the respondents; nearly 60 percent use *Wikipedia* as a gateway to better resources. Nonetheless, 25.4 percent of respondents said that they or their students use *Wikipedia* to gather key project research. Another 20 percent said they "do not use Wikipedia as a source because it is not reliable."[9]

Forty-seven percent of respondents use Flickr and 29 percent use YouTube when researching for NHD. Image and video hosting sites are most helpful in gathering materials for the final projects, especially exhibits and documentaries: one respondent said that he or she "used YouTube for video footage and audio clips." Another student has "taken primary source videos, such as speeches and interviews" from video-hosting sites.

Several students indicated that they use video hosting sites to review other NHD projects: one student stated that he or she uses YouTube "to watch other documentaries." Another added that he or she used YouTube to conduct "general research on performances when not available in other media formats."[10]

Blogs and social networking sites, like MySpace and Facebook, are the least popular Web 2.0 sources for NHD research, with nearly 90 percent of respondents stating they did not use them. The most common reason given for not using blogs and social networking is "because those are more opinion based."[11]

If respondents indicated that they use Web 2.0 resources, they were asked how those resources are helpful. The most popular response—selected by 64 percent of the respondents—was that Web 2.0 tools make finding information easier. Thirty-one percent noted that Web 2.0 sites are the first results that come up when they conduct a Google search. The respondents also gave a handful of other reasons for using Web 2.0, many of which echo this teacher's response: "They provide information not otherwise available through our local sources, especially on recent history topics." Several students added that Web 2.0 tools "were useful for audio or video clips" and "they have multimedia not available elsewhere."[12]

The last few survey questions asked the respondents to suggest how museums, archives, and libraries can use Web 2.0 tools to make their resources more available to History Day teachers and students. Fifty-seven percent of respondents suggested that they use image hosting sites like Flickr to post archival images and documents. Almost 40 percent also recommended that museums, archives, and libraries develop their own wiki and video-hosting sites. Less than 15 percent of respondents felt that social networking profiles/pages or blogs would assist them with their NHD research.[13]

Respondents were also asked in what ways archives can use Web 2.0 tools to make NHD research easier. Most respondents felt that Web 2.0 tools can make navigating existing websites easier, but nearly every response suggested updating existing Web 1.0 resources, specifically institutional websites and online collection databases. One student stated, "[I'd like them to] provide more websites for use. Some museum websites don't tell you information, other than the times of business, location, etc." The most common request from the respondents indicated a need for more primary source information that is easily accessible: "Put links to very good primary sources in an easy to locate format" and "at the very basic, [provide] finding aids [and] highlight key famous people associated with the site and selected digitized documents."[14]

The survey responses suggest that, as our technological world marches forward, History Day participants retain some skepticism about Web 2.0 resources. They continue to express a need for traditional Web 1.0 resources, such as primary source collection databases with finding aids. In addition, young researchers may not be ready for the two-way communication on which Web 2.0 depends. According to the developmental psychology theories of Jean Piaget, teenagers are just beginning to grow out of the cognitive stage defined by concrete levels of thinking. The NHD program can facilitate this change by helping students build the critical thinking skills they need to view the world in more abstract ways, but it is a slow process. Not all History Day students are able to determine which Web 2.0 sites provide reliable information and which are biased. To avoid any potential research missteps, students and teachers are steering clear of blogs and social networking sites, most of which are based on opinion and conjecture. They even view their most commonly used Web 2.0 source, *Wikipedia*, only as a doorway to more reliable resources.

Nonetheless, hope is not lost for the archive or museum looking to use Web 2.0 tools to attract a History Day audience; Americans tend to place the most trust in traditional sources of historical information, specifically museums and historical sites (and by extension, archives).[15] Web 2.0 materials authored or created by these institutions may have an advantage regarding users' views of their authenticity and credibility. The survey responses support this; nearly 50 percent of the respondents encouraged archives and museums to use Web 2.0 tools like wikis and video and image-hosting sites to make their collections materials more easily accessible.

The key to attracting the History Day audience is providing access to primary source materials. Fortunately, a signature trait of Web 2.0 tools is their user-friendly interfaces and their low- (or no-) cost applications. The United States National Archives uses several popular Web 2.0 tools to share its resources with the general public. It most recently started using the Web 2.0 tool Delicious, a free online bookmarking service that allows users to save web links and share them with other people, to create a virtual "index" to primary source documents and other educational resources.[16] At the National Archives Delicious page (http://delicious.com/NationalArchivesEducation/), visitors find a list of links to primary source materials and comprehensive educational websites. Some of the links, such as that for a photo of John Wilkes Booth and the other Lincoln assassination conspirators, take visitors directly to the entry in the Archives Research Catalog where the image can be accessed and downloaded for free. By using Delicious, the National Archives is organizing its vast collections into thematic units that make it easier for researchers of all ages to find. The National Archives has been innovative in other Web 2.0 arenas as well; it has a Flickr page with historical images that can be downloaded for free, a Twitter feed that features a new document each day, a blog called *NARAtions* for information on accessing its online records, a Facebook page with helpful features and links, and a YouTube channel with contemporary promotional and educational films.

The National Archives is only one of many cultural institutions that are trying to repurpose traditional Web 2.0 sources to meet developing needs. However, new Web 2.0 tools are emerging that are designed specifically with collecting institutions in mind. The Omeka project, which was developed by the Center for History and New Media (CHNM) and the Minnesota Historical Society, is a free open-source web publishing platform that brings "Web 2.0 technologies and approaches [to] historical and cultural websites."[17] Omeka not only provides collections database management but also enables users (both internal and external) to create online exhibits and contribute to historical interpretation. As an example, the CHNM and the Smithsonian Institution's National Museum of American History developed an Omeka site called "Object of History" (http://objectofhistory.org/) where visitors can interact with primary source materials, listen to experts discuss the objects through downloadable audio files, and use images to create their own virtual exhibit. New and developing tools like Omeka are helping to refine Web 2.0 and provide more oversight and structure to user-generated content. In addition, they can help meet the missions and goals of cultural organizations.

In conclusion, History Day teachers and students are skeptical of Web 2.0 tools, but they may be open to user-generated web content started and monitored by a reputable historical institution. Archives interested in courting the History Day audience must focus on using Web 2.0 tools to make access to their collections and primary source materials easier. Creative use of Web 2.0 tools, like those by the National Archives and the Smithsonian Institution, can provide the framework needed to alleviate authorship concerns and minimize hurdles to reaching a K–12 audience.

Notes

[1] "What Is National History Day?" National History Day, http://www.nationalhistoryday.org/About. htm (accessed January 17, 2011).

[2] Ibid.

[3] "Web 2.0," *Wikipedia*, http://en.wikipedia.org/wiki/Web_2.0 (accessed May 21, 2009).

[4] New York State Historical Association and SurveyMonky.com, "NYSHD and Web 2.0," http://www. surveymonkey.com/s.aspx?sm=57l_2b1u_2f5gqPHJkTwsBfnoQ_3d_3d (site now discontinued).

[5] New York State Historical Association and SurveyMonky.com, "NYSHD and Web 2.0," http://www. surveymonkey.com/s.aspx?sm=57l_2b1u_2f5gqPHJkTwsBfnoQ_3d_3d (site now discontinued).

[6] Ibid.

[7] Ibid.

[8] Ibid.

[9] Ibid.

[10] Ibid.

[11] Ibid.

[12] Ibid.

[13] Ibid.

[14] Ibid.

[15] Roy Rosenzweig and David Thelen, *The Presence of the Past: Popular Uses of History in American Life* (New York: Columbia University Press, 1998), 91.

[16] "Learn More about Delicious," Delicious, http://delicious.com/help/learn (accessed August 25, 2009).

[17] Center for History and New Media, "Omeka: About," *Omeka*, http://omeka.org/about/ (accessed May 31, 2009).

Waiting for Web 2.0: Archives and Teaching Undergraduates in a Digital Age

Jeffrey W. McClurken

For nearly a decade, I have assigned a research paper in my course on "U.S. Women's History to 1870" that asks students to find a collection of primary sources by or about a woman to use as the basis for their essays. When I first started teaching the course in the late 1990s, my students would look in our school library for published collections of letters, diaries, and other documents. But in recent years the search has been almost entirely online, in part because I've encouraged that, in part because that is where the students look first, and in part because there are so many more primary source collections available online. Digital archival collections at the Library of Congress, National Archives, the Massachusetts Historical Society, New York Public Library, and the Library of Virginia (just to name a few) allow students in the class access to many more perspectives on the history of women in the United States than ever before. But though the sources are plentiful, the spread of the web and myriad accompanying tools have brought about their own set of opportunities and problems for educators in colleges and universities, as well as for archives and archivists.

While Robert Townsend's essay explores the perspective of historians and the historical profession with regard to Archives 2.0, this essay will focus on the impact of digital technologies with regard to teaching with archival materials and will provide some speculation about other ways in which these technologies might be used to more actively engage students and teachers. It is heavily influenced by my own experiences as a U.S.

historian teaching undergraduate history and American studies majors at the University of Mary Washington, a public, mostly undergraduate, liberal arts institution in Fredericksburg, Virginia,[1] and therefore should not be considered broadly representative. Like Dr. Townsend, I am sensitive to the demands of archival users in the digital age and the ways in which those demands can be in tension with the core values of the archival community in terms of collecting, preserving, and sharing the array of materials for which they are responsible. These comments are offered in a grateful spirit for all that archivists do.[2]

Thinking about the ways that those of us who teach history to college students address the question of archives, we can see that much has changed over the last ten to fifteen years. When I began teaching in the late 1990s, teaching with archival records typically meant assigning published document collections, making copies of unpublished materials gathered in my own research and passing them out to the class, or perhaps using transparencies to show a class what nineteenth-century handwriting looked like. Some of my colleagues had carousel after carousel of slides, painstakingly assembled over the years from a variety of archival and published sources. Eventually, I began to scan microfilmed census records or letters between Civil War–era Virginians, using a projector to share those archival materials with my students as part of our lectures and discussions.

When I started teaching, I simply could not expect my undergraduate students to do substantive research in archival materials. Although we have a terrific group of research librarians, schools our size simply do not have the archival collections that larger schools do. Certainly, we had a few students make road trips to nearby archives (UMW is conveniently located between the significant archival collections in Richmond and Washington, D.C.). Still, in the late 1990s I couldn't *expect* research in archives (especially for non-U.S. topics) for undergraduates. Primary source work, which is central to our expectations for our majors, was largely done from the available printed archival materials. When I was a PhD student at Johns Hopkins in the 1990s, my advisor taught me well the importance of talking to archivists about the collections with which they worked—advice I and my colleagues passed on to our students. Realistically, however, undergraduate student interaction with archivists was often limited to phone and perhaps e-mail. Still, an archivist's expert advice was acknowledged and could prove valuable in steering students who took advantage of the opportunity.

Today, of course, we are in the midst of a web-based "Digital Age." Although this book is full of examples of Web 2.0 tools being used by archives and archivists, I would argue that currently the relationship between the college classroom and archives is largely Web 1.0, not Web 2.0. In other words, so far the biggest impact of the digital age on university educators' use of archival materials has been in the area of accessibility to digital and digitized documents, not in the area of interactive social media.

Still, that accessibility has made it much easier to bring primary source documents, videos, and full-color images into the classroom from outside of one's own research. My syllabi now regularly include embedded digital files or links to various sources from across the web.[3] As for student research, although students are even less likely to do research in physical archives than just a decade ago, they now have a wide array of digitized archival collections available to them online. From a professor's standpoint, the physical distance to actual archives matters much less than it once did, especially if educators are just looking for a variety of topics/sources for their students to work on (as opposed to specific sources for a particular advanced research project). Even then, for faculty working on their own projects, or for those who work with graduate students, an incredible array of specialized research can be done using existing digitized collections, as I found out for myself when I was able to access the Library of Virginia's online Confederate pension records to complete my own project on veteran families.[4]

The world of teaching archival research in the digital age is not all flowers and sunshine, however. The abundance of digital archival records can be overwhelming to some students. At the same time, only certain collections are available and often only certain parts of them. In fact, I often hear from frustrated students who expect all materials to be online, and, unfortunately, they often don't seem to understand my explanations of the costs of digitization and online curation. Another issue is that some-times those sources are hidden in the larger array of online information that is not necessarily archival or even scholarly. Partly to combat this issue, my colleagues and I constantly struggle to convince students to search beyond the first page of Google results.[5] Even after students find a digital archival collection, finding individual sources can be a frustrating process. In my experience, many undergraduate students have difficulty locating, using, and citing sources in online collections.

Another issue for educators working with undergraduate students and archival collections has to do with the speed of change online. This issue manifests in several forms. First, there is the simple issue that what is avail-able online is constantly changing as more archival collections are posted to the web, seemingly every day. Generally that's a good problem to have, but it does mean that professors have difficulty keeping up with what's available for their students. Second, educators (and the research librarians who help them) have to spend a great deal of time keeping up with chang-ing user interfaces of databases, repositories, and archives to help students navigate those collections. Finally, the rapidly changing nature of online archival sources (in terms of quantity, interface, even web addresses) is a problem for classes and curriculums. In other words, a syllabus and class lessons (complete with guides to navigating particular online archives, links to specific examples, or online primary documents used for essays) created for one semester may need to be completely revised, perhaps even in the middle of the semester. On several occasions I have been left scram-bling mid-semester because online documents I wanted students to use for a class project were no longer at the same URL as they had been just weeks before. For some professors this instability results in a reluctance to use online archival materials for class work. Perhaps the larger lesson is that we educators need to be teaching (and practicing) adaptability to information retrieval in a variety of ways, rather than focusing on specific databases, archives, or research. In other words, we have seen the problem, and it is at least partly us.

A related problem for educators teaching with digital collections is the occasional loss of access to digital repositories or sources on which we have come to depend. In some cases digital collections drop offline because they are no longer supported by funding streams or even, perhaps, their creators. Even if such "orphaned" collections remain online, they may have outdated software or even digital security issues.[6] In other cases the cost of supporting digital projects might result in a change in ownership and accessibility of resources, causing an effective hiding of materials behind pay walls. To cite one example, I used to assign students in my women's history class a wide array of readings from the Women and Social Movements in the United States history site when it was first available as a freely available array of online edited document projects. Several years ago, however, most of the site became part of a subscription service from Alexander Street Press.[7]

More generally, this issue of accessibility of archival collections behind pay walls can have several key effects from the perspective of educators. First, it creates a digital divide—or more accurately, contributes to an existing digital divide—regarding archival materials because financial resources dictate which institutions can access these collections.[8] Second, it creates a situation in which the material behind the pay wall might as well be hidden or unpublished; because of the restrictions, it does not become part of the larger discussion within history classes or graduate theses, making it less likely to be studied further.

Another issue for those of us who teach with online archival sources concerns the numerous questions raised about source and authority of materials posted on the web. One of the implications of the web's seemingly seamless presentation of its plethora of sources has been the profound blurring of the identity of the institutional home of digitized original documents. Though professional historians pay great attention to the author and source of original documents, it's not always immediately clear, even to us, whether digital reproductions of these documents came from archives, museums, academics, genealogists, or independent researchers. And, though the distance and changes from the original source material obviously matter a great deal (e.g., transcribed versus digitally reproduced, selections versus complete collections), which academic repository hosts it seems to matter much less than it used to.[9] And if that's increasingly true for professional historians, then it is easy to imagine what that blurring might mean for students just being introduced to the basic tenets of the historical profession, despite our constant efforts to make them aware of the need to verify the reliability of online sources.

Of course, primary source documents online are not all published by academic institutions, archival or otherwise. Teaching about sources and authority has become even more important and complicated in the digital age because of the posting of archival sources by enthusiasts, semi-professional historians, students, and for-profit sites.[10] Of course, we all want to see more and more sources available online, and many of these sites are quite well done, with all the scholarly rigor of even the most skeptical of historians. However, the fact is that the quality of these sites is not always as high as scholars and archivists want them to be. Some of them contain typos, poor transcriptions, bad metadata, or unusable scans, or they simply replicate inaccurate or discredited information. Given that this is the case, the blurring of the origins of archival sources that occurs on the web becomes a serious issue for history professors looking to teach their students how to find sources online. My colleagues and I spend a great deal of class time on what has been called "digital literacy" or "information fluency" (among other names), which often amounts to an updated version of the long-held goal for our students to approach all sources with a critical eye.

One particularly revealing example of the potential perils of online sources and the need for a skeptical approach happened in the fall of 2008, with T. Mills Kelly's history course, "Lying About the Past," at George Mason University. Dr. Kelly had the class create an online historical hoax to get the students in the class to think about digital publishing, online sources, authority, and ethics. The fifteen undergraduates chose to create a fake student working on a fake project about a fake pirate, complete with YouTube "interviews," an entry in *Wikipedia*, even a "Last Will and Testament." The hoax took in a number of people, including a few academic bloggers and one from *USA Today*. Importantly, the class and the hoax reinforce the questions raised in the digital age of trust, value, and the potential issues of online sources (not incidentally core components of digital literacy).[11]

Returning to the broader topic of this book, my sense is that, despite the great value of digitally opening many archives, the potential of high level, two-way interactivity between higher education teachers and their students on one hand and archivists on the other, what we might characterize as an essential part of Archives 2.0, is mostly unrealized at the moment. There are certainly efforts by the Library of Congress and other archival institutions to engage the public in Web 2.0-style conversations around documents and images,[12] but these attempts are rarely aimed directly at the university classroom.

One area in which I see an obvious chance to build connections between collegiate classrooms and archives is in the area of increased access to individual archivists themselves. When I was doing my own research as a graduate student, Minor Weisiger at the Library of Virginia and E. Lee Shepard at the Virginia Historical Society were invaluable in directing me to sources critical for my own research. So where is that personal direction toward archival resources in the digital age? In addition to the online collections guides that many archives have available, a number of archival websites have a clear place to contact them for more information.[13] Moving forward, the key is making sure that such features mirror the partnership I felt with archivists when I told them about my research, rather than the flat "book report" style request for "all information on X" that some students use in soliciting help from archivists and librarians. It is, of course, incumbent on educators to help their students understand how to approach archivists in appropriate ways.

In a similar vein, archivists can move further into the realm of digital conversations by using Web 2.0 tools to direct people to archival resources. At this point, however, I am aware of only limited use of social networking aimed at college students (undergraduate or graduate) regarding archives. My students certainly use Facebook, and a few use Twitter, but they rarely see these as tools directly related to their education or their research, nor do they look to such tools for information on their scholarship (unless they are consulting with their fellow students for advice).[14] There is perhaps an opportunity here for careful experimentation.[15] Students at Mary Washington have begun to engage with members of the larger academic community, if not archivists, in the blogs assigned as part of various classes.[16]

Looking forward, I see a number of possible directions for Archives 2.0 and higher education, (with the caveat that predicting the future is something that the study of history tells us we don't do well). First, I have the sense that archives, students, and educators are just beginning to explore the possibilities of targeted crowdsourcing. Admittedly, there are reasons for archivists to be hesitant in having students digitizing or tagging archival collections, and there are limits to how much that often-repetitious process is useful to students from an educational perspective after a certain point, but there are also many reasons to further encourage collaboration between archives and students to enable better archival online resources.[17] Working with local institutions, faculty, and classes to create, present, and improve digital versions of archival materials that the archives don't have the time or resources to create themselves can be a good thing for everyone. Use of free, open-source, content-management tools like WordPress and Omeka, combined with student work, faculty knowledge, and archival expertise, can make more resources available in useful, and yes, rigorous ways.[18]

Second, I think we are close to seeing the democratizing of data-mining for historical purposes. Increasingly, digitized archival collections will be the foundation for broad data-mining projects, not just from specialized academics, but from a broad spectrum of people, including undergraduate and graduate students mentored by a growing group of digitally literate historians.

Third, we need to be prepared for the incipient mobile revolution. Archivists (and anyone working on creating digital versions of archival documents) need to think about how to present material so that it can be accessed and easily consumed on smartphones and other small-screen devices (including ebook readers, netbooks, and slates/tablets). Though I won't presume to predict the specific devices that will be successful in the university classroom of the next five to ten years, it seems clear that we are reaching a kind of critical mass with the number of smartphones and other portable devices owned by students. I see the real possibility of future courses in which my students search and find archival documents on these devices in and out of class.[19]

Fourth, I believe we need to recognize that because of the availability of online sources without the help of archivists (or even the conscious use of archives) there is a potential trend away from involving archivists in education; yet we need to make sure that students and educators keep archivists in the discussion of those archival sources. How? By further encouraging the online presence of archivists who continue to serve as experts, directing scholars and students to digital and analog resources in archives. Web 2.0 is certainly one way to share that expertise, as evidenced by Facebook, Twitter, blogs, and the many examples demonstrated in the other essays in this book. Though these tools can serve as broadcast channels to many, they also provide the opportunity for response from the various communities they serve.

I also see a few areas where archivists can do better at meeting the needs of university history faculty in teaching, and I'd like to offer three specific suggestions. First, it's essential to assure that there are persistent, stable URLs for websites hosting online resources. Certainly it's unavoidable that data is restructured, sites are reworked, and changes must occasionally happen, but as a professor, I can attest that coming back to an electronic syllabus after one semester and finding all the links broken is an incredibly frustrating experience. And it's even more problematic if you're writing anything for print and are attempting to cite sources.[20]

Second, user interface matters a great deal. Students and faculty who can't figure out how to use a site with a little playing around just don't use the site. A colleague of mine at another university uses only one database or archive in a class each semester because learning, and teaching, multiple interfaces for multiple digital repositories is simply not worth it to her. So, time spent on developing the user interface for an archive is time well spent.

Finally, continue to expand on advertising your efforts to open archives through a variety of social media channels. Twitter and blogs seem to be the best avenues at the moment I'm writing this to reach professors and students who are most involved in the online world. It helps that the default for blogs and Twitter tweets is to be searchable in Google. It makes it more likely that archives' hard-fought digitized collections will be seen. Facebook is another option, though it may take some work to convince students and faculty to think of it as a tool for finding out about scholarly resources. Facebook's more than 500 million users makes it hard to ignore (although more and more students are telling me that as their parents are joining, it doesn't matter to them as much as it used to). Still, the larger point here is that archives shouldn't place all their advertising eggs in one technological basket and should be prepared to explore other channels as they arise. Even then, however, such Web 2.0 technologies won't reach all in higher education, so it is incumbent on digitally enabled faculty to help advertise these resources to both our students and our less digital colleagues.

In the end, history educators in university classrooms need to be able to connect with archives, archival projects, and archivists more than we currently do. Certainly, faculty need to do a better job of locating existing efforts at Archives 1.0 and 2.0, and that means staying current with the changes in the field and learning what's available digitally. Teaching faculty need to make themselves and their students more available to archives and archivists for two-way conversations and collaborations, but archives and archivists also need to reach out more to teaching faculty and their students.[21] Doing so would get us closer to the interactive and collaborative promise of Archives and Web 2.0. Going beyond existing efforts with web-based technologies is critically important to the continued relevance of archives in the preservation, creation, and teaching of history.

Notes

1 Formerly known as Mary Washington College, UMW has about 4,000 undergraduates and 1,000 graduate students. Class sizes range from 35 for introductory classes to 25 for upper-level courses like "U.S. Women's History" to 15 for seminars. There is no graduate program in history or American Studies.

2 Much of my thinking has also been influenced by my sister, Kara McClurken, who is head of Preservation Services at the University of Virginia. Thanks also to the advice of my colleagues at UMW. Any errors in this essay are not their fault.

3 Links to all my course websites and syllabi can be found at http://mcclurken.org.

4 These records and many others are available from LVA's terrific new site for its digital collections, http://www.virginiamemory.com/ (accessed September 1, 2010).

5 Even searching better within Google will result in better results. The following web page shows my attempt to point out Google's many search options to a first-year seminar: http://ted2009.umwblogs. org/2009/09/15/research-links/.

6 See "Graceful Degradation," Bethany Nowviskie and Dot Porter's study of digital humanities projects whose funding or support has ended, at http://nowviskie.org/2009/graceful-degradation/ (accessed September 1, 2010).

7 The site was begun in 1997 by Thomas Dublin and Katherine Kish Sklar at http://womhist.binghamton. edu/, while the current site (as of January 2010), with a quarter of the projects still available, is at http://womhist.alexanderstreet.com/.

8 Our libraries regularly have to make tough choices about how many and which digital resources they can afford to subscribe to.

9 The ability to find archival materials through search engines and to link directly to those archival materials (or "deep-linking") without ever needing to consult an institution's own guides or directories exacerbates that blurred sense of archival location.

10 For the last group, I'm thinking of Ancestry.com and Footnote.com, though there are others.

11 T. Mills Kelly, "You Were Warned," edwired, December 18, 2008, http://edwired.org/?p=418; Jen Howard, "Teaching by Lying: Professor Unveils 'Last Pirate' Hoax," Chronicle of Higher Education, December 18, 2008, http://chronicle.com/article/Teaching-by-Lying-Professor/1420 (accessed September 1, 2010); Lying About the Past, course blog, http://chnm.gmu.edu/history/ faculty/kelly/blogs/h389/ (accessed September 1, 2010); Last American Pirate, (fake) blog, http:// lastamericanpirate.net/ (accessed September 1, 2010). The USA Today post seems to have been taken down as of January 2010. The comments on Mills Kelly's post certainly point to the need for skeptical approaches to online materials but also highlight both the power and the fragility of online communities (called "trust networks" by one commenter) built through Web 2.0 tools like Twitter and blogs. Some of the people taken in by the hoax (including me) did so because the people in their network of friends and colleagues "tweeted" about it as if it were a real student project.

12 Here I'm particularly thinking of partnership projects like Flickr Commons, begun in 2008. See http://www.flickr.com/commons/ (accessed September 1, 2010).

13 As of September 2010, the Virginia Historical Society had "Ask a Librarian" and "Ask a Curator" forms at http://www.vahistorical.org/contact_us.htm, while the Library of Virginia used a general contact form at http://www.lva.virginia.gov/about/contact.asp. Some university libraries have begun to offer online "chat with a librarian" capabilities to their patrons as well.

14 This is not to say that some archives have not been using Web 2.0 tools to reach out. I and a growing number of my colleagues use Twitter and blogs to learn more about historical materials in many forms, both from formal archival accounts (e.g., VHS's @vahistorical), but also from

individual scholars, librarians, and archivists at various institutions (e.g., LOC's Susan Garfinkel, @ footnotesrising).

[15] *Careful* because some students may want to keep separate their academic and social online experiences.

[16] UMW has its own WordPress blogging system, known as *UMWblogs.org*, with more than 4,600 users and some 3,600 blogs (as of October 2010). Students use blogs as reflections, journals, project sites, and publishing platforms. For example, one student's reflection on a Revolutionary War soldier's diary led to a comment from an outside scholar. See http://bhupp.umwblogs.org/2008/09/01/private-joseph-plumb-martin-diary/.

[17] I would hope that as collaboration on digital projects and online resources between archivists, librarians, museum professionals, and academics becomes more common, it will become easier to figure out ways to include undergraduate and graduate students in these digital archiving projects. We're experimenting with that at Mary Washington in senior seminar classes like "Digital History." See http://dh2010.umwblogs.org and http://digitalhistory.umwblogs.org.

[18] WordPress is free blogging/publishing software and Omeka is a free digital collections manager and online presentation tool intended for museums and educational institutions. See http://wordpress.com and http://omeka.org.

[19] For more on mobile computing in higher education as a fast-approaching issue, see the 2010 Horizon Report from the New Media Consortium and the EDUCAUSE Learning Initiative at http://www.nmc.org/publications/2010-horizon-report, especially pp. 9–13; see also the *Digital Campus* podcasts from the Center for History and New Media at http://digitalcampus.tv, especially episodes 36 and 50.

[20] This problem, of course, is larger than just archives. It is a general issue of the web. I am concerned that some of the links that I've included here might not work by the time this book comes out. Dan Cohen and Roy Rosenzweig dealt with this by creating a centralized site of cached links for their book, *Digital History*, http://chnm.gmu.edu/digitalhistory/links/.

[21] These conversations can benefit all involved, especially if there are collaborative projects involved. Students learn about how historians and archivists use and think about all kinds of sources. Archivists get feedback, use of their collections, and even some help. Teaching faculty get better-informed students and potentially some meaningful projects for their classes. Everyone wins.

Digging In to Our Mutual Roots: Soliciting the Views of Genealogists, Family Historians, and Companies Providing Access to Archival Documents

Edited by Kate Theimer

Genealogists and family historians are primary user groups of almost all types of archives. From federal census records to local land deeds to college and university yearbooks to records of churches and civic organizations held by local historical societies, virtually every record in an archives documents the life of a person with a family tree. While many archivists were trained to place more value on the work of historians and other scholarly researchers, archivists today increasingly recognize the importance of serving genealogists, family historians, and others seeking knowledge about the past for personal fulfillment.

For this virtual roundtable interview, I sent four experts in the field of genealogy a list of questions via e-mail, and I have assembled their answers here to simulate a group discussion. Because of the key role their firms play in making archival collections accessible online to genealogists, I also sent questions to representatives of Ancestry.com and Footnote.com and then folded their responses into the larger discussion. My goal for this interview was to hear from these experts in their own words about the relationships between their communities and archivists and how the use of social media has changed how today's genealogists conduct research.

Following are the participants in the interview:

Kathryn Doyle *is the director of communications for the California Genealogical Society and Library in Oakland, California. She oversees Internet
presence, including Web 2.0, for the Society, edits its electronic newsletter,
and writes its award-winning blog.*

Dick Eastman *is the author of* Eastman's Online Genealogy Newsletter, *a
daily electronic publication with more than 50,000 readers, and the author
of* Your Roots: Total Genealogy Planning on Your Computer, *published by
Ziff-Davis Press. He is a frequent international lecturer, manager of the
Genealogy Forums on CompuServe, former editor of* Genealogical Computing *magazine, and a former consultant and guest on the* Ancestors *television series on PBS.*

Eric Shoup, *vice president of Product, and* **Loretto Szucs,** *vice president
of Community Relations at Ancestry.com, an online resource for family
history, which has digitized and put online more than 4 billion records
over the past twelve years. Ancestry users have created more than 12
million family trees containing more than 1.25 billion profiles. Ancestry.
com has local websites directed at nine countries, including its flagship
website.*

Thomas MacEntee *is a genealogist specializing in the use of technology
and social media to improve genealogical research and as a means of interacting with others in the family history community. Utilizing more than
twenty-five years of experience in the information technology field, Thomas
writes and lectures on the many ways blogs, Facebook, and Twitter can be
leveraged to add new dimensions to the genealogy experience. As the creator of GeneaBloggers.com, he has organized and engaged a community of
more than 800 bloggers to document their own journeys in the search for
ancestors.*

Justin Schroepfer *is the director of marketing for Footnote.com. Footnote.
com originated in 1999 under the name iArchives, providing digitization
services for historical newspapers and other archival content for leading*

universities, libraries, and media companies across the United States. In January 2007 the company transitioned from using its proprietary systems and patented processes built for digitization to using the iArchives platform to provide online access to these historically significant and valuable collections through the new company website, Footnote.com. Today Footnote. com provides access to more than 62 million original documents from the National Archives and other institutions as well as unique member contributions.

Drew Smith, *MLS, has been the information literacy librarian at the University of South Florida–Tampa Library since 2007. Before accepting this position, he was an instructor for the University of South Florida School of Library and Information Science for more than twelve years. He is currently the secretary of the Association of Professional Genealogists (APG) and in his fourth term as president of the Florida Genealogical Society of Tampa. He has been the co-host of the* Genealogy Guys *podcast since September 2005. Smith is author of the book* Social Networking for Genealogists *(2009).*

What started your interest in family history/genealogy?

Doyle: I think that some people are just born with an inherent interest in their family story. It seems to be one of those traits buried deep in my DNA. I got the gene from my dad, who got it from his mother. But it was a chance conversation with a genealogist that unleashed the researcher in me. Until then I didn't know you could chase documents. My grandmother was a great research partner. When the paper trail got cold, I would pick up the phone and we'd talk about what I had found. Inevitably, she would remember some new bit of information that would send me running in a new direction. Now that she and my dad are gone, I'm waiting to identify "the one" in the next generation.

Eastman: I always had a casual interest, even as a child. However, the thing that inspired me to really start researching was the receipt of a gift: my aunt unexpectedly gave me a family Bible that originally belonged to my great-great-grandmother or possibly to my great-great-great-grand-parents. The Bible was printed in 1828 and someone (my great-great-great-grandparents?) had written in the births, marriages, and deaths back to the 1750s. That was only one branch of the family, but it inspired me to look for information about the other branches. I later extended the information about that original branch documented in the family Bible back into the 1630s.

MacEntee: My first exposure to tracing one's ancestry, like many Americans, was back in 1977 watching the mini-series *Roots,* which was based on the book by Alex Haley. However, I didn't seriously pursue genealogy until 1993, when I was handed a previously published work of an ancestor, which inspired me and set me on the path of tracing my own roots. I was also strongly encouraged by my mother, who always had an interest in genealogy but never took time to pursue it.

After close to seventeen years, I now realize that genealogy is a perfectly suitable career and not just a hobby. So I am transitioning over from the information technology field and working on becoming a certified profes-sional genealogist.

Smith: Growing up in a small town in upstate South Carolina in the 1960s and early 1970s, I found myself surrounded by people who seemed to know how everyone was related to everyone else. From time to time, I would examine the local public library's small genealogy collection to see if I could learn anything about my family earlier than the memories of my living relatives, but it was very difficult because there were so many common surnames in my family. By the early 1990s, my brother and I real-ized that my parents' generation was nearly all gone, and that if he and I were serious about learning our family's history, we would have to waste no more time and begin to do the actual research.

What was the inspiration for your company to get involved in making archival materials available online?

Szucs: Ancestry.com grew out of a small-book genealogy publisher's dream. As a young entrepreneur, John Sittner recognized the strong and growing interest Americans had in tracing their family stories. He founded Ancestry in 1983 while working on the company's maiden publication: *The Source.* For this first book, he enlisted sixteen eminent genealogists to collaborate in a work that would identify, locate, and interpret the volumes of records and little-known collections useful to family historians. Sittner then did what had never been done by a genealogy publisher: he mass-marketed. Handsome promotional pieces were mailed, 100,000 at a time. All over the country, people with an interest in family history read about and purchased *The Source.* The award-winning book that has been revised twice set the standard for excellence for Ancestry, and since its publication, the company has published more than 100 titles. Strong and lasting bonds were formed with libraries (including the Library of Congress), the National Archives, and state and local libraries and archives when Ancestry worked closely with their staffs to produce excellent books that highlighted their respective collections.

The publication of *The Source* brought recognition and respectability to family history research. There are few libraries, large or small, that do not have a copy of it and several other Ancestry titles on their shelves. Scholars, archivists, and librarians were so impressed with the well-documented work that they began to take family historians more seriously. Strong links between these groups were forged, and the Ancestry brand was born. When Ancestry.com went online in 1996, the first database featured on the site was a collection of articles from its books and from *Ancestry Magazine.* Through the years articles written by experts have remained an educational feature at Ancestry.com.

Schroepfer: Footnote.com is part of the company iArchives. For years iArchives has been a provider of digitization services for other businesses and universities. Some of the digitization projects involved historical newspapers and other historical documents. After some time, the CEO of the company, Russ Wilding, had a desire to make historical documents more widely accessible through a consumer website. In addition to making historical documents available on a website, a goal was to create an environment where visitors could interact with the documents and with other people with similar interests.

What was it like to do research when you started? How did you interact with other researchers?

Doyle: I started before census records were digitized, so I spent a lot of time cranking microfilm through a reader at my local Family History Center. The Internet was already becoming a way for family historians to find each other, so I was able to "meet" cousins from all parts of the world using message boards and mailing lists.

Eastman: I started some years before the invention of personal computers or the World Wide Web, so I was restricted to pen, paper, microfilm, and visiting libraries and archives. I must say that I enjoyed the research experience and those who start today miss the fun of digging through old records until they realize that so little information has been digitized. Then they fall back to the "old-fashioned" research methods and I believe they become better genealogists as a result.

When I started researching my family tree, I lived in a rural area in northern Vermont and I had almost no interaction with other researchers. I did talk with librarians and with some archivists at various courthouses, but their expertise varied and my conversations were limited. I do believe that the online world has greatly improved interaction with experienced genealogists. Expertise is available at your fingertips today, something not possible thirty years ago, especially in rural areas.

MacEntee: In 1977, local libraries and archives saw an influx of folks wanting to research their own genealogy. Ask any librarian who was working back then, and you'll understand how ill-prepared facilities were for the surge in interest around genealogy. And back then, the best way to interact and network with other genealogists was by joining a local genea-logical society and attending genealogy conferences—methodologies that still exist and serve a great purpose today.

Smith: Because I was living in a larger city by 1990, I was fortunate to have access to a very good genealogy collection in the downtown public library. Much of my time was spent browsing through rolls of census microfilm and using the somewhat limited print indexes, which listed only heads of household. Because my education and experience was in using computer technology, I was also able to take advantage of the Internet to search for information and to communicate with other researchers using e-mail, mailing lists, message boards, and chat rooms. In many ways, I was a technologist who had discovered genealogy, instead of a genealogist who had discovered technology.

Describe what you thought about archives and archivists when you first started doing research. Did that change as you got more experienced?

Doyle: I learned that archives are magical places on a June day in 2000 when the post office delivered an envelope from the National Archives containing a copy of my great-great-grandfather's Civil War Pension File. I couldn't believe their marriage certificate was safely hidden away in a file in Washington, D.C. Even though I had a copy, it was the first thing I requested when I finally made a research trip to NARA five years later. I just wanted to hold it in my hands.

Eastman: In my "early days," I felt that these archivists were all great experts. Indeed, some of them were. As I have gained more expertise myself, I have become a bit more critical in evaluating the knowledge and expertise of others. Years ago I thought that all archivists were great experts. Today, I think that *some* of them are great experts but others are not. Luckily, I now know where to spend my time: I ask questions of those whose judgment and knowledge I trust and I get better answers as a result. As good as computers are, nothing ever beats human expertise.

MacEntee: I think I was biased by the perception I had of librarians and libraries as I grew up: dark, quiet, musty places staffed by dour people— mostly women—who were helpful to a point. They basically helped you locate what you might need and that was it.

Now, after working for so many years with librarians and archivists, I realize not only has my perception changed but also the field of library and archive science has changed. There are more folks who are willing to share their knowledge, point researchers in the right direction, and even guide genealogists to resources they might not have considered using, like patents and trademark databases, church cookbooks, and more.

Smith: Although I was already very comfortable with using public libraries and academic libraries, I was somewhat intimidated by my first visits to archives. I didn't know what archivists thought about genealogists, and I didn't want to waste the time of archivists with things that I didn't know because I was new to genealogy. I was always a bit afraid that I might violate some rule that I had overlooked. As my experience with using archives increased, the intimidation factor decreased, and I realized that genealogists were some of the most frequent users of archives.

How would you describe your company's relationships with the genealogical community? With archives? Have these relationships changed over time?

Szucs: The relationships that began in the early years between Ancestry. com, genealogical community leaders, librarians, and archivists have grown and strengthened over the years. To this day, experts and authors from each of these groups continue to write for Ancestry publications (magazines and online), and they regularly work with Ancestry.com to come up with ways to further enhance the user experience. As Ancestry. com benefits from their experience with historical records and the public served by librarians and archivists, the record keepers, librarians, and expert genealogists benefit from the tremendous number of records that Ancestry.com has made available to them.

Schroepfer: Our most prominent relationship is that with the National Archives and Records Administration (NARA). Back in January 2007, Footnote.com launched the site in conjunction with the announcement of a partnership with NARA. This was the first time that NARA had entered into this type of partnership, which has flourished over the past three years. Footnote continues to work closely with NARA in order to make some of the most popular and useful documents available on the Internet for the first time. Footnote.com also has a strong relationship with the genealogical community. The genealogical community has been a primary driver on the development of Footnote.com. We have developed an advisory board that is made up of some of the most prominent genealogists in order to help define our future strategies. In a short time period, Footnote is now recognized as one of the most useful tools for genealogists.

How did the web first begin to make things different for you?

Doyle: The web made it possible for me to find family papers residing in archives far from their place of origin. Early on I stumbled upon *The Appleby Family Papers*—a wonderful online finding aid for a collection at the Clements Library at the University of Michigan. It's a detailed description of the 327 Civil War-era letters and documents of one of my collateral families in Western Pennsylvania.

Eastman: I was already running an online genealogy service on CompuServe several years before Tim Berners-Lee invented the World Wide Web in 1991. In my case, the rapid growth of the web opened a huge new audience that had not existed in the earlier proprietary online services.

MacEntee: In the 1990s, there were online bulletin boards (remember those? And the sound of the dial-up modem to connect?) where one could leave messages listing surnames, areas of research, availability for look-ups, and so on.

I was fortunate in that when I started my research, the personal computer was already front and center in the lives of many Americans; however, the Internet was still in its infancy. Working in information technology allowed me to track the development of online resources such as Ancestry, RootsWeb, Cyndi's List, and more.

Unfortunately, all of the resources available from one's personal computer give new researchers a false sense of being able to answer all research questions solely using online resources. The California Genealogical Society and Library has a great "tip of the iceberg" poster (http://blog. californiaancestors.org/2009/08/tip-of-iceberg-poster-buy-three-get-one. html) advocating the use of libraries and archives to help one become a more rounded researcher. Those of us who advocate the use of the Internet for research have a responsibility to give a full picture of what resources are available, including libraries and archives.

Smith: In my first years of using the Internet for genealogical research (the early 1990s), I had to depend a great deal on tools such as Telnet to access library catalogs and ftp to access document and software repositories. As the web became a bigger and bigger part of the Internet, it became easier to locate repositories, search their catalogs, and download documents. Once search engines became more powerful, and archives put more and more of their finding aids on the web, it became easier to determine whether or not an archive's holdings might be relevant for my research.

What about the impact of Web 2.0 and social media? How do you use tools like blogs, Facebook, etc.? What kinds of Web 2.0 resources have made the biggest impact on the genealogy community and why?

Doyle: I use blogs to access information about research techniques and technology. It's pretty much a given that if I have a question or problem, someone else has already dealt with that issue and blogged about it! I keep hoping to find the blog of a cousin who is researching my farmers and coal miners, but so far that hasn't happened. Web 2.0 resources have made the genealogy blogging community a fairly close-knit group. I'm working on a project to create a similar community among genealogical societies.

Eastman: I use very few of the social media services. I do see the value of such services, but I also believe they all need to mature a bit more before they become useful tools. Right now I see far too many problems with privacy issues and with rampant misinformation. I do believe the problems will be solved as we learn to adopt rating systems of peer-reviewed information.

I like the model of eBay ratings: if you are an honest buyer or seller, your customers and vendors will eventually rate you as "reliable." We need something similar in the user-generated information created by tens of thousands of genealogists.

MacEntee: On a personal level, I've used many of the social networking tools to further my own genealogy research. On Facebook, I've managed to contact cousins, many of whom I never knew existed, merely by posting status updates about my work or searching for surnames. On Twitter, I have had offers of assistance from other genealogists to do lookups or take photos of cemetery headstones related to my ancestors. And my blog has been the most important such tool: its content is picked up by Google and other search engines. This allows others researching my ancestral lines to contact me and exchange information.

On a professional level, I can't stress the importance of fully understanding and using social networking tools if you are in the genealogy industry. The genealogy field has a reputation of being slow to embrace new technologies to the point of actually trivializing them without full knowledge of their mechanics and possibilities. If the industry is going to attract more users—especially a younger demographic—they must stop using twentieth-century marketing techniques for what may likely be one of the biggest hobbies of the twenty-first century: genealogy.

Smith: I use blogs quite heavily to keep up with the news in my areas of interest, whether it's related to my work, my hobbies, or my community. Because there are so many genealogy-related blogs, it's difficult to miss any item of news that relates to genealogy. It could be a release of new genealogy software, the publication of a new genealogy book, or the passage of a state law that impacts my access to public records. I use Facebook to keep up with what is going on in the lives of my family, my friends, my colleagues, and even people I had lost touch with decades ago. Although Facebook has certainly made an impact on genealogists, it's been especially interesting to see the dramatic growth of a similar tool just for genealogists, GenealogyWise. Tools such as blogs, Facebook, and podcasts have provided genealogists with new ways to advertise and learn about genealogy-related events.

How have these tools changed the way you work with archives?

Doyle: Many libraries and archives are putting up Facebook pages, which I see as a portal to their websites. A few are starting to use Twitter, but it's still in its infancy. I love how the Massachusetts Historical Society is tweeting the John Quincy Adams diary entries 140 characters at a time [@JQAdams_MHS]. I think that the biggest change is that archives using Web 2.0 have personality. It's brought a friendlier and more approachable "face" to institutions that are sometimes intimidating.

Eastman: I see one huge difference: I can now view images of original documents at my convenience without leaving home. Otherwise, I see little difference. Every scrap of information still needs to be verified by looking at original documents (or images of original documents). Basic genealogy techniques and requirements have not changed a bit. The only difference is in the convenience of doing so. I no longer have to travel long distances to some remote repository. The original document is in England? I can view it (sometimes) at home.

MacEntee: Over the past decade, as more research resources are accessed from the comfort of one's own home, as well, many archives have made their collections available online.

In addition, as I've experienced personally, archivists are willing to interact with researchers and genealogists by answering questions and guiding them to other resources if needed. Also many libraries and archives actively solicit feedback as well as advertise their program of events using tools, especially Twitter.

The number of libraries and archives on Twitter is just amazing. Many do more than just market their upcoming offerings—they actually engage their followers and ask what they want to see from their facility.

Smith: Blogs and other social networking tools have made it easier to find out what's new with archives. It's the fastest and easiest way to learn about new collections, changes in hours, or policy changes. In many ways, these tools have made archives seem a bit more "human" than they would seem otherwise. Archives that use these tools come across as dynamic organizations that adapt to their patrons' needs, instead of unchanging, unresponsive institutions.

Describe how your company initially got involved with using social media tools. How did you think they would be used?

Shoup: By watching our members' site activity and talking to them about what they wanted, it was clear that they wanted what social media tools could offer—the ability to contribute to, collaborate on, and share their family history. Frankly, we have just been following our members' lead. For example, we saw that for the millions of people researching their family history on Ancestry.com, the odds were very high that someone else on the site was researching the same people. That is what led us to add social networking tools such as Member Connect, a feature that makes it easier than ever before to discover and collaborate with other members who are researching the same ancestor. Member Connect was designed to help members learn about other members' research, share discoveries together, and stay up to date on the research they are doing on shared ancestors.

As another example, our members demonstrated a desire to share their discoveries more and in new ways with friends, family, and the Internet at large. As a result, through Ancestry.com, we have enabled members to upload photos and images, record conversations and interviews, and share it all with others via Facebook, Twitter, and e-mail.

Schroepfer: The goal for the Footnote team was to create a website that would utilize the power of social networking. The team knew that the more people you bring into the research process, the easier it becomes to make discoveries. Tools were developed for Footnote users to enhance the content on Footnote by adding their own content and insights and connect with others. Valuable member contributions are added to Footnote on a continual basis. It's the social contributions that add more pieces to the puzzle, thus creating a more vivid picture of the past.

What kind of response has your company had to using your social media tools on your site?

Shoup: The response has been very positive. Due to the nature of family history research, it can often be a solo sport, where one person would spend hours to uncover one small piece of a puzzle in their ancestry. With the integration of tools like Member Connect, Ancestry.com is turning family history research into a team sport, enabling members to connect with each other to share findings on common ancestors.

We hear from Ancestry.com members all the time that some of their most meaningful family history experiences have come from connecting with another Ancestry.com member who has rich information about one of their ancestors.

Schroepfer: The contributions to the site have been amazing. Even from day one, people have added photos, documents, comments, annotations, and other contributions that have increased the value of Footnote. There are some individual Footnote members that have made hundreds and even thousands of contributions to the site. There is a Member Discoveries page on Footnote (http://www.footnote.com/discoveries/) where people can view all the contributions in real time.

How does your company use networks like Facebook and Twitter (or others) and tools like blogs, Flickr, podcasting, etc., outside of your site?

Shoup: We started to connect with our customers on social networks more than twelve years ago, through the creation of our Ancestry.com Message Boards, which are located directly on our website. Since then, we have expanded our social media presence to be on the *Ancestry.com Blog,* Facebook, Twitter, and YouTube, and we also host our very own Ancestry.com webinars on a regular basis. These tools were created with the intent to communicate with our customers, for our customers to connect with each other, and ultimately to provide people with the tools they need to discover their family history.

Additionally, we've added other great tools that make it easy for members to share that thrill of discovery with family and friends through social networks. When on Ancestry.com, members can share historical records or photos via Facebook, Twitter, and e-mail. Once shared, family and friends can click on the link they receive to view the record or photos on Ancestry.com.

Schroepfer: It's encouraging to see the genealogy and history audiences use sites like Facebook and Twitter in order to stay current with the changing world. Footnote has created pages on both of these sites in order to update our followers and fans on a regular basis.

In addition to using these sites as a way to inform the different communities, Footnote has created an application on Facebook called iRemember. Footnote Pages can be shared on Facebook through the iRemember application. This is a great way for people using Footnote to share their discoveries and involve their family and friends on Facebook.

Have there been other changes in the field that have changed how you interact with archives?

Eastman: The METHOD of how I interact has changed tremendously. It is great to stay at home and "visit" distant archives without spending thousands of dollars on airplane tickets and hotels. The online fees I sometimes pay are trivial compared with the expenses I used to incur.

I do miss the personal interaction of conversation with archivists and others employed at that distant archives. However, those people are still generally available via e-mail, if needed. While not as personal, e-mail is a great facilitator. I now hold "electronic conversations" with experts who were simply not reachable before. I believe I have become a better genealogist as a result.

MacEntee: I think archives are becoming more user-friendly, partially due to media exposure, especially television programs such as *Antiques Roadshow* and *History Detectives,* both on PBS. Specifically with *History Detectives,* viewers understand the vital role that archives play in not just preserving history but also solving mysteries. Couple that with Americans' insatiable appetite for *CSI*-style shows where evidence is gathered and reviewed and a puzzle is pieced together—all of a sudden it is cool and hip to be an archivist.

Gone are the days—I hope—when younger people perceived a librarian or an archivist as a vinegary spinster replete with sweater over the shoulders, glasses on a chain around the neck, ready to correct you for ending a sentence with a preposition. Now the role models are folks like Elyse Luray (http://en.wikipedia.org/wiki/Elyse_Luray) and Tukufu Zuberi (http://en.wikipedia.org/wiki/Tukufu_zuberi).

Smith: The biggest change in the past decade in my interaction with archives is in the increase in availability to me of indexed, digital records. The work that ten years ago would have required my planning a long-distance trip to look for and view paper documents has been replaced with the pleasurable and much less expensive alternative of my seeing many of the records I need on my home computer screen. For a busy professional who may find it difficult to block out time to travel to do research, my ability to squeeze in a little time here and there every evening means that I can make some real progress on my personal research that otherwise might wait months or years.

How do you see researchers accessing archival documents in the future? What role will archives play in that vs. your company?

Szucs: Considering the enormous number of historical records housed in archives across the globe, the cost is too great for many archives to digitize the documents on their own. Ancestry.com partners with archives to preserve and digitize these documents and help provide the public with even greater access to the most important family history information available.

Our collaboration with the archives demonstrates the tremendous opportunities that can be created between nonprofit genealogical societies and commercial organizations committed to making family history research easier and more important than ever before. Once records are digitized, Ancestry.com posts them online for its subscribers. Additionally, Ancestry.com offers joint access to the digitized files on-site at the archives, through Ancestry.com.

Schroepfer: The amount of historical content that is now online is staggering. Footnote alone is adding more than a million new documents to the site every month. With this explosion of content, researchers have more access to documents that they may never have been aware of before. Archives, including the National Archives, are working together with Footnote to make their content more accessible and preserving these valuable records. Unlocking this content by putting it on the Internet will lead to new discoveries and bring new life to historical topics and figures. Footnote is leading that charge to provide more content on the Internet and will continue to be a primary research tool in the future.

What do you think genealogists and family historians most want from archives? From companies like yours?

Szucs: What genealogists and family historians want most is to see Ancestry.com continue to acquire and preserve historical records, especially those that hold answers to their own family mysteries. There are still billions of records that are as yet difficult, if not impossible, to find or search elsewhere. Priceless records are hidden away in archives, libraries, and other places, and until these records can be digitized and made available online, they are simply out of reach for most of us. In some cases, untapped record sources may be the only keys to unlock the doors to our past. Family history has become a national passion because the availability of so many different kinds of records make it possible for anyone, regardless of background, race, or ethnicity to find their own family story. And people everywhere are very excited about being able to search so many records at Ancestry.com and the incredible tools on the site that make it possible to build family trees and attach photographs and documents to them. They love it that Ancestry.com has made it possible to connect and collaborate with other family members and researchers. Family historians look forward to the seemingly endless production of new "toys" that

Ancestry.com has made available for them to enjoy and to connect with their loved ones.

Schroepfer: There is a simple answer to this question: more content! There is so much content still to be digitized and genealogists are hungry for more to be made available on the Internet.

What advice would have for the archival profession? What would you most like to see?

Doyle: I would love to see smaller archives put descriptions of their manuscript collections online so researchers can find the hidden gems about their families. The California Genealogical Society recently added a twenty-three-page downloadable (and searchable) document to our website. It is a synopsis of our manuscript collection describing 90 linear feet of loose papers, research, and family histories donated to the CGS Library over our 110-plus-year history.

Eastman: While technologies change and methodologies change rapidly, one thing remains constant: your customer. He or she is the individual who seeks information that is in your possession. That hasn't changed in centuries.

Strive to serve your customer well and use whatever technology is available today. The most valuable service you can provide is one-on-one coaching and assistance. That's true in the case of in-person conversations, of writing letters with a quill pen, or with communication using the latest form of instant messaging. The medium is not important. The customers are always the most important factor.

MacEntee: I think that as more and more of the Baby Boomer generation reaches retirement age (and current data suggests more people are opting for early retirement benefits at age sixty-two), genealogy will become much more popular as a hobby and a family pastime. Add to that the increase in television programs focused on genealogy (*African American Lives, Find My Family, Who Do You Think You Are*, etc.), librarians and archivists should prepare now for the next wave of newcomer to genealogy and to research facilities. Despite the existence of the Internet as a convenient means of starting one's research, many will and should still turn to libraries and archives to help them get started. They should be welcomed and feel welcomed. This is an opportunity to convert these patrons and users of archival resources into donors and advocates for the importance of libraries and archives.

Smith: I think the biggest challenge facing the archival profession is that it needs to tackle the issue of long-distance outreach and instruction for the general public in the use of its resources. Once rare or unique materials have been collected, preserved, organized, digitized, and made accessible online, they still aren't truly usable unless those who might want to use them know they exist and can be shown how to use them. Outreach and instruction for individuals ranging in age from middle-school students to retirees needs to be designed and implemented using the latest technologies. There need to be more instructional blogs, wikis, podcasts, videocasts, screencasts, and webinars of all kinds.

Going to See the Elephant: Archives, Diversity, and the Social Web

Terry D. Baxter

Who doesn't remember this childhood poem?

> It was six men of Indostan
> To learning much inclined,
> Who went to see the Elephant
> (Though all of them were blind),
> That each by observation
> Might satisfy his mind . . .[1]

Written in 1864 by John Saxe as an interpretation of a variety of Asian Indian proverbs, it goes on to describe the blind men's attempts to accurately describe the elephant through an investigation of its constituent parts—trunk, tusk, leg, tail, ear, and side. They, of course, come to poor conclusions based on incomplete evidence. (See Figure 1.) The meaning of the story varies through its historical iterations, but it generally admonishes people to be wary of believing that the piece of information that they understand to be the entire truth and encourages them to seek to understand the entire elephant.

In many ways, trying to apprehend concepts like diversity or Web 2.0 can be as frustrating as describing an elephant to the proverbial six blind men. There are mountains of descriptive material about both concepts, much of it coming from differing perspectives and much of it anecdotal

Figure 1: Blind monks examining an elephant, Itcho Hanaguxa, 1888. *Wikimedia Commons.*

in nature. To further complicate things, both concepts are continually evolving.

The very use of the term *Web 2.0* implies a Web 1.0 and a Web 3.0. In fact, by the time this book is published, Web 2.0 may have already moved into the historical footnote category. On the surface, it often appears that the web is constantly changing. Just look at browsers themselves. Since 1991, there have been more than fifty browsers released to the public. Who remembers Netscape, Mosaic, America Online (AOL), Compuserve, or Prodigy?[2] Bulletin boards, Internet relay chat, and Doom have been replaced by blogs, instant messaging, and World of Warcraft.

If one takes a closer look, though, how exactly is something like AOL, a proto-social networking site created in the 1990s, that much different from Facebook? Both could be described as member-only networks designed to be one-stop-shopping for information and fun using internal messaging systems and relying on friend referrals for growth. Of course, there are significant differences, too, but conceptually they are more similar than not.

Diversity is also a concept that has changed significantly. It initially related to the gradual coalescence of a variety of identity politics groups. Diversity was about the need for *groups* of people, historically disenfranchised and underrepresented within power structures, to assert their equal rights. It has gradually morphed into a conceptual framework that seeks to assert individuals' needs for respect, acceptance, and equal and fair treatment, regardless of their individual characteristics. More and more, the term *inclusiveness* is used to describe what used to be called *diversity*.

Once again, however, this evolution has not radically changed the underlying needs and premises. Both diversity and inclusiveness look to reformulate the world into a place where people, whether in groups or as individuals, are not constrained or inequitably treated in their "pursuit of happiness."

As with the blind men, there is more going on than what is immediately apparent. There is a sense that *something* is happening, that it can't quite be apprehended, but that we need to understand what it is.

If neither diversity nor Web 2.0 are elephants in their own rights, but parts of some larger animal, then what kind of parts are they and how can one come to describe this creature? This essay is not a definitive description, of course. What it is, however, is an attempt to look clearly at what diversity is, how our current web increases our awareness of the world's diversity, and how Web 2.0 can help archivists tap into a broader set of resources, attract a wider variety of users, and create a more representative profession.

What Is Diversity?

Scratch a Google search and you will find a million definitions of diversity (more than 2 million, actually). Many of them focus on similar concerns. They acknowledge that individuals have differences. They often enumerate these differences—gender, race, religion, ethnicity, and orientation are a few of the categories. They encourage people to "embrace" these differences and to "celebrate" them.[3]

This type of definition is certainly an advance over some of the earlier efforts to diversify society. Those efforts generally focused on identifying

groups who had suffered discrimination, creating systems of legal protec-
tions for those groups and attempting to create representative ratios of
these groups in societal structures such as schools, the workplace, and
governance bodies. While this body-count mentality was a necessary step
in the creation of a diverse society, it was a crude tool at best. It assumed
uniformity among members of protected classes and was often seen by
opponents as arbitrary and unfair. In fact, some members of protected
classes became increasingly wary of definitions and standards imposed by
outsiders without much consultation with the affected groups.

As diversity efforts began to take hold, the definition and conceptual-
ization of diversity expanded. Diversity was no longer seen as a requirement—something that needed to happen because it was the right thing to
do—but as an inherently useful attribute. Definitions of diversity began to
focus not so much on the fair representation of protected classes of people
but on the sense that all people have differences and that these differences
have value to groups and organizations.

Recent literature has begun to replace the concept of diversity with a
variant called *inclusion*. This conceptual evolution focuses more on the
removal of barriers to individuals' participation in whatever group, activity, or service interests them. It operates from the premise that it is a false
position to consider groups of people having the authority to "allow" other
people to participate in societal structures.[4]

Diversity in Society

Regardless of the changes in nomenclature, it is clear that the measurement of diversity in society is still based in statistics and the participation
of protected groups in various phases of society. For instance, one can
easily find statistics on the percentage of African Americans in the U.S.
Congress (7.8) and compare that to the percentage of African Americans
in the United States (12.8). Or that women earn nearly 60 percent of all
master's degrees in the United States, while constituting only 51 percent of
the population. Or that 67 percent of the U.S. Supreme Court identifies as
Catholic and 22 percent identifies as Jewish, compared with 25.1 percent
and 1.2 percent, respectively, in the general population. One can also track

statistical changes through time and compare those changes against organizational goals.

This statistical analysis of societal diversity is invaluable. In many respects it is the foundation on which all other diversity initiatives are built. Without an understanding of both the current makeup of society and how it has changed and is continuing to change through time, it would be difficult to measure the effectiveness of different strategies to encourage diversity in organizations and institutions.

The discussion of diversity in the United States is far too broad and complex a study to be undertaken here. By looking at the diversity values of the archival profession, however, one can at least view societal diversity as seen through that discrete lens. The Society of American Archivists (SAA) identifies the following groups in its policy on nondiscrimination: "age, color, creed, disability, family relationship, gender identity/expression, individual life style, marital status, national origin, race, religion, sex, sexual orientation, or veteran status."[5] The following is a brief, *impressionistic* look at each of these categories.

Age: One in four Americans is under the age of eighteen. Forty percent of the population is under the age of thirty (the age often associated with the first digital natives), and 12.5 percent of the population is over the age of sixty-five.

Color: This is a term often used as an equivalent for race. *See below.*

Creed: This term implies that personal beliefs can be openly held without discrimination. *See* religion *below.*

Disability: The U.S. Census identifies 16.3 percent of the U.S. population as having a disability. There is much discussion about what this number means, because it includes all types and levels of disability.[6]

Family relationship: This term implies that a person's status in a family, say as an adoptee or a stepfather, can be openly expressed without discrimination.

Gender identity/expression: There are no reliable statistics for this group; however, it is an important category, especially in an online world where representation is a key component of interaction.

Individual lifestyle: While this is impossible to analyze (Any lifestyle? Legal lifestyles?), it is an important recognition that people want to live openly as they see fit and should not suffer discrimination for personal lifestyle choices—like smoking or being a vegan, for instance.

Marital status: Just over half of all Americans over the age of fifteen are married. Thirty percent have never been married. Twelve percent are divorced or separated, and six percent are widowed.[7]

National origin: This term implies that a person can claim a country or area as his or her heritage openly without discrimination.

Race: The following table shows information from the U.S. Census Bureau.[8] As will be seen later, the categories do not match precisely with the A*CENSUS, the first (2004) truly comprehensive nationwide survey of the archives profession.[9] Of special note is the categorization of Hispanics. The category is counted in addition to race (e.g., black *and* Hispanic). It is predicted that by 2050, non-Hispanic whites will total 49 percent of the population, and the segment of the population that is Hispanic will have grown to 30 percent.

Table 1

Group	Percent of U.S. Population
White	80
White (Non-Hispanic)	66
Hispanic	15.1
Black	12.8
Asian	4.4
American Indian and Alaska Native	1
Native Hawaiian and Pacific Islander	0.2

Religion: The religious affiliation of the United States is strongly Christian, a group constituting 75 percent of the population. Half of all Americans identify with a Protestant denomination and a quarter identify themselves as Catholics. Fifteen percent identify as nonreligious. All other identified religious practitioners total 5 percent, and another 5 percent refuse to provide information.[10]

Sex: As with most of the world, the United States is close to a half-and-half split of males and females, with the latter making up 50.7 percent of the population.

Sexual orientation: Statistical sources are notoriously unreliable, often due to imprecision in survey language, under/overreporting, and the fluid nature of human sexuality. The most common numbers indicate roughly 4 to 5 percent of the U.S. population is gay or lesbian.[11]

Veteran status: Veterans constitute about 7.6 percent of the U.S. population. This number is expected to steadily decline in the next twenty-five years.[12]

One category that is not included but is vital for a discussion of both archives and of Web 2.0 is adult literacy in the United States. Both rely heavily on textual bases, and that requires literacy to be useful. While there are claims that the United States has a rate of 99 percent basic literacy, other sources indicate that roughly 14 percent of Americans perform at below basic standards for literacy. For adult Hispanics and blacks, that number is 39 percent and 20 percent, respectively. Eighteen percent of Americans speak a language other than English at home.[13]

These snapshots only provide some basic starting points for a conversation on diversity in the United States. They can easily be used without context or history to make all sorts of claims, but they also can provide a way to gauge the success of initiatives and to measure changes in large groups of people through time.

Diversity and Archives

Like much of the rest of society, the archives profession considers diversity a central focus.[14] The arc of this concern follows general societal concerns in the United States. For instance, the SAA began a long series of diversity initiatives in the early 1970s. In 1981, it created a Task Force on Minorities that operated for six years and effectively established a broad array of minority-based roundtables to act as advocates for their respective members. A Task Force on Diversity was formed in 1997 and issued its final report and recommendations in 1999. Partly in response to this report, SAA Council updated a resolution prohibiting discrimination based on a number of minority classifications (and this list continues to grow—the definition was most recently expanded in February 2009). In 2003, a standing Diversity Committee was created, and in 2005, diversity was identified as one of three strategic priorities for the profession.[15]

One should note, however, that evaluating diversity across a profession can be a tricky endeavor. A professional organization has authority over its own organization and can provide leadership to its members but has little authority to make substantive changes within the organizations that make up its membership—a high carrot-to-stick ratio, so to speak. That said, most public institutions (government agencies and colleges and universities) as well as many companies have similar diversity programs in place.

Having a program in place does not necessarily equate to a diverse environment. Nearly every organization in the United States talks the diversity talk pretty well. The jargon and policy structure has become nearly universal. Walking the walk, on the other hand is much less uniform. Part of this stems from the fact that so much of the focus of diversity efforts is on process issues instead of vision. Rather than identifying what a diverse society and profession would look like, most of the policies are reactions to issues as they occur. Consequently any discussion of diversity and the archives profession will necessarily swing back and forth between generality and anecdote.

So what are the key issues that archivists should consider? Elizabeth Adkins identifies three broad diversity categories on which to focus:

diversity in the historical record, diversity in the archival profession, and diversity in the Society of American Archivists as an organization.[16]

Diversity of the historical record is the conceptual child of several movements in historical theory. Social history and history from below were popularized in the 1960s. At the same time, postmodern theory revolutionized the way that archives were viewed, especially in their relationship to history. These movements created a need for different archival sources, notably those documenting transient social movements, marginalized communities, the poor, and other "voiceless" groups. Archivists began to call for the preservation of all sorts of different records—both in format and media and in subject matter.

As detailed in the section "Using Web 2.0 to Increase Diversity in the Archival Profession," archivists have also gone through changes in the last twenty-five years. The gender shift is perhaps the most striking, with women now constituting more than two-thirds of archivists. But other changes have occurred as well. The percentage of non-white archivists, while still extremely low compared to the general population, has more than doubled, from 2.8 percent to 7 percent. Archivists are also more educated, with nearly half of the profession holding a master's degree, compared with less than a third in the past.

While these three categories are important in any discussion of archives diversity, there is a notable absence. Where is the user of archives in this picture? The archives profession has historically been inwardly focused—on processes (like appraisal or description) or things (like manuscripts or series). While this focus has been shifting in the last two decades, there is still a critical lack of acceptance of the centrality of the user. The absence of users in a discussion of archival diversity points toward an old-school view of the archival transaction—a view that sees information flowing in one direction, from archival experts to information consumers.

This might have described the situation in the recent past, but an adequate description of the current world requires the user to have an equal stake in the information transaction. Users are demanding more and varied ways to locate, describe, and use information.

Web 2.0 and Diversity

Jack Dorsey, the creator of Twitter, tweeted the following on his way to the 140 Characters Conference: "Headed to #140conf to talk about approachability, transparency, and immediacy. Beautiful morning in NYC."[17] Twitter is one of many Web 2.0 tools currently enjoying high use levels. But people often forget that the same things that are said about Twitter or Facebook or Second Life were also said about AOL, e-mail, and Internet relay chat.[18] Web tools are usually here today, gone tomorrow. But what they do often remains through a number of iterations.

It's important to remember, as we talk about different "versions" of the web, that the mix of systems and services that make it up are in constant flux and evolution. People often date the beginnings of the web to 1992, when graphical interfaces and "What's New" listings (just imagining a daily listing of *all* new web pages is mind-boggling) came into being. The web of 1992 would not be completely unfamiliar to people today. The key concepts of linking, bookmarking, searching, and presentation have all remained. They have evolved and been augmented, but they are clearly recognizable. Change on the web is not really done in quanta; it is incremental and often in fits and starts.

There are four underlying concepts, however, that seem to drive the evolution of the web. They are key to understanding why the web matters, especially why it matters in the context of diversity. Scale, ubiquity, interactivity, and creativity are attributes of one of the largest connective mechanisms in the world. As these attributes increase, the value of that mechanism, especially as a tool for individual inclusion, increases as well.

Take scale, for instance. When it comes to networks, size really does matter and bigger is definitely better. There are a variety of laws that govern network growth. While not really laws, like Boyle's Law or Gauss's Law, they act as "rules of thumb" as David Post describes them in *In Search of Jefferson's Moose*.[19] For instance, Sarnoff's Law states that the value of a one-way communication network (in which information flows from sender to recipient) is proportional to the number of members. So as the number of members increases, the value of the network increases at the same rate (network value = n).

Metcalfe's Law proposes that this proportion in a two-way network (one in which members can be both sender and recipient) is geometric; when membership doubles, network value quadruples (network value = n^2).

And finally Reed's Law, which states that the value of a "group-forming network" (which has both two-way communication among individuals, but also multi-way communications among groups of various sizes) is hyper-geometrical (network value = 2^n). The following table illustrates the relationship between network value and member growth for the three types of networks.

Table 2

N	N^2	2^N
1	1	2
10	100	1024
50	2500	1,125,899,907,000,000
100	10000	126,765,600,000,000,000,000,000,000,000

The Internet is a hyper-geometric network. The laws above, as well as experience, explain how in less than twenty years, it has become the most valuable network in the world. As it got bigger and more valuable, more people wanted to join. The more people that joined, the bigger and more valuable it got, which caused even more people to join.

A great example is the growth in the social networking site Facebook. Formed in 2004 by a Harvard student and limited to students at high schools and universities, Facebook grew slowly at first. In 2006 it was opened to any registrant, and by early 2008 had reached 50 million users worldwide. In the next eighteen months, it grew by *200 million users* and continues to grow rapidly. Facebook has clearly benefited from growth.[20]

There are more than 250 million Internet users in North America, which is nearly 75 percent of the population.[21] While this is an immense number, the previous discussion would suggest that the Internet could become much more valuable if it expanded even further, incorporating individuals and groups who have to date not joined in for one reason or another. The value of a network is based on being as diverse (having as many unique members) as possible. In effect, network *value* is a function of network *diversity*.

Another is ubiquity. Until recently, the use of the web was restricted to computers, mostly desktop configurations, with a hardwired connection to a network. But the advent of wireless networks, and especially web-enabled cell phones, has allowed people to connect to the Internet at all hours and in most places. With the expansion of Internet services in libraries, free wireless access in a number of public and retail areas, and newer systems aimed at providing wireless access in travel vehicles like planes, trains, and buses, even people without a personal computer, a personal Internet connection, or both can now become connected to the web.

What does this mean for users? Because so many companies and organizations have stepped forward to take advantage of the mobile web, it has clearly expanded and will continue to expand the types of and availability of information and services. Anyone looking for just the right Thai restaurant in an unknown city knows how valuable it is to use a phone to look up restaurants, read some reviews, look at a map, find a transit schedule, and see where he or she is and needs to go using the global positioning feature.

Almost all major services are web-based now, and for an increasing number of people, access to these services comes via cell phone. This expanding access has the potential to increase the value of the network in general (by making the overall network larger).

Some populations, like Rwanda's, for example, are trying to build on this potential. A small land-locked country, relatively poor compared to its neighbors, Rwanda is consciously creating a communications network to include all of its citizens—based on cheap cell phones, laptops, fiber networks, and a growing technically trained cadre. It sees the key to creating a modern self-sufficient community as ubiquitous and reliable communication.

> . . . the cell phone connection works everywhere—even on winding dirt roads where there's no electricity. We could get a connection on safari in the middle of nowhere,

but we can't seem to get a good connection in our living room in the middle of San Francisco. Who's the developing nation now, America?[22]

What this really translates into is participation, or at least the opportunity for participation. Processes that were once limited by the need for a physical presence or a hardwired connection to a desktop computer can now be joined by anyone connected to the network, and that can mean almost anyone from anywhere in the world.

The third concept is interactivity. In its early days, the web was primarily used to publish static information that could be read by users. As the web matured, it increasingly supported user interactions. Today's web is heavily interactive. Commenting, tagging, user reviews, polls, and any number of technologies allow the user to participate in the information environment instead of merely viewing it.

Once again the theme here is participation. Of all of the changes that the modern web brings to archives, this one is perhaps the scariest. Archives theory is based on control. Accessioning, description, reference–these can all be seen as highly controlling actions, but it's not control for control's sake. The theory behind this control is to attach authenticity to archives, to provide users with confidence that the records used are what they purport to be.

Making this case in a world where faceless users are allowed to interact with the description of archives, or perhaps even the archives themselves, changes the nature of that authority. As Howard Rheingold points out, using the modern web requires a highly refined "crap detector."[23] Allowing people to interact with information instead of just consuming it can enhance the process, bringing new value to individuals and networks, but it can also muddy the network, reducing authority and authenticity and, perhaps, value. It certainly introduces complexity.

Consider the differences between two online encyclopedia models– *Wikipedia* and the Oregon Encyclopedia Project. In the first case, content is open for adding, editing, revising, sourcing, illustrating, and a host of other actions. In the second, articles are assigned to content experts and then edited by a small editorial board before being posted online. The first is nimble, up to date, and diverse but sometimes inaccurate, biased, and

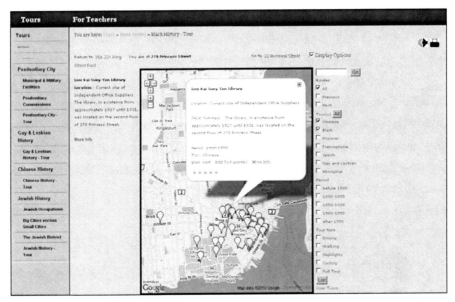

Figure 2: A screen shot of the location description for the Low Kai Suey Yen Library, at http://www.stoneskingston.ca.

incomplete. The latter is authoritative and complete but slow, prone to outdatedness, and biased in its own way. Both models work, but in a large network looking for diversity, the open model of *Wikipedia*, with its focus on interactivity and recursive user revision, is much more useful.[24]

And finally, the web is more and more about creativity. Some of this creativity is in the content itself. There are a lot more people populating it with blog posts, tweets, pictures, audio, and video (the variety of content created for YouTube alone warrants an essay of its own). But even more so are the creative ways in which people use and present the information.

Take, for instance, the mashup "Stones: A Guide to the Social History of Kingston." (See Figure 2.)[25] It uses a mix of archival documents and images, Google map technology, audio recordings, and text to create both an instructional tool and a tour guide to the history of Kingston, Ontario. Available in both English and French, it especially focuses on the histories of four minority groups: blacks, Chinese, gay people and lesbians, and Jewish people. A person could access this on a smart phone and walk through the city viewing locations from any or all of the tours, while listening to the audio tour guide, and reading background documentation. The creative use of sources and maps allows people to access information useful to them from varied contexts and detail.

You can see how scale, ubiquity, interactivity, and creativity have increased the usefulness and value of the web to an increasingly diverse population. So return to the three general areas where archives and diversity hold common course—archival sources, archival users, and the archival profession. What is the web doing to expand diversity in these areas and what more could it be doing?

The Challenge of Web 2.0 for the Archives, or Diversity in the Historical Record

For much of this country's history, the sources that mattered to historians were usually the records of literate, propertied, white men. This was especially true of the records collected by the nascent archives profession at the end of the last century. These were primarily the records of either government or the records of "great men." The people collecting them were looking to preserve the history of the United States as they knew it—a history of the people in power and the institutions they established.

Of course, there were records that had been collected and preserved by all sorts of organizations, institutions, and individuals documenting a broad range of American life and culture that did not fit this description—religious groups, minorities, the counter-culture, and pop culture, to name a few. But their records were unknown to and unused by all but a few mainstream researchers.

The mainstream view, while challenged by professional historians in the aftermath of World War II, was still dominant as late as the bicentennial celebration in 1976. That perception and bias has been changing. As it has changed, the need to identify, collect, preserve, and promote archives of different types and of different sources has become crucial, both for the adequate and accurate documentation of the full breadth of American society, as well as making the records useful to a much broader audience.

What Web 2.0 has done is to increase the number, volume, and influence of the "voices" archives need to capture. One of the most poignant examples is the role that Twitter played in Iranian protests over voting issues associated with the June 2009 presidential election. As the current regime attempted to regulate media coverage, Iranian protestors turned to Twitter to make their case known to both the outside world and to each other. An *Al Jazeera* report details the methods protestors used to circumvent governmental blockages of social networking tools. As one commentator noted, calling this the first "Twitter Revolution" diminishes the personal courage taken by people to protest. But the role of social media in *documenting* those protests and *communicating* their message cannot be understated.[26] In fact, the role of Twitter was seen as so crucial as to cause the U.S. State Department to call for Twitter to postpone a planned upgrade so that its service would not be interrupted.[27] And it is not just Twitter that served in this particular context—blogs, Facebook, and cell phone texting were equally vital in telling the story.

Another example of a "voice" given volume by Web 2.0 tools is Chris Crocker. The twenty-one-year-old Internet "edutainer" is the eighteenth most viewed YouTube vlogger (or video-blogger) ever, with more than 153 million views. He has used the Internet as a way to both inform about the nature of his world, respond to attacks on his lifestyle, and connect with others with similar sensibilities.[28] And while the jury is still out about whether Chris will escape from a place "which he hates, and which hates him," it is clear that the web has given him a voice, a way to record what he sees and to share that voice with the rest of the world:

> There was a time, not so long ago, when even Chris Crocker could not have been Chris Crocker—could not have sat in the Bible Belt and downloaded news of the wider, gay-tolerant world and, in response, uploaded his singularly bizarre and angry take on gay life and his intolerant town.
>
> In that time before YouTube and MySpace and Internet connections in rural America, this, too, could not have happened: I could not have become one of Chris Crocker's MySpace friends, which I did shortly after watching "Bitch, Please." I could not, the next day, have sent Chris a MySpace message in an attempt to figure out who the heck he was. And I could not have learned, heartbreakingly, that Chris is not some art

student in Manhattan, as I'd initially guessed—and, I suppose, on some level, hoped—but rather a 19-year-old trapped in a stifling Southern town that he hates, and which seems to hate him.[29]

This story is repeated every day from nearly every combination of human attributes one could imagine. The web has moved to more fully democratize the human record than any invention since the printing press. While it is not complete—witness the number of people who are not online—it has allowed individuals to both locate information of value to them and to create and present unique and personal information.

To create an accurate record of the times in which we live, archivists must develop methods for both the identification and preservation of these new types of records. If the Chris Crockers of the world are to be heard beyond this generation, archivists must begin collecting this information and preserving it so that future generations will also be able to see and understand these times.

"We have the power to make voices heard that have never been heard before," said Stacey Monk, founder of Epic Change and TweetsGiving.[30] These voices are coming from different people than those usually involved in the documentation of society. There are as many as 12 million active blogs in the United States. These aspiring Pepys are creating a record far more diverse than any that has existed to date. The Storycorps program has digitally recorded more than 50,000 stories told by everyday Americans across the country and broadcasts selected stories through podcasting and a regular feature on NPR.[31] These examples are part of a larger trend to create and preserve stories from a much broader group of people than has ever been done before.

The reality is that the combination of diverse tools and diverse people is creating a record that allows almost any story to be told. Seth Godin states, "The word *blog* is irrelevant. What's important is that it is now common, and will soon be expected, that every intelligent person (and quite a few unintelligent ones) will have a media platform where they share what they care about with the world."[32]

But if this expanding chorus of voices is to be heard by future generations, it must be preserved, and so archivists need to be more aggressive in their efforts both to identify new sources of relevant materials and in their efforts to collect and preserve them. Even more so than with traditional records, archivists will have to be proactive in these efforts. In addition to the existing issues inherent with electronic records—media and format stability, metadata standards, and descriptive methods—Web 2.0 brings its own set of issues. For example, commercial sites like Flickr and YouTube are great at doing the things they were built to do, like sharing, commenting, saving favorites, and uploading, but they provide no guarantees ensuring long-term preservation, providing context, and identifying records with long-term value. That is the job of archivists.

Archivists' commitment to diversity requires them to include Web 2.0 records in their collection policies, their documentation strategies, and their appraisal guidelines. The inclusion of the new forms in the documentary record is crucial in presenting a true and whole picture of our society and culture.

Leveraging the Power of the Web, or Increasing the Diversity of Archives Users

As any good archivist will tell you, archives are meaningless in their own right. They only have meaning in their relationships to human beings. In other words, people using archives is the existential act that justifies their preservation. A central tenet of archival ethics relates to access:

> Archivists strive to promote open and equitable access to their services and the records in their care without discrimination or preferential treatment, and in accordance with legal requirements, cultural sensitivities, and institutional policies. Archivists recognize their responsibility to promote the use of records as a fundamental purpose of the keeping of archives. Archivists may place restrictions on access for the protection of privacy or confidentiality of information in the records.[33]

While this clearly puts access into a central role for archivists, it does not indicate how (beyond the somewhat platitudinal nod to "open and equitable" and "without discrimination or preferential treatment") that access should occur.

In the past, many archivists saw their role as providing the basic information necessary for "serious researchers." Historians, graduate students, journalists—anyone performing traditional scholarly tasks—were often seen as the best examples of why archives existed. There is certainly nothing wrong with this role. The use of archives to underpin formal stories provides a factual and authoritative foundation to central cultural narratives.

As awareness and understanding of archives has increased in recent years, other users and uses of them have appeared. Many of these uses are neither scholarly nor traditional. There is a thriving business in graphical reproductions of archives, especially public archives. Photographs, trademarks, letterhead, maps, and other image-friendly records have been converted to picture books, notecards, and frameable art.

In a provocative article in *Harper's Magazine*, Jacques Barzun discusses the use of pop culture as a necessary element in the development of "high" culture. In discussing Demotica, the muse of popular culture, he concludes that

> In any case, "the world of knowledge" is not something in a warehouse. Knowledge lives by being known, not stored. Like religion, like popular culture, it is a possession held in common as widely as possible.[34]

The movies and jazz are seen as nonthreatening, broadly used "lowbrow" arts that can create awareness of and interest in more sophisticated forms of art.

In a similar vein, McMennamins, a company in Portland, Oregon, that restores and repurposes historic properties, recently held a ninety-fifth birthday bash for the Crystal Ballroom. The all-day event included wine, beer, and spirits tastings; a variety of local bands playing while people of all ages danced on the historic dance floor; scavenger hunts for kids; and exhibits of old rock posters and other ephemera. But they also had tours led by their historian, handouts detailing the history of the property, and information about specific historic preservation techniques used on the property. All of this was their way of complying with their opening day requirements as a landmark on the National Historic Register.

So what do art in a casino and parties in a bar have to do with diversity in the users of archives? And how does this relate to the web in any way?

In very different ways, Barzun and McMennamins present the case that you can use nontraditional, fun ways of presenting culture to the general public as a sort of gateway drug to a deeper and more meaningful way of seeing its relevance to their lives. By couching art as casino decoration and historic preservation as a way to have fun with your kids, these institutions are bringing a whole new set of people into the world of culture.

Archivists can take a cue from this. There has long been this underlying assumption that archives, because of their unique nature and importance to our society, are also wrapped in a certain gravitas. All one has to do is see the semi-religious nature of something like the National Archives' Charters of Freedom exhibit to see a fairly traditional method of treating them. Much of this often translates into online web presences that mirror traditional views. *Important information is presented to a receptive audience in the hopes that they will learn something.* While not a bad thing and often well done, this is mostly preaching to the choir. The people using these services already understand and value archives and culture. If archivists want to expand and diversify their user bases, however, they need to start thinking of new ways to interact with people.

The uses of social networking tools, blogs, Flickr, and YouTube by archivists and archives discussed throughout this book are clear attempts to bring archival collections to the attention of new audiences. But archivists and archives can do more. The web is brimming with people familiar with nontextual sources—pictures, videos, podcasts, and other audio-visual materials. Archivists have been pretty good about putting these materials online as resources (via tools like Flickr and YouTube). Archivists have not been as good at using these methodologies to bring a new generation into the archives. The people growing up today are dependent on cell phones, like free media, spend a lot of time on Facebook (or similar social networking sites), enjoy gaming, and find viral marketing the only acceptable kind.

Archivists can ignore these kinds of trends and try to enforce their conceptions of the proper way to conduct outreach, advocacy, and marketing. But that will only bring in the usual suspects. To bring in a new generation of users, archivists need to be willing both to monitor new web technologies but to expand their expertise to Internet marketing, cell phone applications, and even gaming. This requires work and an openness to change that is unsettling, but the rewards are the inclusion of a large segment of users that can use the resources archives have to more fully participate in society.

Building on the Web 2.0 ethos, archivists must strive to not only bring new users into the archives but also to support efforts of communities to document their own history and build their own archives. Take the Manilatown Archival Project, a community archives dedicated to San Francisco's Manilatown neighborhood specifically and to the Filipino diaspora generally. The project promotes its collections via a blog (hosted at no cost by Blogger), which enables the project to publish not only basic contact information and blog posts (with commenting capabilities) but also link to digitized archives, finding aids, and "solidarity sites," as well as links to Manilatown materials on YouTube and Facebook—a plethora of resources for anyone looking to connect to this small, precise community. The connection it provides for community members, as well as a window for to the community for outsiders, would have been difficult, if not impossible, in a pre-web world and rudimentary at best in the early "push-only" versions of the web.

The website for the Royal Australian Air Force School, Penang, site is another example of the creation of a virtual community.[35] The RAAF School site is based on building connections among people with ties to the now-closed school. The site hosts a forum where people can reminisce or plan reunions or discuss the weather. It allows uploading photos as well as commentary. It provides institutional history and personal contacts. Some might claim that it is not an archives and certainly not a professional one. Maybe not, but the creation and preservation of a body of documentation about an organization and its members, describing it, and making it accessible sounds very archives-like. The tools of the modern web allow the creation of collaboratively documented history by a community that does not have to be physically proximate; it encourages, by its very nature, diverse participation.

A key component of these sorts of community-sponsored representations, as well as many of the Web 2.0 tools used by archives, is their interactive nature. People are free both to write and to comment on blog posts, start discussions on social networking sites, post documents, and engage in dialog about the archives that are presented there. A great example of this is the use of tagging/folksonomy, seen most prominently on Flickr but also appearing on a growing number of online catalogs. By allowing users to directly participate in the description of archives, they are expanding its searchability to groups who might not normally find material that has been meticulously cataloged using professional thesauri. While some do not believe this is useful and that allowing user tagging clutters up and devalues archival collections,[36] this is exactly the kind of participation that archives should encourage to both expand the use of collections (through the creation of additional access points) and also to foster more engaged window users.

While this can offer a sense of being some sort of passing fad or "feel good" activity, there are very tangible benefits to both the users and the archives. Many users, unfamiliar at first with archives, see how they can be used to support their individual and community histories and meet their own needs, both personal and professional. And the archives gains an army of people who want to help them describe, contextualize, repurpose, and consume the information in their records. Working *with*, not *against*, people who want to contribute to the archives and create their own collections allows archivists to more fully realize their professed goal of fully documenting the human story.

Using Web 2.0 to Increase Diversity in the Archival Profession

If a person were to rely on generalities, the average archivist would be a middle-aged white woman, similar to the stereotypical cardigan-and-glasses-wearing librarian, or maybe even Jocasta Nu, head librarian of the Jedi Archives.[37] Of course, generalities like this don't present a complete picture of the archival profession, the demographics of which are constantly changing. It does however, point toward one of the key issues facing the profession—the continual need to make the profession relevant to the public it serves.

As mentioned earlier, there are a number of statistical realities that have been documented in recent archival literature, most notably the A*CENSUS.[38] While there is too much detail to report here, there are several key concepts that emerge.

First, the profession is overwhelmingly white. In the A*CENSUS, 87.8 percent of respondents self-identified as white. But even this number is misleading. The total percentage of archivists who self-identified as Native American, Pacific Islander, Latino/Hispanic, African American, Alaska Native, and Asian combined totaled 8.3 percent. No one category in this group exceeded 3 percent.

Compare this with the current census number for the United States. Whites make up 80 percent of the U.S. population. Non-Hispanic whites make up two-thirds of the population. Hispanics (15.1 percent), blacks (12.8 percent), Asians (4.4 percent), and Native Peoples (1.2 percent) make up the remainder.[39]

The thing that jumps out is just how white the profession is, including nine out of ten archivists. This comes at the expense of significant underrepresentations of both blacks and Hispanics—12.8 percent and 15.1 percent of the U.S. population, respectively, but only 2.8 percent and 2.1 percent of the population of archivists. More importantly, these sectors of the population are growing quickly. Within 25 years, these two groups will constitute nearly 45 percent of the American population or roughly the same percentage as non-Hispanic whites.

In addition to being largely white, the profession is also predominantly female, educated, and middle-aged. One of the most startling changes in the profession reported by A*CENSUS is the flip in gender prevalence. Fifty years ago one-third of archivists were women. Twenty-five years ago that number had risen to about half. Currently, that number is around two-thirds.[40] And of the archivists surveyed under age thirty, this number moves toward 80 percent.[41] This shift in the composition of the profession has been an important and underexamined change, especially when compared to the roughly equal number of men and women in the United States.

Of the archivists surveyed in the A*CENSUS, nearly 80 percent have a master's degree of some sort. This compares with roughly 10 percent of the American public. Many see the requirement of a master's degree as fundamental to the creation and maintenance of a professional class of archivists. On the other hand, Tony Greiner in a 2008 *Library Journal* article makes the case that the requirement of an advanced degree as the entry-level degree for the library profession may be an impediment to diversity. His case is backed in part by numbers in a 2009 AFL/CIO fact sheet on library workers that shows that while 13.8 percent of librarians are minorities, more than 20 percent of library technicians are. [42]

The fact that only 7 percent of archivists are under the age of 30 is not really surprising, given the requirement in many settings for an advanced degree. It is, however an important number. If you peg the birth year of digital natives at 1980, you get just over 40 percent of the U.S. population— and only 7 percent of its archivists. Add to this the fact that the A*CENSUS identified the median age of archivists *entering* the profession as 44.3 years old (and the median age of archivists in general as nearly 50).

Clearly, the archival profession does not mirror the characteristics of the population. If archival programs really want to compete with other information professionals in an increasingly bleak budgetary environment, they had better figure out effective ways to recruit archivists with diverse perspectives, able to relate to the 40 percent of the population that is under 30, to the person of color majority in the making and to the broad individual variety that exists in the United States today.

But how can the archival profession make itself more diverse? Just hoping for and talking about the need for a more diverse profession will not make it happen. While there is a complex set of factors that work together to determine populations of professions, I propose three areas, all supported by the application of Web 2.0 tools, which would make a good start.

First, the profession should look closely at its recruitment methods. As recently as 2008, SAA intended to recruit minority students to graduate programs using a paper brochure distributed to college and university recruitment officers. Feedback from students and staff indicated that these would be virtually ignored—that students would prefer online and interactive information. In fact, it would make even more sense to work toward attracting students at the undergraduate and even high school level. Using social networking tools that relate archives to the active and important maintenance of minority communities could direct students toward careers in archives at an earlier age.

Second, and closely related, the profession should seek to expand its notion of what an archivist is. There are a large number of people working in community-based settings, paraprofessionals whose duties include managing archival records and often providing a broad array of reference services to them. The profession could choose to embrace this highly diverse group as fellow archivists. While this would challenge some notions of professionalism, it would also immediately provide broad diversity to the profession as well as a wealth of expertise about highly specialized and geographically focused collections. The use of social networking sites, like the Lone Arrangers site,[43] for instance, could be used to allow interaction among both professional and paraprofessional archivists—broadening subject expertise but also allowing for more creativity in collection development, access strategies, exhibits, and other archival activities.

Third, the profession should seriously consider the impediment to diversity inherent in the requirement of graduate degrees for entry-level positions. While not negating the importance of graduate archival education in the development of archival theory and practice, this would consider the reality that there is much archival work that can be performed by a person with a general education and a commitment to ongoing training by hiring institutions. The idea of using a variety of Web 2.0 tools as inexpensive, or even free, tools for continuing education is a direct challenge to the university system, but recent surveys indicate that online education is as successful or more so than traditional schools. It's not hard to imagine the application of open-source software models to educational paradigms.

Again, this would challenge conceptions of professionalism. In a variety of other American professions with very popular graduate degrees—education, business, health, public administration, and engineering—however, an undergraduate degree can also be used as entry point to the profession. It is hard to see what qualities archivists need that differentiate their educational requirements from these other professions.

Flexible, open to user needs, collaborative, malleable, dynamic—if this is the type of professional desired, it makes sense to look for them in this kind of environment.

Community and Connection

Archives, and especially archivists, are connectors. In their best incarnations they help connect people to themselves, to their pasts, and to each other. As noted above, archives can provide people with the resources to see who they are and to help present that self to the world. But archives also can put that knowledge into historical perspective. Humans do not drop into this world fully formed.

The web is designed, both by intent and by action, as a means for connection. As mentioned earlier, its value is proportional to the number of people it can connect. But the reality is so much more human than numbers and network laws.

Multnomah County (Oregon) chair Ted Wheeler has worked to use Web 2.0 tools as a means both of creating government accountability and transparency and as a means of community building. In an interview following a series of negative reporting on his posting of a job for a social networking (SN) coordinator, he had the following comments, which I think are just as relevant for archives as for government:

> For many of these so-called "Digital Natives," social networking isn't just a tool—it's a lifestyle. As one young Facebook fan recently told me, "It's where we are. If you want to talk with us, you better be here." . . . Government leaders need to reach out to people where they are. And increasingly, they are in SN communities.
>
> The future is here. I say let's embrace it.[44]

This is a clear blueprint for change, and it really isn't so much about the technology. What it is about is the sense that decision making, diversity, and community are not things that politicians or religious leaders or government officials or *archivists* can impose on people. They are all the by-products of a new social compact that sees all voices as important.

Archivists that embrace this view and open their processes and products to a community custodianship with all their constituencies will have a much better chance for success than those who continue to try and hold on to control over them. The diversity of voices makes for a more complete record. The diversity of users means more use of archives and consequently more demand for archives and archivists.

While connective technologies are important tools, it is up to people—in this case, archivists—to actively use these tools to create and participate in communities.

Seeing the Elephant

The elephant is not a rope. Nor is it a spear. As has been seen above, diversity and Web 2.0 (and a host of other pieces, like spirituality, environmentalism, literature, peace, economics, love, etc.) are merely parts of a larger whole. It doesn't mean that they aren't important in their own right, just that they have their most complete meaning as part of something larger.

Consider another elephant. Lord Ganesha, the elephant-headed god, is the deva of intellect and wisdom. He is honored at the beginning of rituals and ceremonies and invoked as Patron of Letters during writing sessions. The *Ganesha Sahasranama* describes Ganesha's thousand names and provides an encyclopedic review of Ganesha's attributes and roles. Of these, Ganesha's most important role is as the remover of obstacles; his task in the divine scheme of things, his dharma, is to place and remove obstacles. It is his particular territory, the reason for his creation. He removes obstacles to help us achieve success and places obstacles to block negative actions.[45]

Humans have a deep-seated need to order and find meaning in their own lives. In the Declaration of Independence it's called the "pursuit of happiness." Psychologists call it *self-actualization*. Lifestyle coaches call it *empowerment*.

The evolution of both the web and diversity has been toward an empowered individual. But the future of that evolution is toward a *community* of empowered individuals. Community, like Lord Ganesha, has a variety of attributes. Archives, diversity, and the web are some of its connective attributes. Archives connect through time, diversity connects through space, and the web provides the connective tissue. When added together with other attributes, the community elephant is not a jumble of unmatched parts, but the remover of obstacles to individual fulfillment.

Notes

[1] John Saxe, "The Blind Men and the Elephant," *Clever Stories from Many Nations* (Boston: Ticknor and Fields, 1865).

[2] "List of Web Browsers," *Wikipedia*, http://en.wikipedia.org/wiki/List_of_web_browsers (accessed September 17, 2009).

[3] While somewhat dated (1999), this example from the University of Oregon is representative, even down to the water droplet background, of the general tenor of many diversity definitions. "Definition of Diversity," University of Oregon Multicultural Office, http://gladstone.uoregon.edu/~asuomca/diversityinit/definition.html (accessed September 17, 2009).

[4] The Inclusion Network provides a good background on the use of the term *inclusion*. Inclusion Network, http://www.inclusion.com/inclusion.html (accessed September 17, 2009).

[5] Society of American Archivists, "Equal Opportunity/Non-Discrimination Policy" (February 2009), http://www.archivists.org/governance/handbook/app_b.asp#equal (accessed September 17, 2009).

[6] U.S. Census Bureau, "USA State and County Quickfacts," http://quickfacts.census.gov/qfd/states/00000.html (accessed September 17, 2009). For a discussion of what that actually means, see Center for an Accessible Society, "Identity, definitions and demographics of disability," http://www.accessiblesociety.org/topics/demographics-identity/ (accessed September 17, 2009).

[7] U.S. Census Bureau, "America's Families and Living Arrangements: 2008," http://www.census.gov/population/www/socdemo/hh-fam/cps2008.html (accessed September 17, 2009).

[8] U.S. Census Bureau, "USA State and County Quickfacts," http://quickfacts.census.gov/qfd/states/00000.html (accessed September 17, 2009).

[9] A*CENSUS results, data, and a variety of reports and interpretive materials can be found at Society of American Archivists, "Archival Census & Education Needs Survey in the United States," http://www.archivists.org/a-census/ (accessed September 17, 2009).

[10] "Religious self-identification of the U.S. adult population: 1990, 2001, 2008," *Wikepedia*, http://en.wikipedia.org/wiki/Demographics_of_the_United_States#Religious_self-identification_of_the_U.S._adult_population:_1990.2C_2001.2C_2008 (accessed September 17, 2009).

[11] GLBTQ, "Demographics," http://www.glbtq.com/social-sciences/demographics.html (accessed September 17, 2009).

[12] U.S. Department of Veterans Affairs, "Veteran Population 2007," http://www1.va.gov/vetdata/page.cfm?pg=15 (accessed September 17, 2009).

[13] U.S. Department of Education, "National Assessment of Adult Literacy," http://nces.ed.gov/naal/kf_demographics.asp (accessed September 17, 2009).

[14] The use of the term "archives profession" in the context of this essay primarily includes U.S. archivists; much of the statistical information in this essay is based on work done either through the A*CENSUS project or by the Society of American Archivists (SAA), the largest professional archivist organization in the United States.

[15] This is a compression of the outstanding review of diversity in SAA written by Elizabeth Adkins, "Our Journey Towards Diversity—and a Call to (More) Action," *American Archivist* 71 (Spring/Summer 2008): 21–49.

[16] Adkins, "Our Journey," 24.

[17] Jack Dorsey tweet, Twitter, June 16, 2009, 5:30 a.m. PDT.

[18] Listserv, a trademarked software for running e-mail lists whose name is often used to refer to the lists themselves, was once a "killer app" that tempted many professors to try the Internet in the first place.

[19] A detailed review of networks can be found in David G. Post's *In Search of Jefferson's Moose: Notes on the State of Cyberspace* (New York: Oxford University Press, 2009), 46–49.

[20] "The Road to 200 Million," *New York Times*, http://www.nytimes.com/imagepages/2009/03/29/business/29face.graf01.ready.html; and "Press Room Statistics," Facebook, http://www.facebook.com/press/info.php?statistics (both accessed September 17, 2009).

[21] "World Internet Users and Population Stats," Internet World Stats, http://www.internetworldstats.com/stats.htm (accessed September 17, 2009). Web usage is a little trickier. Parks Associates has shown a decline in households without Internet access but still shows one in five heads of U.S. households has never used the web. Parks Associates, "One in Five U.S. Households U.S. Has Never Used E-mail," http://www.parksassociates.com//blog/article/one-in-five-u-s--households-has-never-used-e-mail- (accessed September 17, 2009). Pew reports similar numbers in a variety of reports at http://www.pewinternet.org/Static-Pages/Data-Tools/Download-Data/Trend-Data.aspx (accessed September 17, 2009).

[22] Sara Lacy, "How to Cross the Digital Divide, Rwanda Style," *TechCrunch*, http://www.techcrunch.com/2009/06/24/how-to-cross-the-digital-divide-rwanda-style/ (accessed September 17, 2009).

[23] Howard Rheingold, "Crap Detection 101," *City Brights*, http://www.sfgate.com/cgi-bin/blogs/rheingold/detail?blogid=108&entry_id=42805 (accessed September 17, 2009).

[24] See *Wikipedia* at http://www.wikipedia.org/ and Oregon Encyclopedia Project at http://www.oregonencyclopedia.org/ (both accessed September 17, 2009).

[25] The term *mashup* refers to a web page or application that combines data or functionality from two or more external sources to create a new service. "Mashup," *Wikipedia*, http://en.wikipedia.org/wiki/Mashup_(web_application_hybrid) (accessed September 17, 2009). The Stones mashup is located at http://www.stoneskingston.ca/publisher/articleview/frmArticleID/81/.

[26] Riz Kahn, "Iran's Internet Revolution," *Al Jazeera*, http://english.aljazeera.net/programmes/rizkhan/2009/06/200962281940160238.html (accessed September 17, 2009).

[27] Monica Guzman, "State Dept. to Twitter: Iran to Important, Site Fix Can Wait," *PI Blogs*, http://blog.seattlepi.com/thebigblog/archives/171381.asp (accessed September 17, 2009).

[28] "Chris Crocker (Internet Celebrity)," *Wikipedia* http://en.wikipedia.org/wiki/Chris_Crocker_(Internet_celebrity) (accessed September 17, 2009).

[29] Eli Sanders, "Escape from Real Bitch Island," *The Stranger*, http://www.thestranger.com/seattle/escape-from-real-bitch-island/Content?oid=232684 (accessed September 17, 2009).

[30] Shana Glickfield, "NextGenWeb Celebrates 'The Power of Now' at the 140 Conference," *NextGenWeb*, http://www.nextgenweb.org/home/nextgenweb-celebrates-%E2%80%9Cthe-power-of-now%E2%80%9D-at-the-140-conference (accessed September 17, 2009). Epic Change is located

at http://www.epicchange.org/.

[31] *Storycorps*, http://storycorps.org/ (accessed August 30, 2010).

[32] Seth Godin, quoted in the slideshow "What the F*ck is Social Media?", http://www.slideshare.net/mzkagan/what-the-fk-is-social-media-one-year-later# (accessed September 17, 2009).

[33] Society of American Archivists, "Code of Ethics, Section 6," http://www.archivists.org/governance/handbook/app_ethics.asp (accessed September 17, 2009).

[34] Jacques Barzun, "The Tenth Muse: Who Is Demotica, What Is She?", *Harper's Magazine* (September 2001): 73–80.

[35] *The Story of RAAF School, Penang* is a school blog located at http://www.raafschoolpenang.com/index.html. There are thousands of school sites, but the author of this essay has a connection to this one; that's really how Web 2.0 often works.

[36] Larry Cebula, "Lick This: LOC, FLickr, and the Limits of Crowdsourcing," *Northwest History*, http://northwesthistory.blogspot.com/2009/06/lick-this-loc-flickr-and-limits-of.html (accessed September 17, 2009). Larry Cebula's post is representative of a stream of thought related to the value of tagging.

[37] "Jocasta Nu," *Wikia*, http://starwars.wikia.com/wiki/Jocasta_Nu (accessed September 17, 2009).

[38] For an analysis of the results of the A*CENSUS, see the Fall/Winter 2006 issue of *American Archivist*.

[39] U.S. Census Bureau, "USA State and County Quickfacts," http://quickfacts.census.gov/qfd/states/00000.html (accessed September 17, 2009).

[40] Adkins, "Our Journey Towards Diversity," 26.

[41] Victoria Irons Welch, "A*CENSUS: A Closer Look," *American Archivist* 69 (Fall/Winter 2006): 331.

[42] Tony Greiner, "Backtalk: Diversity and the MLS," *Library Journal*, http://www.libraryjournal.com/article/CA6551177.html (accessed September 17, 2009). Greiner is making the case for the librarian profession, but given the similarity in demographics and degree requirements, it isn't a stretch to make a similar case for archivists. See AFL-CIO statistics at http://www.dpeaflcio.org/programs/factsheets/fs_2009_library_workers.htm#_edn13 (accessed September 17, 2009).

[43] The Lone Arrangers social networking site is at http://lonearrangers.ning.com/.

[44] See the full interview at http://www.blueoregon.com/2009/06/can-twitter-social-networking-lead-to-a-renaissance-in-civic-engagement.html (accessed September 17, 2009).

[45] For a basic overview of Ganesha, see "Ganesha," *Wikipedia*, http://en.wikipedia.org/wiki/Ganesha (accessed December 22, 2010).

Archives 101 in a 2.0 World:
The Continuing Need for Parallel Systems

Randall C. Jimerson

The exciting promises of Web 2.0 applications have already begun to change how many archivists engage a new generation of researchers. However, the legacy of archival theory and praxis remains central to *why* we practice our craft and how archives benefit people throughout society. The lessons learned through traditional archival education remain valid, and the description and access systems employed in the past continue to be needed to provide services for many users of archives. Although Web 2.0 represents tremendous opportunities, we must remember that these resources will not solve all needs and are not available to everyone. The Internet and its many social networking features still do not provide access to all available sources of information. Many people lack the motivation or the connectivity to become active participants in online culture. As archivists begin to embrace new 2.0 technology and to explore its possibilities, it remains essential to focus on our central purposes: ensuring adequate documentation of institutions, people, and society and serving the needs of a wide variety of users. While archivists must become skillful users of the tools we need to keep in touch with tech-savvy online audiences, we must also be cognizant of the groups who are not represented in this online world. We can embrace the new 2.0 world without abandoning our professional heritage and roots.

Technology Is Only a Tool

The promises of new technology systems such as Web 2.0 applications offer seemingly irresistible temptations to archivists to enter this world of blogs, wikis, social tagging, Flickr, and social networking. As the essays in this volume demonstrate, many archivists already embrace these methods for responding to the brave new world of twenty-first-century technology. This is still a time of experimentation, testing boundaries, thinking creatively, and seeking new ways to improve the profession's responsiveness to its audiences. Using these tools, archivists can reach new constituencies, particularly the younger "digital natives" who generally bypass traditional forms of information gathering and research. As archivists respond to these challenges and opportunities, they need to think clearly about the purposes of archives, the societal needs they meet, the clienteles they serve, and the impact of new tools and new methods on the central principles of archival theory and praxis.

It is essential for archivists to remember that Web 2.0 technology is a tool, not a goal. As intriguing and addictive as these Web 2.0 apps may be, archivists must regard them as professional tools, not toys.[1] It is fine to play with blogs, Facebook, and other apps in our personal lives. But using them in the archives should be done in mindful recognition of their usefulness in achieving professional goals.

Technology has always driven the forms of human communications, records creation, and access to information.[2] The computer age, Internet revolution, and Web 2.0 have each transformed our methods of recording and transmitting information and knowledge. News reports often present the Internet revolution as unprecedented in human history. Yet significant eras of technological change—as profound and pervasive as the computer age—also occurred with the origins of writing, the development of cuneiform symbols and clay tablets, the introduction of the codex as an early form of the modern book, the invention of movable type and printing, and the Industrial Revolution.[3] Each new form of communication technology created disruption and transformed how people communicated. However, the purposes served by these changing technologies have remained relatively constant. Since ancient times, human beings have felt a compelling need to remember legal, financial, operational, and historical transactions and events. Electronic records and Web 2.0 applications are simply a new generation of tools with which people record, organize, and manage their interactions and ideas.

The Societal Purposes of Archives

The starting point for considering adoption of any of these Web 2.0 applications and the social and intellectual philosophy underlying social networking should be a reanalysis of the societal purposes of archives and the needs they meet for people of all backgrounds and social groupings. What is the role of archives in society? What benefits do they (or should they) provide? To whom? How can technology support these goals? If records were simply aggregates of data or information, information technology experts could manage them effectively. However, when records are needed for long periods of time as evidence or as historical documentation, archivists and records managers need to contribute their knowledge of authenticity, reliability, and context.

Services and Benefits

Archives provide essential services and benefits for society. Individually, archival repositories may meet only one or more of these needs, but collectively, the diversity of archival institutions ensures that a broad array of goals can be met. To demonstrate the significance of archives to society, archivists need to be able to explain the purposes of archives, which they have not yet done effectively. "If society is to believe in their importance, archivists must be able to articulate their purpose clearly and meaningfully," Kent Haworth declared in 1992. "In order to communicate their purpose meaningfully archivists must first understand its meaning themselves."[3] Haworth recognized the essential value to society of the archival record, which provides "the impartial and authentic evidence of transactions, decisions, and information necessary for the sustenance of democratic societies."[5] By preserving such evidence, archives protect the legal rights of citizens and enable them to hold their public leaders—governmental, corporate, academic, religious, and institutional—accountable for their actions. When archivists support the goals of access to information, open government, and accountability, they contribute to the quest for social justice.[6]

In addition to these legal and accountability purposes of archives, they also contribute to the human need for culture and meaning. According to information scientist David M. Levy, documents enable us to create culture and "help us exert power and control, maintain relationships, acquire and preserve knowledge."[7] He declares that "documents—*all of them*—address the great existential questions of human life," by serving "as sources of stability, providing meaning, direction, and reassurance in the face of life's uncertainties."[8] This gives all documents "a sacred quality."[9] Perhaps this perspective will give archivists slogging through mountains of records or terabytes of digital data some inspiration for the work of preserving such documents.

By contributing to the care and management of cultural resources, archivists work in parallel with librarians, museum curators, and other cultural heritage professionals. They provide both secure preservation for irreplaceable documents and access by a wide range of users. Archivists thus contribute to preserving culture and enabling people to enjoy its bene-fits. This is a fundamental public interest. As the Universal Declaration of Human Rights stated in 1948 (Article 27): "Everyone has the right freely to participate in the cultural life of the community, to enjoy the arts and to share in scientific advancement and its benefits."[10] Culture is thus an essential human right. As part of each society's cultural resources, archives thereby represent part of the lasting legacy of society, which all people have a right to enjoy. "We know that we each individually will die. . . . But we have an overarching shared interest that the world of ideas will go on without us," Richard Heinberg stated in October 2009. "Cultural death— the passing of the wisdom, artistic creations, and practical knowledge of an entire people, painstakingly built up over many generations—is a loss almost too wrenching to contemplate." As Heinberg concludes, "If we want future generations to have the benefit of our achievements, we should start thinking more seriously about what to preserve, and how to preserve it."[11] This is precisely what archivists do. It is one of their most important functions—both within their repositories, and for society as a whole.

Constituencies

As archivists define the purposes that their repositories serve, they must also determine which constituencies they serve. An institutional archives might serve primarily the legal and administrative needs of the larger organization, with most of its users and clients coming from within the institution. Government archives serve both the agency staff and the public, including legal researchers, genealogists, individual citizens, among others. Manuscript collecting repositories, on the other hand, typically serve an external audience, which might comprise one or more constituent groups, such as local historians, genealogists, students, or other researchers. All too often, archivists take for granted that potential researchers will find their way to the repository or that identifying a collecting policy or archival mission statement will be sufficient to ensure public knowledge and support. However, as Timothy Ericson declares, "it is important to keep our focus on the records we are preserving and the impact they have (or may have) on the lives of people who would benefit from using them. We should bear in mind that if people do not know what archivists are, or what they do, it is simply because archivists have not touched their lives in any meaningful way."[12] Essential to this process is the archivist's effort to reach out to active constituencies and to identify and target new potential users of archival resources. The purpose of each repository derives in part from the nature of the records it manages and in part from the groups of people who use or otherwise benefit from the archives.

Goal and Policies

Once archivists have identified the purposes fulfilled by their repositories and the constituencies they serve, they develop policies and procedures to help achieve their goals. In regard to Web 2.0 applications, this is the point at which archivists must decide how technology can support the repository's mission, purpose, and objectives.

As they consider the options for adopting Web 2.0, archivists should weigh carefully the promised benefits and the potential limitations of these technologies. Because these 2.0 apps are still very new, they have only recently begun to be tested. Much of what we have to say about archival use of Web 2.0 is either speculative or based on very limited experience and small evidential samples of current practice. As Steve Bailey states, in considering how to apply Web 2.0 strategies and systems, "not only do we not currently know the answers, we are only just beginning to understand the questions."[13] Because most of the essays in this volume extol the benefits of Web 2.0, it is useful here to provide additional context and to consider some of the cautionary flags raised about the digital divide, and the challenges of applying these new technologies in archival repositories.

Promised Benefits of Web 2.0 for Archives

Accessibility and Democracy

First, some good news: Building on the concepts and applications labeled Web 2.0, using these tools promises important benefits. When (or if) realized, these benefits could greatly improve the levels of service, responsiveness, immediacy, and relevance of archives in modern society. The reorientation in archival thinking and practice proposed by those who embrace these new technologies prepares the way for a more inclusive and democratic approach to archival systems. Tim O'Reilly, an early pioneer of Web 2.0 applications, sees the Internet as a platform for "delivering software as a continually-updated service that gets better the more people use it, consuming and remixing data from multiple sources, including individual users, while providing their own data and services in a form that allows remixing by others, creating network effects through an 'architecture of participation.'"[14]

Applying Web 2.0 to archives could expand social connections directly, with minimal mediation by external experts or gatekeepers. At heart it is a democratically inspired approach to Internet use. The key concepts underlying these applications, according to Dutch-Canadian archival entrepreneur

Peter Van Garderen, are usability, openness, and community. By *openness*, he means nonproprietary software, architecture, standards, content, and sources. The concept of community emphasizes people connecting to each other, taking responsibility and ownership of web services, technology, and content.[15] Because Web 2.0 offers new ways for people to interact and to share information, it offers the possibility of reaching a more diverse audience of archives users. This can enhance social diversity by promoting a culture that is more open, creative, participatory, and nonhierarchical. Societal groups that had been marginalized by traditional approaches to archives, libraries, and museums could then employ archival resources to participate actively and contribute to the creation, preservation, and use of community memory and history.

Web 2.0 could thereby contribute to the further democratization of access to information, records, and knowledge. This is particularly true for young people, who are less and less likely to use print and documentary sources, which are the predominant staples in libraries and archives. If archivists are to connect with such an audience—both now and as they begin to reach the age at which archival sources might be more useful— archives must meet them where they are—that is, online. A 2007 marketing report found that 96 percent of U.S. teens and tweens used social networks, linking them to each other and to the only information sources they are likely to use.[16] Archivists have already seen changes in public expectations regarding access to sources and services, as researchers demand ready access to archival information, available at any time and any place.[17] As a 2004 library research report discovered, "users want granular pieces of information and data, at the moment of need, in the right format. . . . The mantra will be: 'Everything, everywhere, when I want it, *the way* I want it.'"[18] If archivists can meet these expectations, they can position their repositories to become vital hubs in the information and research networks employed by Internet-savvy users.

Empowerment

Such expanded access to archival resources can help to empower people and enhance their control over vital information and social connectivity.

In both the marketplace of consumer goods and the marketplace of ideas, people have come to expect a greater measure of control over their social interactions. According to Jeff Jarvis, this has been a central factor in the success of companies such as Google. The new relationship between customers and service providers requires openness, collaboration, and conversation.[19] Jarvis cites Google's key concepts from the company's website: "Focus on the user and all else will follow. . . . It's best to do one thing really, really well. . . . You can make money without doing evil. . . . There's always more information out there. . . . The need for information crosses all borders. . . ."[20] Adopting such concepts would change the culture of any organization, "to finally make it customer-focused and mean it," Jarvis states.[21] These observations could easily be adapted for archival repositories seeking to redefine their orientation to the public. People will only perceive archives to be relevant to their needs if archivists pay attention to their needs and interests and seek to develop good relationships with researchers and potential users.

In the public marketplace, particularly with Web 2.0, traditional approaches and the status quo are being challenged and overthrown by popular demand. This is also true in libraries, museums, archives, and records management. "Technology has profoundly shifted the balance of power away from the organization and towards the individual," English records manager Steve Bailey declares. Web 2.0 "is a technology that strips away many of the fundamental building blocks on which records management has traditionally been based and its influence is rapidly expanding beyond the walls of the organization to pervade virtually every sphere of our cultural, social and economic life."[22] The "wisdom of the crowd" has become one of the leading mantras of Web 2.0. Social networking advocates seek to replace taxonomies of information, imposed by organizations and authorities, with "folksonomies"—"bottom-up tagging done by strangers rather than expert-designed and -applied canonical classifications like the Dewey Decimal System or the Library of Congress schemes for sorting books."[23] This returns control to users of information resources. It also presumes that collectively, at least, users can provide each other with more appropriate and helpful information than can information professionals.[24]

Creativity

As archivists participate in Web 2.0, they join an online culture that breaks down barriers—or more accurately leaps across them—marked by entitlement, authority, and privilege. According to David Bollier, the Creative Commons community established through the Internet "enlivens democratic culture by hosting egalitarian encounters among strangers and voluntary associations of citizens." Web 2.0 systems "have democratized creativity on a global scale, challenging the legitimacy and power of all sorts of centralized, hierarchical institutions." Bollier contends that Internet-based innovations "proliferate with astonishing speed."[25] He sees great promise in this new approach to social networking and information exchange. "Through an open, accessible commons, one can efficiently tap into the 'wisdom of the crowd,' nurture experimentation, accelerate innovation, and foster new forms of democratic practice." Bollier adds that these online networks "capture and project people's everyday feelings, social values, and creativity onto the world stage. Never in history has the individual had such cheap, unfettered access to global audiences, big and small."[26] Behind the inflated rhetoric of such grandiose claims, however, there is a real promise of empowerment and democracy. The question is whether the proponents of this new online world can achieve their lofty goals.

Advocates of Web 2.0 celebrate its potential to foster creativity and new ways of conceptualizing human interactions. Daniel Pink proclaims that right-brain thinkers will rule the future, because their qualities of "inventiveness, empathy, joyfulness, and meaning" meet the needs of the emerging Conceptual Age better than the left-brain qualities that powered the Industrial Revolution and the Information Age.[27] This new way of thinking emphasizes synthesis rather than analysis, detects broad patterns rather than providing specific answers, identifies relationships between seemingly unrelated ideas, and combines elements to create something new.[28] Creativity and forging new relationships with others drive the new generation of thinkers. For the most part, these are the young people who grew up with computers and the Internet, often referred to as "digital natives."[29] They don't remember a time before cell phones and online communications. Multitasking comes naturally to those who spend much of their lives

online, creating "a 24/7 network that blends the human with the technical."[30] Such new forms of interaction could provide a valuable stimulus
to intellectual life and to the information professions if their promised
benefits can be realized.

Thinking Differently

Although advocates of Web 2.0 celebrate the new ways of thinking fostered
by the online environment, skeptics wonder, as Nicholas Carr asks, "Is
Google making us stupid?" The values and habits developed over centuries
of textual literacy seem to be eroding in the face of web surfing and hyper-
texting. "I'm not thinking the way I used to think," Carr lamented in a 2008
Atlantic essay. "The deep reading that used to come naturally has become
a struggle."[31] As Marshall McLuhan observed in the 1960s, media not only
supply the information for thought but also shape the process of thinking. Carr cites evidence that online reading leads to superficial scanning
for data rather than detailed examination and consideration of complex
ideas. This overturns the traditional process of scholarly research. It also
potentially undermines the archivist's emphasis on the need to understand
context and how (and why) documents and information were created.

On the other hand, Jeff Jarvis argues that blogging and other Web
2.0 systems foster creativity, collaboration, and peer review. "Thinking
differently is the key product and skill of the Google age," Jarvis asserts.[32]
Archivists contemplating the future of Web 2.0 need to consider these
factors, both in how they think about their own work and how it affects
the users of archives and hence the reference process.

Potential vs. Real Benefits

This is the key issue as archivists experiment with Web 2.0. Can we harness
the potential benefits of this new technology to achieve the promises being
made for it? As with the advent of every new technology introduced since
ancient times, there are both advocates and skeptics for Web 2.0. As Alecia
Wolf stated a few years after the Internet first reached widespread use,
"the Internet represents an exciting potential. However, at this stage in
its evolution it remains just that—only the potential to move us toward a

more egalitarian society."[33] In examining Web 2.0, as well, for now one must conclude that emphasis should be placed on the term *potential* as we consider the preliminary reports of the new technology's applications to archival practice. The promises being made for these initiatives may well produce revolutionary changes with tremendous advantages, but at the end of 2010 these results are still largely untested.

Concerns and Limitations of Web 2.0

The Digital Divide

Even more significant than concerns about how the Internet affects patterns of thought and behavior is the argument that it widens a "digital divide" between those who have access to this powerful technology and those who do not. In 1998 Bosah Ebo stated that some critics claimed that the Internet's "architecture of technology harbors an innate class bias and other nuances of power entitlements," creating a cyberghetto that trapped women, minorities, the poor, and rural residents in a technology backwater.[34] The impact of this new technology on social justice concerns remained unclear. On one hand, the Internet promised "a windfall of publicly accessible information and a barrier-free terrain of social associa-tions." Yet it could also result in "the marginalization of the underclass, the subliterate, minorities, and women."[35] Alecia Wolf likewise warned of the emergence of two technologically separate societies and stated that the disfranchised had little voice in shaping policies beneficial to themselves. The Internet's promise as a social equalizer seemed "only to equalize the differences among young, college-educated, middle-class white males."[36]

Those with the education and abilities to use computer technology clearly possess significant advantages in the online environment. Yet rapid changes in technology require funds to upgrade equipment and continu-ous learning to keep pace. Poor households will find it ever more diffi-cult to remain plugged in to online resources. In 1998 Rebecca Carrier warned, "unless measures are taken to increase information access to non-elite members of society, the distance between the information-rich and -poor will continue to grow."[37] More than a decade later, the emerging technologies of Web 2.0 raise some of the same concerns, with the answers still unclear.

In 2002 Marilyn Deegan and Simon Tanner argued that although the Internet provided significant benefits for many people and transformed modern libraries, the promise of cheap access for all still could not reach many social strata and many parts of the world due to political, financial, and cultural barriers. "The digital divide exists and could further disadvantage the poor, the undereducated and those in developing countries as the better-off, the better educated and the economically developed race into the digital future," they asserted.[38] Deegan and Tanner found some hope in creative efforts to bridge the digital divide. For example, in India, where only 2 percent of the population had access to computers, the post office had set up more than 200 e-post centers linked to more than 500 distribution centers. In many developing countries Internet cafés offered low-cost access, although they were mainly confined to cities. However, the authors concluded, "The digital divide will not just be about access but also about the resources available at each access."[39] Providing computers would be only a first step. Training, tech support, and other resources must also be available to those on the margins of the technological society.

It is impossible to obtain precise measurements of the percentage of the world's population that has adequate access to and ability to use the Internet or the newer and more sophisticated Web 2.0 applications. The same is true for access to libraries and, even more, to archives. Jean-Claude Guédon of the University of Montreal estimates that only 20 percent of the world's population benefit from good distribution of the world's available knowledge.[40] There have been several projects designed to provide computers for schoolchildren in poor districts in the United States and in developing countries around the world. For example, in addition to the initiative in India cited by Deegan and Tanner, in 2005 Nicholas Negroponte, former director of the MIT Media Lab, announced the One Laptop Per Child project. The project's goal is to provide 1 million hardy, portable computers to children in the developing world. However, as Jonathan Zittrain points out, several such prominent and well-funded projects designed to bridge the digital divide—including the Volkscomputer in Brazil, the VillagePDA, the Ink, and the Simputer in India—have "fared poorly, stuck at some phase of development or production." Furthermore, there seems to be a possibility that, as computer scientist Gene Spafford warns, "Access to eBay and YouTube isn't going to give them clean water and freedom from disease. But it may help breed resentment and discontent where it hasn't been before."[41] Thus, there may be significant unintended consequences from the introduction of advanced technology in underdeveloped countries, further widening the digital divide. However, mobile devices such as cell phones may make web access, including social networking media, more affordable in the third world.

As archivists consider adopting or expanding their use of Web 2.0 applications, they should consider both the promised benefits and opportunities and also the potential consequences of new technologies. "Web 2.0 presents great opportunities for archivists to appraise/document/acquire voices from those sectors in a society whose stories never before got to archives," Canadian archivist Terry Cook states. "But even Web 2.0 platforms still leave the voices of those without access to or comfort with the technology outside this new world, as indeed their voices (not as they might be heard/reflected in government or church reports) were absent in the traditional paper archival world."[42] Cook does not discourage using Web 2.0 applications, but he does offer a valuable reminder that archivists should remain vigilant to prevent such technology from further separating the information haves from the have-nots.

The Role of Gatekeepers

A second challenge of applying Web 2.0 to archives is finding a balance of power between archivists as gatekeepers and users of archives who seek direct accessibility and control over what they see, when, and how. Despite signs of progress toward greater access, "web pages are nonetheless a very powerful form of mediation and gatekeeping," according to archival educator Helen Tibbo.[43] Many researchers will access archival information through the website rather than visiting the physical archives repository. To understand archival sources fully, they need to be seen in relation to other documentation, not as isolated bits of information. Reliance on websites for research access makes archives available to "new generations of users, with fundamentally different perspectives on the past, who will approach archives through computer interfaces rather than visiting physical archives and interacting with tangible documents."[44] The context provided in archival finding aids and the reference guidance required for evaluating digitized documents are difficult to provide on websites.

The essays in this volume highlight creative approaches to using Web 2.0 systems and applications for archival outreach and user services. This alters the role of archivists in the reference process and creates challenges for providing context and guidance in those using virtual archives rather than tangible sources. Elizabeth Yakel observes that archivists who employ interactive access tools "have ceded some control over these core archival functions to their visitors" and are "reimagining the ways in which researchers can interact with the archival record and with fellow travelers in the virtual archives."[45] This partial surrender of power is not easy for many archivists, but it offers some hope for improved accessibility and use of archives by people from all walks of life, including those who have seldom used traditional archives in the past. To employ archival sources effectively, however, researchers need to understand archival systems, principles, practices, and institutions—what Yakel calls "archival intelligence."[46] Terry Cook also advocates ceding some of the gatekeeping power to users, while at the same time recognizing the potential dangers of unmediated access to and use of archival sources. "As for Web 2.0 and description and reference, the interactivity possibilities are exciting, and archivists will need to let go of the monopoly power they have (and often deny!) over these processes," he argues, "as well as adopt monitoring/policing roles to make sure abuse and abusive comments (neo-Nazis, racists, etc.) are not permitted to be socially tagged to descriptions and finding aids."[47] Even in the open, user-oriented Archives 2.0, some of the archivist's traditional gatekeeper role must still persist. Archival institutions cannot allow abusive behavior or unchecked hate speech.

These discussions about the gatekeeping role of archivists echo debates throughout the field of information technology. In *The Cult of the Amateur: How Today's Internet Is Killing Our Culture*, Andrew Keen complains about politicians using YouTube to trash their opponents and media companies using the same web service to broadcast "reviews" of their own products. "The irony of a 'democratized' media is that some content producers have more power than others," he warns. "In a media without gatekeepers, where one's real identity is often hidden or disguised, the truly empowered are the big companies with the huge advertising budgets. In theory, Web 2.0 gives amateurs a voice. But in reality it's often those with the loudest, most convincing message, and the most money to spread it, who are being heard."[48] Some form of gatekeeping is necessary to filter public messages and protect consumers. In a *Wall Street Journal* debate with Keen, David Weinberger agreed that on the web "because anyone can contribute and because there are no centralized gatekeepers, there's too much stuff and too many voices." However, he argued that instead of imposing external gatekeeping mechanisms and powers, we can rely on site managers such as Amazon, eBay, and *Wikipedia* to provide internal policing of web-based information sources. If such commercial systems are not adequate, then community-based "trust mechanisms" such as comments from other web contributors, bloggers, and the "massness" of the Internet will root out bad information.[49] Thus, rather than rely on external authorities, Web 2.0 advocates argue that "the crowd" will determine which information and opinions are acceptable and which are not.

The assumption behind crowd-based program services such as *Wikipedia* is that errors will be corrected by the collective wisdom or knowledge of the masses. Sometimes this works. Often it does not. David Levy found this out in a relatively trivial situation. Unsure how to spell "Caribbean," he did a web search and found thousands of hits for his spelling, "Carribean." As he discovered, many others didn't know how to spell the word either. "I should have known better," Levy concluded. "Authoritative knowledge, unlike elective office, isn't simply established by a show of hands."[50] Archivists can gather valuable information from public users regarding their collections, such as identifying photographs. By relying on such crowd knowledge, however, they may also end up with inaccurate information, false identifications, and "knowledge" that is not reliable. We need to be judicious in soliciting such user responses and cautious in relying on the information thereby gained. This does not mean keeping the gates locked. But archivists who solicit comments from the crowd need to become fact checkers and ensure that the information presented in, for example, finding aids is trustworthy. One can never eliminate all errors, but it is important to retain some aspects of the gatekeeper approach to provide information that is as accurate as possible.

The Web Does Not Tell Us All We Need to Know

Frequent users of the web sometimes assume that all the information they need is available on the web. With the seeming ubiquity of Internet information, it is easy to assume that anything one needs to know can be found online. This common fallacy can be dangerous. As archivists know, even with the best knowledge, resources, and good intentions, the vast documentation available in even the smallest archival repository will likely never be entirely accessible on the web. The web has already transformed how many researchers locate and use information. If it cannot be located online and accessed quickly, it is unlikely to be incorporated into research projects. "The web has become the ubiquitous starting point for discovering all types of information and conducting a wide array of research," according to Richard Szary. Web users "expect a level of access and service that repositories are not, and never have been, expected to provide."[51]

Archivists have already seen changes in public expectations regarding access to sources and services. What we need to explain to potential users is the limitations of what they can find online. It is possible for researchers to find a lot of useful information from archival sources without entering the repository. But in almost every instance, this is only the smallest sampling of the rich resources that can be accessed in person. In *From Gutenberg to the Global Information Infrastructure: Access to Information in the Networked World*, Christine Borgman states: "The claim that the Internet will replace libraries often is based on questionable assumptions. Three common misconceptions are that all useful information exists somewhere on the Internet, that information is available without cost, and that it can be found by anyone willing to spend enough time searching for it."[52]

As archivists vigorously apply Web 2.0 systems to reach nontraditional audiences, they need to avoid perpetuating these misconceptions.

Technological Obsolescence

Another caution in adopting Web 2.0 applications is the rapidity of changes in technology. Commentaries on the speed of technological obsolescence have become commonplace and do not need to be recited here. Yet it is important to remember that these changes will continue to affect any applications that rely on current systems and services, including those in libraries and archives. Information science expert David Levy reminds us that this not only entails economic costs but also adjustments to our altered relationship to documents themselves. "The financial implications of making this global infrastructure work are staggering: the cost of networks, of computers, of upgrades and maintenance, of training, of the reorientation and rethinking of work," Levy states. "In addition, however, we now live with certain deep confusions and uncertainties about the nature of these new documents, what they are and how they are to be preserved."[53] Digital documents depend on a complex technical system. The same is true with Web 2.0 applications. Who is responsible for maintaining YouTube videos, blogs, Flickr images, or other documentary evidence once it is uploaded to a commercial site? Can archives rely on such services for long-term preservation or only for temporary public access and use?

These concerns (among others) cause French historian Lucien Polastron to warn about the limitations of the mass digitization efforts under way in Europe and North America. The Google project to create a comprehensive digital "library" of the world's great books, launched in 2005, raises concerns about maintaining cultural heritage and access to such resources. Who will own the digital heritage if Google goes bankrupt?, Polastron asks. It seems "likely that the partner libraries will not be authorized to cooperate with Google's competitors" nor to distribute content that actually resides in the public domain. As he states, "it is currently impossible to measure the weight, the cost and the maintenance know-how sought by the planetary memory in the process of shaping itself." Rapid technological change further complicates the problem. "The other indisputable fact of the electronic world is its own obsolescence," Polastron adds: "in ten years, none of the computers today will be compatible with the systems yet to come."[54] To the extent that it depends on hardware and software to maintain its presence and usefulness, archival use of Web 2.0 will be susceptible to this potential for technological obsolescence.

What archivists will need to do is to plan for change. The Web 2.0 tools available for use in today's archives will inevitably change, evolve, or disappear. They are likely to be replaced by new systems and innovations. Archivists themselves may in fact engage in adapting current tools or creating new ones for specific archival applications. Above all, any archivist who participates in the 2.0 environment must be comfortable with the inevitability of change and remain "open to learning about the next generation of tools."[55] Such flexibility, after all, is an essential component of the mind-set for all Web 2.0 practitioners and adopters. Changing technology is a limitation for Web 2.0, but it also presents opportunities for creativity and experimentation.

Preserving a Virtual Medium

Beyond the limits imposed by rapid technological change, digital media pose serious problems for long-term preservation. Archivists using wikis, blogs, Facebook, and other 2.0 apps need to consider how any information or documents needed for future use can be backed up, emulated, or otherwise protected from deterioration and loss. One of the significant changes brought by digital formats is that text and physical format "have been pulled apart," so that the stability of documents must be established and maintained virtually rather than tangibly.[56] Another prominent difference is the instability of digital documents, which have been created on hardware and software platforms that are volatile and quickly become obsolete.[57]

Richard Heinberg, a leading expert on peak oil and the energy crisis, warns that this dependence on technology makes our very culture "evanescent" and insecure. Librarians and archivists need to respond to these threats. "Preservation of digitized knowledge can become a problem simply because of obsolescence," he warns. Billions of floppy disks produced and used to store data between 1980 and 2000 cannot be accessed on today's computers. In an era of looming climate catastrophe, the worldwide information system becomes vulnerable to an even greater danger. "Ultimately the entire project of our digitized cultural preservation depends on one thing: electricity. A soon as the power goes off, access to the Internet goes down," Heinberg asserts. "It is ironic to think that the cave paintings of Lascaux may be far more durable than the photos from the Hubble space telescope."[58] Responding to Heinberg's article, an anonymous writer added that "what we see happening is digitization being embraced with little regard for its technical and structural limitations, much like the fossil-fuel energy system that powers it."[59] Heinberg's doomsday scenario may seem extreme, but it highlights just how vulnerable our information infrastructure has become. Librarians, archivists, and others need to ensure the long-term viability of our cultural heritage.

Privacy Concerns

One of the most significant impacts of Web 2.0 on the way people think and behave is its tendency to blur the line between public information and privacy. This should be a concern for many users of the new technology, who often seem to pay no attention to the consequences of posting intimate and private information about themselves. As Jonathan Zittrain observes, "the Net enables individuals in many cases to compromise privacy more thoroughly than the government and commercial institutions traditionally targeted for scrutiny and regulation."[60]

Privacy concerns are not new for archivists. When we engage users and potential researchers in online exchanges or encourage user postings and commentaries about finding aids or archival websites, there need to be mechanisms or policies to ensure both user privacy and the protection of third parties whose documents may become part of an online access system. Privacy concerns need not prevent archivists from using such new methods of outreach and communication, but these systems do raise new requirements for privacy protection.

Becoming a 2.0 Archivist

Learning from Other Disciplines

The new challenges posed by electronic records have altered the record-keeping landscape. Similarly, the opportunities promised by Web 2.0 require archivists and other information professionals to develop and adopt new methods to meet the rapidly changing needs of their users. The new technologies employing Web 2.0 applications and related methods require archivists to modify some of their long-held assumptions about archival sources, reference services, and research strategies. Similar changes are simultaneously taking place in libraries, museums, records management, and other information professions.

Archivists, librarians, and records managers need to reconceptualize their roles for the digital future. What makes libraries distinctive, for example, is "linking information to people, managing collections, providing cohesiveness of provision and service, sustainability, preservation, authenticity and quality," according to Deegan and Tanner. "Digital preservation is the cutting edge of digital librarianship and information management technology," they add. "The future librarian's role will be to find and promote islands of simplicity, and create secure harbours of stability, trust and authenticity, in this fluid world of information turmoil."[61] These considerations could just as easily be attributed to archivists, whose roles also include preservation, trust, and authenticity. The new generation of "digital natives" expect creative methods for gathering information. This has led librarians to re-imagine their role: "Instead of primarily organizing book titles in musty card catalogs and shelving the books in the stacks, they serve as guides to an increasingly variegated information environment."[62] Librarians, like archivists, are becoming more active as guides to information resources. This requires engaged participation to assist users in the research process.

Contemplating the possible loss of vast cultural resources in the event of a massive electricity grid failure, Richard Heinberg turns to librarians for a solution. His admonitions could as easily—perhaps even more so—be addressed to archivists. In recovering from a widespread blackout, he declares, "it is important that the kinds of information that people would need are identified, and that the information is preserved in such a way that it will be accessible under extreme circumstances, and to folks in widely scattered places." Essential information must be identified, preserved, and retrieved. "There is a task that needs doing: the conservation of essential cultural knowledge in non-digital form," Heinberg concludes. "Librarians catalog, preserve, and make available accumulated cultural materials, especially those in written form. That's their job. What profession is better suited to accept this charge?"[63] These functions are also central to the mission of archivists. This should be a shared responsibility.

Libraries also have a tradition and a mission of providing free access to vast information resources. As a 2008 American Library Association conference report suggested, libraries should be "more and more a place to do stuff, not just to find stuff. We need to stop being a grocery store and start being a kitchen."[64] Heinberg observes that one of the "primary practical functions" of libraries is "the provision of free public Internet access, with computer included."[65] Although increasingly difficult due to shrinking budgetary resources for libraries, this is one of the most commonly suggested solutions to overcome the digital divide. People who cannot afford to buy a computer or pay for Internet access fees, many writers argue, can access Web 2.0 through their local libraries. At best, though, this is only a partial stop-gap solution. There simply are not enough computers in enough libraries to accommodate the potential demands.

Records managers face similar challenges. In his provocative book *Managing the Crowd: Rethinking Records Management for the Web 2.0 World*, English records manager Steve Bailey declares that the rise of Web 2.0 "strips away many of the fundamental building blocks on which records management has traditionally been based." Yet he asserts that "the core values and objectives of records management are still hugely relevant and necessary in this new world—provided we are willing to fundamentally rethink the way in which we strive to achieve them."[66] Bailey reaffirms the importance of guaranteeing the quality and accuracy of organizational records, based on "authenticity, completeness, reliability and fixity." The growing complexity of record keeping, however, demands greater concern for "the broader picture of information creation and use."[67]

Bailey argues that Records Management 2.0 must be scalable to an (almost) infinite degree, comprehensive, and able to absorb new priorities and responsibilities as they change. This requires records management to be "a benefits-led experience for users, that offers them a positive incentive to participate." To do so, records managers need to be "self-critical and willing to embrace challenge and change."[68]

These criteria could apply just as well to archives. Bailey strongly urges records managers to accept the spirit and culture of the Web 2.0 approach to information and cooperation. Many of his suggestions would also make sense for archivists, particularly those working within institutional or governmental repositories. Such qualities will enable archivists to participate in the 2.0 environment, while maintaining their core mission and purposes.

Promoting Essential Archival Principles

The essays in this volume indicate the scope of innovative approaches and new models currently being test-driven by archivists. These are necessary and valuable new methods of archival practice, based on changing demands and circumstances. As archivists move forward in the 2.0 world, however, they need to remember the principles and concepts on which modern archival practice has been based and to acknowledge that not all users or potential users of archives will have access to or knowledge about how to use these innovative tools.

Archivists who embrace the new technologies need to recognize the distinction between using the tools of Web 2.0 and allowing the new techniques to determine their professional direction and goals. Although there will be radical changes in the methods employed and the environment in which archivists work, the essential purposes and core principles of the archival profession must remain essentially intact. Institutions will continue to need authentic and reliable records for legal, evidential, accountability, administrative, and documentary purposes. Individuals will still require documentation to protect their rights as citizens, to hold public

and corporate leaders accountable, and to gain access to valuable information resources. Ultimately, society—all of us—must retain both legal records
and cultural resources to maintain a surrogate for memory by which accurate knowledge of the past can be protected, leaders charged with carry-
ing out the people's governance or with providing goods and services can
be held accountable, and the rights and identity of the diverse groups
within society can be protected. Focusing on these archival purposes amid
the rapidly changing technological environment requires creativity and
inspiration. "Now is not the time for designing pre-formed, ultra-detailed
methodologies but, instead, for thinking more in terms of adaptable, reusable and extensible concepts," Steve Bailey declares.[69] As archivists experiment with their new tools, they should keep their attention focused on the
goals they seek to achieve and on the fundamental purposes served by
archives.

Web 2.0 offers archivists both new tools to conduct description, reference, outreach, and other services and also new challenges to manage the
records created in this new medium. Since the introduction of electronic
record keeping, archivists have debated whether it would transform and
overturn their traditional methods and concepts or merely require some
adjustments to keep up with new developments. This is still an openly
contested issue.

Most of the core concepts of archival practice continue to be useful in
utilizing and managing digital resources. "The introduction of electronic
records does not appear to have changed in fundamental ways the underlying meaning of 'recordness,' at least not yet," stated information management expert Richard Barry, even though dramatic changes in record-making
technologies will change how organizations conduct their record keeping.[70]
These characteristics remain unchanged, whatever the medium of record.
With electronic information, the essential archival functions of ensuring
trustworthiness, reliability, and accountability through record keeping can
be documented using metadata, according to Minnesota state archivist
Robert Horton.[71] This is also true for Web 2.0-generated materials.

Maintaining Analog Options

As archivists embrace the opportunities offered in the Web 2.0 environment, they will also need to maintain many of their traditional "analog" systems and services. Finding aids, reference and access services, and outreach programs still need to serve those who do not have access to or means of using new technological tools. Thus far few radical changes have occurred in archival praxis. Already a decade into the twenty-first century, archivists as a profession are still beginning the process of adapting to the digital age. Many archival concepts remain valid. The technology shift from paper to electronic records has altered how we create archives, how we use them, and how we think about archives. Yet archives have always been products of technology. "The web is infinitely more flexible than the clay tablet," observed historian of technology Steven Lubar, "but similar in its recording of the structures of power."[72] Record keeping has always depended on technology, from clay tablets and parchment to paper and photographic film, from wax seals and codices to filing cabinets and digital video discs. Each new form of technology solved some problems of the old technology and created some new ones. As John Seely Brown and Paul Duguid have observed, new technologies typically "augment or enhance existing tools and practices rather than replace them."[73] In efforts to ease the transition from old to new systems, digital technologies adopt conventions and terminology from their analog predecessors. The World Wide Web, for example, mimics books and paper documents, borrowing from the older technology terms such as *web pages, bookmarks, indexes*, and *tables of contents.*[74]

One interesting experiment in employing the possibilities of Web 2.0 to enhance archival finding aids showed that researchers are not yet ready to exploit the full range of interactive options. In 2005 students and faculty in the University of Michigan School of Information conducted an ambitious effort to apply a combination of social media tools to create an interactive finding aid for the Bentley Historical Library's Polar Bear Expedition Collections. The project's central goal was to demonstrate a more transparent, user-centered, and need-based approach to archival finding aids. Researchers who did use these enhanced features reported being very

satisfied with their experience. Unfortunately, the overall result was very
limited use of some of these new features, perhaps because researchers did
not know how to exploit new methods of access and research.[75] Despite
limited success, the project illustrates both the possibilities for creative
approaches to archival access and also the need to continue providing traditional access systems. While archivists may want to accept and promote
such technological tools, it is important to note that they may bear a steep
price tag, that they may promise more than they can deliver, and that there
remain many people unable to use these tools because they cannot afford
access or cannot learn the necessary techniques.

Archives 2.0 and Society

The ultimate measure of the value of Web 2.0 tools will be how well they
contribute to meeting the essential goals and purposes of archival services.
It may be tempting to disparage or dismiss Web 2.0 applications because
they cannot solve all of our professional problems. Yet it is important to
allow archivists to experiment with these new tools and to find appropriate
applications. Dire predictions of technology run amok have permeated one
strand of social criticism for two centuries. During the early disruptions
of the Industrial Revolution, for example, English Luddites destroyed the
machinery that threatened to eliminate their jobs, threaten their liveli-
hood, and disrupt traditional society. Internet critics such as Andrew Keen
may overstate the dangers of new technologies, such as Web 2.0, but their
message needs to be heard and considered.

Archivists should employ the new technologies of Web 2.0 to meet the
needs of the younger generation of tech-savvy researchers. Using these
tools they can connect in new ways with new groups of potential users.
Yet archivists must also continue to provide traditional services and access
systems to serve the interests of the many people who do not have access
to newer technologies or the knowledge or interest to use these new tools
and methods of Web 2.0. Ultimately, archives will be judged by how well
they contribute to the fundamental purposes served by the archival record.
Web 2.0 can be an effective tool in achieving these objectives as long as
archivists do not confuse it for the goal itself.

In the larger context of the role of archives in society, it is essential to distinguish between these technological tools and the actual purposes, goals, and values provided by archives. The concept of Archives 2.0 centers on the distinction between methodology and theory, between *what/how* and *why*. This requires a new mind-set, a new orientation to archival practice.[76] Archives 2.0 will prove a welcome and liberating force if it enhances the contributions of archives and archivists to social needs, such as legal evidence, accurate documentation of the past, accountability, and representation of the diversity of cultural heritage. Archivists need to watch the horizon for important trends and changes, to embrace technology, to find creative and practical approaches to new Web-based tools, and to plan and evaluate methods to meet patrons' needs. Core archival principles remain valid. *How* archivists perform their responsibilities will change to meet the demands of the digital age, but *why* they do it will remain the same.[77] Archivists can bring to these discussions their expertise based on centuries of archival development, the growing awareness and understanding of society's need for reliable evidence and documentation, and techniques developed out of necessity and refined by practice and experimentation.

With a wary eye on the future and a firm grounding in principles based on past experience, archivists can and should embrace Web 2.0 technologies as one part of a new reorientation toward an approach to archival practice that is open, transparent, user-centered, and flexible. The innovative orientation of Archives 2.0 thus takes us away from a passive gatekeeper mentality and enables archivists to assert the power of archives, their essential value for society, and their capacity to contribute to the public interest. By providing both traditional and new social networking options for users, archivists can better serve the needs of all members of society. Using such tools for the public good, archivists can use their power within the information sphere to provide essential public benefits, including evidence, documentation, historical memory, accountability, and protection for the rights and interests of all people. Archives 2.0 opens the archives to new voices, new needs, and new constituencies. It can thus have a liberating impact for society.

Notes

1 Kate Theimer, "Introduction to Web 2.0 in Archives: What You Need to Know in a Nutshell" (web seminar), Society of American Archivists, October 13, 2009, p. 9.

2 Ian F. McNeely and Lisa Wolverton, *Reinventing Knowledge: From Alexandria to the Internet* (New York: W. W. Norton & Company, 2008), 271–272.

3 Charles M. Dollar, *Archival Theory and Information Technologies: The Impact of Information Technologies on Archival Principles and Methods* (Macerata, Italy: University of Macerata, 1992), 35.

4 Kent Haworth, "The Principles Speak for Themselves: Articulating a Language of Purpose for Archives," in *The Archival Imagination: Essays in Honour of Hugh A. Taylor*, ed. Barbara L. Craig (Ottawa: Association of Canadian Archivists, 1992), 94.

5 Ibid., 91.

6 See Richard J. Cox and David A. Wallace, *Archives and the Public Good: Accountability and Records in Modern Society* (Westport, CT: Quorum Books, 2002); Verne Harris, *Archives and Justice: A South African Perspective* (Chicago: Society of American Archivists, 2007); and Randall C. Jimerson, *Archives Power: Memory, Accountability, and Social Justice* (Chicago: Society of American Archivists, 2009).

7 David M. Levy, *Scrolling Forward: Making Sense of Documents in the Digital Age* (New York: Arcade Publishing, 2001), 159.

8 Ibid., 183–184, emphasis in original.

9 Ibid., 194.

10 Universal Declaration of Human Rights, 1948, quoted in Lucien X. Polastron, *The Great Digitization and the Quest to Know Everything* (Rochester, VT: Inner Traditions, 2006), 118.

11 Richard Heinberg, "Our Evanescent Culture and the Awesome Duty of Librarians," Post Carbon Institute, October 7, 2009, p. 1, http://www.postcarbon.org/article/40397-our-evanescent-culture-and-the-awesome-duty-of-librarians (accessed December 14, 2010).

12 Timothy L. Ericson, " 'Preoccupied with Our Own Gardens': Outreach and Archivists," *Archivaria* 31 (Winter 1990–91): 120.

13 Steve Bailey, *Managing the Crowd: Rethinking Records Management for the Web 2.0 World* (London: Facet Publishing, 2008), xi.

14 Tim O'Reilly, quoted in Mary E. Samouelian, *Embracing Web 2.0: Archives and the Newest Generation of Web Applications* (Master's thesis, University of North Carolina at Chapel Hill, April 2008), 2–3.

15 Peter Van Garderen, "Web 2.0 and Archival Institutions," *Archivematica*, May 8, 2006, http://archivemati.ca/2006/05/08/web-20-and-archival-institutions/#more-34 (accessed December 18, 2008).

16 Jeff Jarvis, *What Would Google Do?* (New York: Collins Business, 2009), 231.

17 Richard Pearce-Moses, "Janus in Cyberspace: Archives on the Threshold of the Digital Era," *American Archivist* 70 (Spring/Summer 2007): 13–22.

18 Quoted in Nicholas C. Burckel, "Academic Archives: Retrospect and Prospect," in *College and University Archives*, ed. Christopher J. Prom and Ellen D. Swain (Chicago: Society of American Archivists, 2008), 20.

19 Jarvis, *What Would Google Do?*, 11.

[20] Ibid., 4.

[21] Ibid., 22–23.

[22] Bailey, *Managing the Crowd*, xiii–xv.

[23] Jonathan L. Zittrain, *The Future of the Internet and How to Stop It* (New Haven: Yale University Press, 2008), 214.

[24] "Full Text: Keen vs. Weinberger," *Wall Street Journal*, July 18, 2007, http://online.wsj.com/article/SB118460229729267677.html (accessed October 8, 2009).

[25] David Bollier, *Viral Spiral: How the Commoners Built a Digital Republic of Their Own* (New York: The New Press, 2008), 1–3.

[26] Ibid., 6, 8.

[27] Daniel H. Pink, *A Whole New Mind: Why Right-brainers Will Rule the Future* (New York: Riverhead Books, 2006), 3.

[28] Ibid., 130.

[29] "What Is the Digital Natives Project?", *Youth and Media*, http://www.digitalnative.org/wiki/Main_Page (accessed September 24, 2009); John Palfrey and Urs Gasser, "Excerpt," *Born Digital: Understanding the First Generation of Digital Natives*, http://borndigitalbook.com/excerpt.php (accessed October 5, 2009).

[30] Palfrey and Gasser, *Born Digital*.

[31] Nicholas Carr, "Is Google Making Us Stupid?", *Atlantic* (July/August 2008), http://www.theatlantic.com/doc/print/200807/google (accessed October 2, 2009).

[32] Jarvis, *What Would Google Do?*, 234–235.

[33] Alecia Wolf, "Exposing the Great Equalizer: Demythologizing Internet Equity," in *Cyberghetto or Cybertopia?: Race, Class, and Gender on the Internet*, ed. Bosah Ebo (Westport, CT: Praeger, 1998), 29.

[34] Bosah Ebo, "Internet or Outernet?", in *Cyberghetto or Cybertopia?*, 6–7.

[35] Ibid., 8–9.

[36] Wolf, "Exposing the Great Equalizer," 26–30.

[37] Rebecca Carrier, "On the Electronic Information Frontier: Training the Information-Poor in an Age of Unequal Access," in *Cyberghetto or Cybertopia?*, 158–160.

[38] Marilyn Deegan and Simon Tanner, *Digital Futures: Strategies for the Information Age* (New York: Neal-Schuman Publishers, 2002), 4.

[39] Deegan and Tanner, *Digital Futures*, 239–240.

[40] Jean-Claude Guédon, cited in Polastron, *Great Digitization*, 118–119.

[41] Zittrain, *Future of the Internet*, 235–240.

[42] Terry Cook, e-mail to author, June 16, 2009.

[43] Helen R. Tibbo, "The Impact of Technology on Academic Archives in the 21st Century," in *College and University Archives: Selected Readings* (Chicago: Society of American Archivists, 2008), 38–39. See also Margaret Hedstrom, "Archives, Memory, and Interfaces with the Past," *Archival Science 2*, nos. 1–2 (2002): 21–41.

[44] Hedstrom, 24.

[45] Elizabeth Yakel, "Inviting the User into the Virtual Archives," *OCLC Systems and Services 22*, no. 3 (2007): 163.

[46] Elizabeth Yakel, "AI: Archival Intelligence and User Expertise," *American Archivist* 66 (Spring/ Summer 2003): 51–78; and Elizabeth Yakel, "Managing Expectations, Expertise, and Effort While Extending Services to Researchers in Academic Archives," in *College and University Archives*, 270.

[47] Cook, e-mail to author, June 16, 2009.

[48] Andrew Keen, *The Cult of the Amateur: How Today's Internet Is Killing Our Culture* (New York: Doubleday, 2007), 92.

[49] David Weinberger, in "Full Text: Keen vs. Weinberger," *Wall Street Journal*, July 8, 2007, 2 at: http:// online.wsj.com/article/SB118460229729267677.html (accessed December 14, 2010).

[50] Levy, *Scrolling Forward*, 170.

[51] Richard V. Szary, "Encoded Finding Aids as a Transforming Technology in Archival Reference Service," in *College and University Archives*, 247, 252.

[52] Christine L. Borgman, *From Gutenberg to the Global Information Infrastructure: Access to Information in the Networked World* (Cambridge, MA: MIT Press, 2000), 194.

[53] Levy, *Scrolling Forward*, 152.

[54] Polastron, *Great Digitization*, 63–65.

[55] Theimer, "Introduction to Web 2.0 in Archives," 9.

[56] Levy, *Scrolling Forward*, 56–57.

[57] Catherine O'Sullivan, "Diaries, On-line Diaries, and the Future Loss to Archives; or, Blogs and the Blogging Bloggers Who Blog Them," *American Archivist* 68 (Spring/Summer 2005): 54; Levy, *Scrolling Forward*, 119.

[58] Heinberg, "Our Evanescent Culture," 2.

[59] Anonymous response, in Heinberg, "Our Evanescent Culture," 7.

[60] Zittrain, *Future of the Internet*, 200.

[61] Deegan and Tanner, *Digital Futures*, 241–242.

[62] Palfrey and Gasser, *Born Digital*.

[63] Heinberg, "Our Evanescent Culture," 5–6.

[64] Quoted in Heinberg, "Our Evanescent Culture," 2.

[65] Ibid., 2.

[66] Bailey, *Managing the Crowd*, xiii–xv.

[67] Ibid., 59–60.

[68] Ibid., 126–127.

[69] Ibid., 125.

[70] Richard E. Barry, "Technology and the Transformation of the Workplace: Lessons Learned Travelling Down the Garden Path," in *Effective Approaches for Managing Electronic Records and Archives*, ed. Bruce W. Dearstyne (Lanham, MD: Scarecrow Press, 2002), 16.

[71] Robert Horton, "Obstacles and Opportunities: A Strategic Approach to Electronic Records," in *Effective Approaches for Managing Electronic Records and Archives*, 64–65; see also Levy, *Scrolling Forward*, 178.

[72] Steven Lubar, "Information Culture and the Archival Record," *American Archivist* 62 (Spring 1999): 11, 20 (quoted passage found on p. 20).

[73] John Seely Brown and Paul Duguid, *The Social Life of Information* (Boston: Harvard Business School Press, 2002), xii.

[74] Ibid., 182–183.

[75] Magia Ghetu Krause and Elizabeth Yakel, "Interaction in Virtual Archives: The Polar Bear Expedition Digital Collections Next Generation Finding Aid," *American Archivist* 70 (Spring/Summer 2007): 285–286, 306–312.

[76] For a fuller definition and explanation of the concepts of Archives 2.0, see Kate Theimer's "Conclusion" in this volume (p. 334-346), and her essay. "What Is the Meaning of 'Archives 2.0'?," in *American Archivist* 74 (Spring/Summer 2011).

[77] Pearce-Moses, "Janus in Cyberspace," 20–21.

Conclusion

Archivists and Audiences: New Connections and Changing Roles in Archives 2.0

Kate Theimer

The case studies and essays in this collection reflect one or more aspects of an archival profession that is substantially different from that of twenty, ten, or even five years ago. While no profession stands still in its evolution, the scale of the changes in the archival profession in recent years, taken as a whole, reflect a fundamental shift that is analogous to the changes seen between Web 1.0 and Web 2.0. The concept of an Archives 2.0 has been discussed and debated within archival circles on the web for some time, but it has only recently been formally defined.[1] The term is often used, even in this volume, to refer to implementations of Web 2.0 tools by archives. While this usage is certainly appropriate, it benefits us more to think about Archives 2.0 as having a much larger scope. The kinds of attitudes, tactics, and philosophies that characterize Archives 2.0 are demonstrated by all the authors in this collection, including the most important characteristic of our profession today: a different kind of engagement with our users.

Defining Archives 2.0

Archives 2.0 is more than simply "Archives + Web 2.0."[2] Archives 2.0 is an approach to archival practice that promotes openness and flexibility. It is an approach in which archivists are user-centered and embrace opportunities to use technology to share collections, interact with users, and improve internal efficiency. Archives 2.0 employs measurement and assessment as regular tools of our practice and assumes that archivists base their work on established professional standards and practices. It requires that archivists are active and engaged rather than passive and neutral, resulting in effective advocacy for archival programs and the profession.

Another way of explaining what Archives 2.0 means for the profession is by contrasting it with Archives 1.0:

Archives 2.0	Archives 1.0
Open	Closed
Transparent	Opaque
User-centered	Archivist- and record-centered
Technology-savvy	Technology-phobic
Archivist as facilitator	Archivist as gatekeeper/authority figure
Open to iterating products	Focused on "perfect" products
Innovative and flexible	Adhering to tradition
Looking for ways to attract new users	Relying on interested users coming to the repository on their own

While these lists of characteristics are by nature generalizations of more complicated issues, they do provide a means of quickly illustrating what is different about Archives 2.0, and I will use them as a framework for discussing the initiatives described in the case studies in the context of Archives 2.0 and new relationships between archivists and our audiences.

Open Spaces

Previously, access to many archival collections was restricted based on the qualifications or associations of the researcher, and, where it was not restricted by policy, access may have been restricted by practices or physical spaces that were intimidating to inexperienced researchers. Physical or intellectual access was often granted to those researchers who "deserved" it.[3] Today, archives strive to make their physical spaces and access policies as welcoming and fair as possible to ensure the broadest possible use of their collections.

The use of Web 2.0 "spaces" by archives is an extension of this trend to create physical spaces that are open and accessible to all. Using popular social media tools and participating on these sites where users already feel comfortable makes the resources of the archives available outside of any restrictive policies or physical setting. We see this demonstrated in the experiences of Syracuse University using *Wikipedia*, the Library of Congress using Flickr, Iowa State University using YouTube, Stanford University using Second Life, the University of Alabama using Facebook, and the Jewish Women's Archive using Twitter. In all of these examples, archives are making their collections and resources available to any user of the host site. By participating in these popular commercial sites, these archives provide a virtual invitation to visit the archives in person or online to learn more.

Transparent Organizations

Believing in the value of professional neutrality, archivists in the past often strove to make their own activities and influence on their collections invisible to researchers. In contrast, today archivists are increasingly realizing that their own decisions regarding appraisal, processing, and description should themselves be documented and made available to researchers.[4] Additionally, archivists are beginning to appreciate that making the work we do visible to users can contribute to an increased public understanding of the value of the profession and so has an important advocacy function.

We see evidence of this kind of transparency in processing blogs such as *A View to Hugh*, which share with readers first-person accounts of archival processing. Tools such as Flickr and catablogs like the University of Massachusetts Amherst's *UMarmot* allow users to contribute information to supplement existing descriptions, further opening the process of description, showing that it is iterative. Although not specifically documented in this book's case studies, many archives are using tools such as Facebook and Twitter for informal communication with fans and followers about the daily activities of processing, description, and reference.[5] We are also beginning to see evidence of institutions making a deeper commitment to transparency by involving the public in discussions about priorities and policies. The most prominent example of this has been the National Archives and Records Administration's use of the Open Government Idea Forum to solicit input on its Open Government Plan and its use of blogs to interact with researchers.[6]

User-centered Practices

In the past many archivists saw their primary responsibility as serving their collections, and they created policies and practices that were not always "user-friendly." They produced descriptions and access systems that were designed to serve people who understood archival systems, such as other archivists and experienced researchers. Today's archivists understand that their mission should be serving researchers, not records. They seek ways to provide descriptive information in ways that meet their users' needs, employing systems and tools that users can more easily understand.

Much of this movement is typified by a desire to provide descriptive information in ways other than the traditional online finding aid or library catalog entry. By creating catablogs such as *UMarmot* and contributing information to *Wikipedia* articles, archives are providing users with access to descriptive information in formats that are easy to understand and discover. Initiatives such as Dickinson College's reference blog capitalize on users' desire for specific, item-level or name-based access points rather than description of a collection or series. By participating on popular social media sites such as Flickr, YouTube, Facebook, and *Wikipedia*, many archives are going where the potential users are already looking for information; they are focusing on what users want and are comfortable with, rather than relying on traditional forms of access that focus on presenting descriptive information about the records.

Technology-savvy Archivists

While it is true that the archival profession has always had members who embraced technology, it is also true that until recently those members were probably in the minority. However, the stereotype of an archivist who is more comfortable confronting papers than a computer is fading away as more archivists are becoming visible participants in online culture, becoming proficient at working with and modifying open-source software and even producing their own software products (such as Archon and the Archivists' Toolkit).

While most of the social media tools used by the case study authors are not particularly technologically challenging, for many members of the public the mere fact that archivists are using tools like Second Life, wikis, and Drupal would be a revelation. The stereotype of the archivist as a shy, retiring Luddite is being dismantled by the many archives and archivists sharing information on blogs, Facebook, and Twitter and adding images and data to Flickr and YouTube.

Archivist as Facilitator

If in the past archival spaces were "closed," they were kept that way by archivists who functioned as gatekeepers between prospective users and the collections. Archivists controlled all aspects of access to collections, deciding how they would be viewed, how they were described, and, to some extent, what use could be made of them. Increasingly, archivists are seeing their primary role as facilitating rather than controlling access.

Using social media tools, archivists also invite user contributions and participation in describing, commenting, and reusing collections, creating so-called participatory archives.[7] This subject is discussed at length by Elizabeth Yakel in her essay on the Library of Congress on Flickr, and in the case studies for The National Archives' *YourArchives* wiki, the National Archives of Australia's Mapping Our Anzacs, and Syracuse University's use of *Wikipedia*. Indeed, the work demonstrated in all the case studies shows a movement toward using resources to facilitate access as broadly as possible, rather than using resources to restrict or filter access to collections.

The efforts of nonarchivists Patrick Peccatte and Michel Le Querrec in the PhotosNormandie project represent an important example of what many archives may face in the future—the adoption and co-opting of their materials by an interested community of users. In this example, archivists from Library and Archives Canada and the U.S. National Archives, the custodians of the archival materials, would be just one set of voices among many experts. While such communities of interest have always existed and made use of our collections, social media and social networking allows them to create more sophisticated, accessible, and geographically diverse communities around materials that they do not in fact own. As Yakel discusses in her essay, this is a new role for many archivists, and the rules for operating in these environments have yet to be determined.

Open to Iterating Products

Traditionally, there has been something in the personality of most archivists that makes them want their work products, such as finding aids and processing of collections, to be perfect and final. But in the face of mounting backlogs and increasing user expectations, most archivists have come to realize that "the perfect is the enemy of the good," or perhaps, that something is better than nothing. Probably best characterized by the embrace of the "More Product, Less Process" (MPLP) approach to processing, as well as the more informal approach to information sharing that is common in Web 2.0 products, more and more archivists have come to expect and accept that the work they do will be revisited, revised, and corrected.[8]

The use of wiki software is built around an iterative approach to creating documents, with each page of a wiki being a work continually in process. The *YourArchives* wiki and the College of William and Mary's *SCRC Wiki* are predicated on ongoing updates from users. Using tools such as the *UMarmot* catablog, Flickr, and processing blogs, archivists are openly sharing their information about collections before it is necessarily complete or "final," often in the hopes that users will be able to help add to it.

Innovation and Flexibility

I don't think anyone who has worked in an archives can have escaped hearing the justification "but we've always done it that way." Just as localized practices for processing and cataloging have fallen by the wayside, so has unquestioning adherence to tradition in the face of changing work practices and user needs. The need to work efficiently, collaboratively, and responsively has resulted in more openness to new ideas and flexibility (illustrated again by the largely positive response to MPLP).

All the case studies discussed by James Gerencser–the Dickinson College reference blog, the *UMarmot* catablog, and the College of William and Mary wiki–demonstrate this willingness to create new tools and innovate, as does the general sense expressed by many of the other case study authors that an experimental approach to using social media was acceptable and even necessary. Those archives who were early adopters of specific Web 2.0 tools, such as the Library of Congress on Flickr and Stanford University on Second Life, may have been seen by their peers as wasting time on a "frivolous" site, yet now their efforts are seen by many as groundbreaking. All of the projects described in the case studies show a willingness to try something new that is essential to the meaning of Archives 2.0.

Looking for Ways to Attract New Users

Formerly, many archives were confident that their predefined audience of professional historians, genealogists, and "hobbyist" researchers would find their way to the archives. That philosophy may be summed up as "if we describe it, they will come." The more popular philosophy today might be, "go where your users are," even if this means making digital collections available in spaces the archives don't control, such as Flickr, YouTube and Facebook.

Again, all of the case studies demonstrate a proactive rather than passive approach to promoting collections. Perhaps the most dramatic example of this is the Mapping Our Anzacs project, which took records that had great historic value and built tools that helped visitors visualize and comprehend the information held in the records, as well as contribute their own information and thoughts about the people represented in those records. Syracuse University's efforts to insert links in relevant *Wikipedia* articles to alert researchers to materials of interest is another example of taking additional steps to promote the use of collections. One of the most valuable aspects of the Dickinson College reference blog is that the detailed, often item-level descriptions of the materials used to answer research questions are now themselves discoverable by future researchers via web searches.

The Challenges and Opportunities of Archives 2.0

Just as the case studies provide examples of the qualities of Archives 2.0, the essays show us the challenges and opportunities inherent in this new environment. While considering the role of Web 2.0 tools in archival outreach, Joy Palmer and Jane Stevenson raised questions about the assumptions archivists make about our audiences and how we value different kinds of users. Web 2.0 tools provide the means of reaching new kinds of audiences and becoming part of their social networks, but this raises new issues of the role of traditional archival authority and how to maintain an authentic "voice" in social networks while still protecting the personal privacy of the archivist. They conclude: "Increasingly, we are not going to be directly serving the user but enabling the user to serve him- or herself" (p. 18). This increased emphasis on the role of archivist as facilitator, as community builder, and as participant may require a different skill set and present management challenges that have yet to be fully explored.

The challenge of how to balance necessary archival authority with encouraging user contributions was the focus of Elizabeth Yakel's essay. How successfully can archivists participate in the emerging "peer production" environments spawned by Web 2.0? How will authority be judged when there are multiple voices contributing? On what basis should the archives moderate user participation? Examining the opportunities presented by authority as "non-rivalrous good," Yakel concludes, "This leads me to think that there are more types of authority and more possibilities to extend archival authority through the social web than we have yet imagined." (See pp. 95–96.) While this is "perhaps the scariest time," Yakel observes that it is also one of great opportunity, as archivists determine what the role of archival authority should be in the new "social web of archives."

The opportunities presented by social media to archival managers constitute the central theme of James Gerencser's analysis. Building on Archives 2.0 themes such as flexibility and the embrace of technology, Gerencser argues for the integration of social media capabilities into archival processes such as appraisal, arrangement, and reference. While Web 2.0 tools have been readily embraced for archival outreach, it is still rare to see them adopted by archival managers to increase internal efficiencies, as they have done in the case studies in this section. Incorporating the needs and opportunities of social media earlier in archival processes takes the incorporation of user needs and a desire for transparency to a new level.

As Yakel observed in her essay, an opportunity exists for the creation of a research agenda that considers issues such as how the archival profession should best move forward in the world of Archives 2.0. Perhaps this kind of inquiry is already beginning to take place, as graduate students who are themselves products of this new environment formulate their research topics.

Any new Archives 2.0 research agenda would have to include studying the needs and practices of the users (and non-users) of archives. Indeed, it seems virtually impossible for anyone writing about archival theory or practice today to do so without mentioning the importance of putting the needs of our users first. The need to conduct user studies and usability testing of archival products has long been recognized, and indeed much of the drive for implementing Web 2.0 tools in archives has been to better meet the needs of our users. But how successful have we really been in achieving these goals?

The need for archivists to hear the views of users presented in their own words has never been greater, and yet how often do we have a chance to hear them? In his essay Robert Townsend reviewed the history of the relationship between archives and their users, primarily their historian users, and presented some views from the user perspective about how archives should be employing Web 2.0 tools. Focusing on the areas of discovery, dissemination, and advocacy, Townsend argues that "Digital media create an opportunity to diminish the gap between archivist and user in a way that can revitalize that relationship—making the users participants in the work of the archives and stakeholders in their ongoing vitality and health." (See p. 229)

The information shared about the needs of National History Day participants, undergraduate history students and faculty, family historians, genealogists, and companies that provide access to archival materials provide a chance to hear what our users want. Just as important in some ways is their inclusion in a book of this kind. While the need for systematic formal user studies is as strong as ever, Townsend's observation about the opportunity for revitalizing the relationship between archives and our users is an essential element of Archives 2.0. We should not only be studying our users, we should be consulting with them and encouraging them to participate in dialogues such as these. An essential part of any Archives 2.0 research agenda should be considering how to best establish an ongoing conversation with our various user communities about what they want from the archival community.

Just as no discussion about the future direction of archives on the web is complete without asking our users what they want, no discussion should take place without considering the wider impacts of our actions. In taking on the assignment of writing about archives, Web 2.0, and diversity, Terry Baxter employed the metaphor of the blind men examining an elephant to illustrate the difficulty of grappling with nebulous concepts such as "diversity." Difficult, yes, but necessary, as there can be no advancement of understanding without such grappling. If the goal of the archival profession is to make its members, its collections, and its users as diverse as the people of our communities, we must continually ask how well we are achieving that and what tools we can use to do a better job. Much like Townsend, Baxter concludes that the opportunities presented by the social web for inclusion and participation are the key to ensuring that the participation of archivists on the web embraces and encourages diversity:

> The evolution of both the web and diversity has been toward an empowered individual. But the future of that evolution is toward a *community* of empowered individuals. Community, like Lord Ganesha, has a variety of attributes. Archives, diversity,

and the web are some of its connective attributes. Archives connect through time, diversity connects through space, and the web provides the connective tissue. When added together with other attributes, the community elephant is not a jumble of unmatched parts, but the remover of obstacles to individual fulfillment. (See p. 300.)

But if participation is the key, we need to remember those who cannot participate. In the final essay of the volume, Randall Jimerson provides several necessary cautions. Jimerson reminds us about the necessity to continue serving audiences who do not have access to social media, as well as the need to consider preservation issues related to Web 2.0 materials and other forms of electronic records. He closes his essay by observing that though the tools may have changed, the goals and accumulated knowledge of the profession remain the same. The tools of Web 2.0 will be successful if they help us achieve those goals, but using them should not be a goal in and of itself. Jimerson's essay reminds us that Archives 2.0 builds on the responsible principles of our archival traditions. We need to build on our strengths while embracing new opportunities.

New Roles, New Relationships

Taken together, the case studies and essays in this volume present an argument that the role of archivists on the web has changed significantly with the rise of Web 2.0 tools. The ways we present information about our collections have changed, the ways our users expect to locate and interact with our collections have changed, and the ways we interact with our users have changed as well. These changes raise fundamental questions. How do we want to define our relationships with our users and our collections? What should be the primary role of the archivist? Is it even possible for us to "define" our relationships or our roles? What is the function of an archives on the web? How can we best add value and promote the use of our collections? What kind of authority should the archivist have, and how should that be established and maintained?

The premise of defining Archives 2.0 as more than just "Archives + Web 2.0" is that it promotes discussion of the broader, deeper, interrelated changes that are affecting the profession. It acknowledges that the changes we are discussing are based on far more than just technology. Among the most important of these changes is our continuously evolving relationship with our users. Today we are indeed faced with "a different kind of web," but it is an exciting one that gives archives the opportunity to engage more directly with their audiences, forging new kinds of relationships and leading more people to understand the value and role of archives in our society.

Notes

[1] A definition and supporting arguments were proposed in Kate Theimer, "What Is the Meaning of 'Archives 2.0'?", *American Archivist* 74 (Spring/Summer 2011). Much of the online conversation about the concept has taken place on the *ArchivesNext* blog, most prominently in "Archives 2.0?", October 21, 2008, http://www.archivesnext.com/?p=203#more-203. Relevant posts, including those referencing other conversations on related blogs, can be accessed by selecting posts tagged "Archives 2.0." This discussion also references concepts from "Archives 2.0: An Introduction," presented at "The Real Archives 2.0: Studies of Use, Views and Potential for Web 2.0," August 13, 2009, Austin, Texas, available at http://www.slideshare.net/ktheimer/archives-20-an-introduction (accessed December 11, 2010).

[2] This statement is not intended to discount the value of social media. Web 2.0 tools have been instrumental in helping many archives achieve the kind of interactivity with their users that they have long wanted to embrace. They have brought the goals of Archives 2.0 within the reach of almost all archives and in so doing have helped propel those goals forward. But if the sophistication and desire to use them had not already been present in the profession, Web 2.0 tools alone would not have brought about Archives 2.0.

[3] As noted by Elizabeth Yakel in her essay, these issues are discussed in T. R. Schellenberg, *Modern Archives: Principles and Techniques* (Chicago: University of Chicago Press, 1956), 232–235, and Howard H. Peckham, "Aiding the Scholar in Using Manuscript Collections," *American Archivist* 19 (July 1956): 221–228.

[4] For a discussion of the values of neutrality vs. objectivity and the value of transparency, see Randall C. Jimerson, *Archives Power* (Chicago: Society of American Archivists, 2009), 290–295 and 309–314. The most cited example of the call for increased transparency in processing is Michelle Light and Tom Hyry, "Colophons and Annotations: New Directions for the Finding Aid," *American Archivist* 65 (Fall/Winter 2002): 216–230.

[5] See the examples cited in Kate Theimer, *Web 2.0 Tools and Strategies for Archives and Local History Collections* (New York: Neal-Schuman Publishers, 2010), or J. Gordon Daines III and Cory L. Nimer, eds., *The Interactive Archivist* (Chicago: Society of American Archivists, 2009), http://lib.byu.edu/sites/interactivearchivist/ (accessed October 19, 2010).

[6] NARA's Open Government Idea Forum can be found at http://www.naraopengov.ideascale.com/ (accessed October 15, 2010). NARA hosts several blogs for communicating with researchers, including David Ferriero's *AOTUS* blog, http://blogs.archives.gov/aotus, and *NARAations*, http://blogs.archives.gov/online-public-access/ (both accessed October 15, 2010).

[7] One definition of a participatory archive was proposed in Isto Huvila, "Participatory Archive: Towards Centralised Curation, Radical User Orientation, and Broader Contextualization of Records Management," *Archival Science* 8, no. 15 (2008): 15–35. My usage of the term is broader.

[8] Mark A. Greene and Dennis Meissner, "More Product, Less Process: Revamping Traditional Archival Processing," *American Archivist* 68 (Fall/Winter 2005): 208–263. For a more recent example of this kind of iterative approach, see Robert S. Cox, "Maximal Processing, or, Archivist on a Pale Horse," paper presented at the New England Archivists' meeting, March 20, 2010, http://www. newenglandarchivists.org/meetings/maximal_processing_cox.pdf (accessed April 6, 2010).

Contributors

Terry Baxter has been an archivist for nearly twenty-five years, first at the Oregon State Archives and then at Pacificorp. He has worked at the Multnomah County (Oregon) Records Program since 1998. He has also served in a variety of elected and appointed positions in the Society of American Archivists (SAA) and Northwest Archivists and has been a member of the Academy of Certified Archivists since 2004. He lives in Portland, Oregon, and blogs at *Beaver Archivist*.

Michele Christian is the collections archivist and university records analyst for the Special Collections Department of the Iowa State University Library. Before working at Iowa State, she was the labor archivist at the State Historical Society of Iowa. She has written articles on various topics, including managing artifacts in archives and using oral histories in collection developments. She received her MA in history and MLIS from the University of Wisconsin-Milwaukee.

Michele Combs is librarian for manuscripts processing at Syracuse University's Special Collections Research Center, with primary responsibility for EAD encoding and publishing. She is a co-author of the Online Computer Library Center (OCLC) paper, "Over, Under, Around, and Through: Getting Around Barriers to EAD Implementation" and an ex officio member of the Society of American Archivists' (SAA) Technical Subcommittee for Encoded Archival Description. She has been a *Wikipedia* editor since 2006 and has made more than 4,000 edits. Michele is also a freelance writer, editor, and indexer.

Robert Cox began as head of Special Collections and University Archives at the University of Massachusetts–Amherst after stints at the American Philosophical Society and the William L. Clements Library of the University of Michigan. A one-time paleontologist, he has six academic degrees, including an MLS and a PhD (history) from Michigan and is author of *Body and Soul: A Sympathetic History of American Spiritualism* (Charlottesville: University of Virginia Press, 2003) and author and editor of *The Shortest and Most Convenient Route: Lewis and Clark in Context* (Philadelphia, PA: American Philosophical Society, 2004).

Stephen J. Fletcher has served as the North Carolina Collection photographic archivist at the University of North Carolina at Chapel Hill since 2003. He holds a BFA in photography from Rochester Institute of Technology and an MA in museology from the John F. Kennedy University's Center for Museum Studies. He previously held positions as the curator of Photographs at the California Historical Society and curator of Visual Collections at the Indiana Historical Society. As a member of the Society of American Archivists (SAA), he has twice served as Visual Materials Section chair and is on the Steering Committee of the Metadata and Digital Objects Roundtable.

James Gerencser is the college archivist at Dickinson College in Carlisle, Pennsylvania, heading up the Archives and Special Collections Department since 1998. During the 2005–2006 academic year, he also served as interim director for Academic Technology Services. He holds an MLS from the University of Pittsburgh and an MA in history from Shippensburg University. A focus of Jim's work over the past decade has been providing greater access to unique resources via the web, and he has managed numerous digital projects highlighting special collections. He has taught workshops on digital project management and has been a frequent conference presenter, primarily speaking on issues of reference, access, and digital collections.

Guy Grannum joined the Public Record Office, now The National Archives, in 1988. He has worked in a variety of roles, but for most of his career he has worked in public facing departments providing advice and guidance to researchers. For three years he managed the *Your Archives* wiki. Guy is the author of *Tracing Your West Indian Ancestors* (Public Record Office, 2002) and "Sources for the Study of the Transatlantic Slave Trade and

Slavery" at The National Archives (UK) in *Slavery, Abolition and Social Justice, 1490–2007* (Adam Matthew Digital) and has written many articles on Caribbean genealogical research.

Randall C. Jimerson is professor of history and director of the Graduate Program in Archives and Records Management at Western Washington University in Bellingham, Washington. He is a Fellow and past president of the Society of American Archivists (SAA). He is author of *Archives Power: Memory, Accountability, and Social Justice* (Chicago: Society of American Archivists, 2009), editor of *American Archival Studies: Readings in Theory and Practice* (Chicago: Society of American Archivists, 2000), and author of *The Private Civil War: Popular Thought During the Sectional Conflict* (Baton Rouge: Louisiana State University Press, 1988).

Danielle Kovacs has served as the curator of Collections at the University of Massachusetts–Amherst since 2004. A New England native, she held positions at the Morgan Library and Museum and the New Jersey Historical Society before returning to Massachusetts, where she is currently restoring a Victorian home from butler's pantry to housemaid's quarters. She received her MA in English at the University of Virginia and her MLIS at Simmons College; she joined the adjunct faculty of the latter program in 2006 and has taught courses in information organization and archival methods and services.

Jessica Lacher-Feldman is the curator of Rare Books and Special Collections and an associate professor at the W.S. Hoole Special Collections Library at the University of Alabama. She is a native of the state of New York and holds an undergraduate degree in French Studies and history, an MA in history, and an MLS with a concentration in archival studies from the University at Albany in Albany, New York. Jessica is active in the Society of American Archivists (SAA) and the Rare Books and Manuscripts Section of ACRL/ALA. She is the author of *The University of Alabama Trivia Book* (Athens, GA: Hill Street Press, 2007) and is currently writing a monograph on exhibit development for SAA. Jessica served as project manager for "Publishers' Bindings Online, 1815–1930: The Art of Books," an IMLS National Leadership grant-funded collaborative digital project.

Jeffrey W. McClurken is associate professor and chair of history and American studies at the University of Mary Washington. His research areas include the history of veterans, families, gender, the Pinkertons, mental institutions, the nineteenth-century American South, and the digital humanities. He teaches classes on a wide array of U.S. history topics, including American technology and culture, digital history, women's history, history and film, and *TED.com*. His first book, *Take Care of the Living: Reconstructing the Confederate Veteran Family in Virginia*, was published by the University of Virginia Press in 2009. He is a contributing author for the *ProfHacker* group blog (http://chronicle.com/blog/ProfHacker/27) at the *Chronicle of Higher Education*. Links to his classes and presentations can be found at http://mcclurken.org/.

Andrea Medina-Smith has an MLS with a concentration in archival management from Simmons College, where her focus was on digital collections, digital preservation, and online access to archival collections. Currently, she is the metadata librarian at the National Institute of Standards and Technology where she works with materials from both the archival and library worlds. She worked with the Jewish Women's Archive's archival collections and implemented new tools that promote their mission. She also holds a BA in history from the University of California at Santa Cruz.

Dr. Joy Palmer is the senior manager of Library and Archive Services at Mimas (http://mimas.ac.uk). She is responsible for the strategic direction of the Archives Hub and Copac and negotiating the funding and stakeholder environment. Part of her work involves developing proposals, initiating new projects, and collaborating with stakeholders across the sector—from local cultural heritage institutions to national and international organizations. Joy has a diverse range of experience, including fifteen years of teaching and research at the university level. She lived in the United States during that time, and it was at Michigan State University that she became involved in digital humanities project development and management.

Patrick Peccatte is an information scientist. After studying mathematics and computer science, he worked in scientific documentation and in the press. In recent years he has specialized in XML technologies applied to text and digital images. He has produced many software products for metadata management. He is also a consultant, author, and translator in analytic philosophy and an associate researcher in LHIVIC-EHESS (Laboratoire d'histoire visuelle contemporaine/École des hautes études en sciences sociales) on visual studies. His blog can be read at http://culture-visuelle.org/dejavu/.

Amy Schindler is the university archivist at the College of William and Mary. She has primary responsibility for collection management activities for the university archives and records management. In addition to the activities typical of the position, she coordinates the institutional repository and collections database and is active in access and outreach functions. Before her current appointment, she was curator of Manuscripts at the University at Albany–SUNY (2002–2007) where she was responsible for the Archives of Public Affairs and Policy. She previously held contract positions in corporate and local government archives. As a member of the Society of American Archivists (SAA), she served as chair of the Reference, Access and Outreach Section. She earned an MLIS and MA from the University of Wisconsin–Milwaukee and a BA in history and a certificate in Asian American studies from the University of Wisconsin–Madison.

Tim Sherratt is a digital historian, web developer, and cultural data hacker who has been developing online resources relating to archives and history since 1993. He has written on weather, progress, and the atomic age and has developed resources, including Bright Sparcs and The History Wall. Tim created Mapping Our Anzacs for the National Archives of Australia in 2008. He is currently employed by the National Museum of Australia and is an adjunct associate professor in the Digital Design and Media Arts Research Cluster at the University of Canberra. Tim blogs at http://www.discontents.com.au and is @wragge on Twitter.

Michelle Springer is a project manager of digital initiatives within the Office of Strategic Initiatives at the Library of Congress. Her work is focused on web policy; particularly the identification, development, intra-agency coordination, and documentation of policies addressing Library initiatives related to the use of social media. She began her career at the

Library twenty-five years ago as an information research specialist in the Congressional Research Service focused on legislative initiatives in the arts and education. She received her MLS from the University of California–Los Angeles and a BS in education from Northwestern University.

Jane Stevenson is the manager of the Archives Hub service at Mimas (http://mimas.ac.uk). She is the line-manager for the team and is responsible for the day-to-day running of the Archives Hub. She oversees the technical development of the service and works closely with Dr. Joy Palmer to translate ideas into practical goals. A trained archivist, Jane has expertise in metadata standards for archives and issues around interoperability and particularly EAD. She is a Teaching Fellow at the University of Dundee and is active in the UK Archives Discovery Network and Archives and Records Association (ARA) Data Standards Group.

Mattie Taormina is the head of Public Services and is a processing manuscripts librarian for Stanford University's Special Collections and University Archives. Her career in archives began with an archival internship at the Archdiocese of San Francisco in 1993, and she has worked continuously in our field since then. Motivated to become familiar with all facets of information management, she has worked in records management, political research, museums, and various other archival and library repositories. Before coming to Stanford in 2006, Mattie worked at the California State Library for nine years for then-State Librarian Dr. Kevin Starr. She holds an MA in public history from Sacramento State University and an MLIS from San Jose State University, which she completed in 2005.

Kate Theimer is the author of the popular blog *ArchivesNext* and a frequent writer and speaker on issues relating to archives and the use of social media. She is the author of *Web 2.0 Tools and Strategies for Archives and Local History Collections* (New York: Neal-Schuman Publishers, 2010) and has contributed chapters about Web 2.0 to the edited volumes *The Future of Archives and Recordkeeping* (Facet, 2010) and *Many Happy Returns: Advocacy and the Development of Archives* (Society of American Archivists, 2011). Beginning in spring 2011, she became a Teaching Fellow on the University of Dundee's distance-learning MLitt for Archives and Records

Management, teaching on the impact of Web 2.0 on archives and record keeping. Before starting her career as an independent writer and blogger, she worked in the policy division of the National Archives and Records Administration in College Park, Maryland. She holds an MIS degree from the University of Michigan and is currently a member of the Council of the Society of American Archivists.

Robert Townsend is the assistant director for research and publications at the American Historical Association, where he serves as senior staff assistant to the Association's Research Division, maintains databases and statistics on the historical profession in the United States, and oversees print and online publications produced at the AHA Headquarters office. He is the author or co-author of more than 200 articles on various aspects of history, higher education, and electronic publishing in *Perspectives on History, AHA Today, Chronicle Review,* and the American Academy of Arts and Sciences' Humanities Resource Center. He received his PhD from George Mason University in 2009 and is currently revising his dissertation under the working title "Making History: Scholarship and Professionalization in the Discipline, 1880–1940."

Malinda Triller serves as special collections librarian at Dickinson College in Carlisle, Pennsylvania. She has contributed to a number of digital projects, including the *James Buchanan Resource Center* and the *Slavery and Abolition in the U.S.* sites, both LSTA-funded projects involving the digitization of nineteenth-century publications. Triller has also been involved in an initiative to make special collections images available through Flickr and most recently supervised a team of student researchers in the creation of a *Women's Experiences at Dickinson* blog. She holds an MLIS from the University of Pittsburgh and an MA in applied history from Shippensburg University.

Tobi Voigt served as the coordinator for the National History Day program in New York State from 2006 to 2010. Voigt earned her MA in history museum studies at the Cooperstown Graduate Program in 2006. Shortly after, she was hired as the manager of statewide programs for the New York State Historical Association, which has sponsored NHD in New York since

1980. In addition to History Day, Tobi worked on education programs and wrote curriculum materials that promote state and local history in K-12 classrooms across New York State. In October 2010, Tobi accepted the position of director of education at the Detroit Historical Society, where she has become involved with the National History Day program in Michigan.

Elizabeth Yakel, PhD, is an associate professor at the University of Michigan School of Information, where she teaches about archives and preservation. Before joining the Michigan faculty in 2000, she taught at the University of Pittsburgh; earlier, she was an archivist and records manager for fifteen years. Yakel's research interests include access to primary sources and user information behavior in archives, particularly digital archives. The essay in this volume is a reflection on research investigating how social computing/Web 2.0 applications affect access to archives through the Polar Bear Expedition Digital Collections. Her other major research project, funded by the Andrew W. Mellon Foundation and the National Historical Publications and Records Commission concerns archival metrics and creating standardized assessment and reporting tools for archivists. Yakel is active in the Society of American Archivists (SAA) and has served on its governing council. She became an SAA Fellow in 1999.

Tanya Zanish-Belcher received her BA (1983) in history from Ohio Wesleyan University and an MA (1990) in historical and archival administration from Wright State University in Dayton, Ohio. She worked as a special collections archivist at the Alabama Department of Archives and History in Montgomery, Alabama, from 1989–1994. In 1995 she became the curator for the Archives of Women in Science and Engineering at the Iowa State University Library, and in 1998 she was promoted to head of the Special Collections Department and head of the University Archives.

Helena Zinkham began working with photographic collections in 1977 at the Maryland Historical Society and is chief for the Library of Congress Prints and Photographs Division. She served on the design team that developed Encoded Archival Description (EAD) for finding aids and enjoys teaching the visual materials cataloging course at the Rare Book School. Her publications include *A Guide to Print, Photograph, Architecture and*

Ephemera Collections at The New-York Historical Society (New York: The New-York Historical Society, 1998) and the essay "Finding and Researching Photographs" for *Working in the Archives* (Carbondale: Southern Illinois University Press, 2009). She received her MLS from the University of California, Berkeley, and a BA in German from Pomona College.

Index

Boldface indicates illustrations

CPSIA information can be obtained at www.ICGtesting.com
Printed in the USA
LVOW131600051012

301651LV00004B/14/P